Praise for *Almost a Woman*

"A courageous memoir . . . One witnesses the blessings, contradictions, and restraints of Puerto Rican culture."
—*The Washington Post Book World*

"An exquisite memoir . . . deserves a place among the classic American coming-of-age stories"—*Detroit Free Press*

"Richly evocative . . . [Santiago has] the skill to render the most minute details of her before and after lives."
—*The Los Angeles Times*

"Santiago writes with a flair for detail, humor, and complex emotion that draws readers into a delightful . . . if sometimes heart breaking, personal journey."—*The Orlando Sentinel*

"A universal tale . . . made special by Santiago's simplicity and honesty."—*Miami Herald*

"Santiago spares no feelings but lays out the truth as she sees it, taking the reader on compelling trips to other worlds."
—*Dallas Morning News*

"Santiago's descriptive prose and lively dialog draw the reader in."
—*Library Journal*

"Not only for readers who share [Santiago's] experiences but for North Americans who seek to understand what it is to be the other."—*Boston Globe*

almost a woman

ALSO BY ESMERALDA SANTIAGO

When I Was Puerto Rican

América's Dream

almost a woman

Esmeralda Santiago

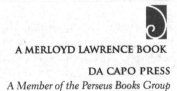

A MERLOYD LAWRENCE BOOK

DA CAPO PRESS

A Member of the Perseus Books Group

Copyright © 1998 by Esmeralda Santiago

All rights reserved. No part of this publication may be reproduced, stored in a retrieval system, or transmitted, in any form or by any means, electronic, mechanical, photo-copying, recording, or otherwise, without the prior written permission of the publisher. Printed in the United States of America. For information, address Da Capo Press, 44 Farnsworth Street, 3rd Floor, Boston, MA 02210.

Cataloging-in-Publication data for this book is available from the Library of Congress.
First Da Capo Press paperback edition 2012
ISBN 978-0-306-82082-3 (paperback)
ISBN 978-0-306-82111-0 (e-book)
Library of Congress Control Number 2012935752

Published as a Merloyd Lawrence Book by Da Capo Press
A Member of the Perseus Books Group
www.dacapopress.com

Da Capo Press books are available at special discounts for bulk purchases in the U.S. by corporations, institutions, and other organizations. For more information, please con-tact the Special Markets Department at the Perseus Books Group, 2300 Chestnut Street, Suite 200, Philadelphia, PA 19103, or call (800) 810-4145, ext. 5000, or e-mail special.markets@perseusbooks.com.

10 9 8 7 6 5 4 3 2 1

contents

⁓

"Martes, ni te cases, ni te embarques, ni de tu familia te apartes."

In the twenty-one years I lived with my mother, we moved at least twenty times. We stuffed our belongings into ragged suitcases, boxes with bold advertising on the sides, pillowcases, empty rice sacks, cracker tins that smelled of flour and yeast. Whatever we couldn't carry, we left behind: dressers with missing drawers, refrigerators, lumpy sofas, the fifteen canvases I painted one summer. We learned not to attach value to possessions because they were as temporary as the walls that held us for a few months, as the neighbors who lived down the street, as the sad-eyed boy who loved me when I was thirteen.

We moved from country to city to country to small town to big city to the biggest city of all. Once in New York, we moved from apartment to apartment, in search of heat, of fewer cockroaches, of more rooms, of quieter neighbors, of more privacy, of nearness to the subway or the relatives. We moved in loops around the neighborhoods we wanted to avoid, where there were no Puerto Ricans, where graffiti warned of gang turfs, where people dressed better than we did, where landlords didn't accept welfare, or didn't like Puerto Ricans, or looked at our family of three adults, eleven children and shook their heads.

We avoided the neighborhoods with too few stores, or too many stores, or the wrong kind of store, or no stores at all. We circled around our first apartment the way animals circle the place where they will sleep, and after ten years of circling, Mami returned to where we began the journey, to Macún, the Puerto Rican barrio where everyone knew each other and each other's business, where what we left behind was put to good use by people who moved around less.

By the time she returned to Macún, I'd also moved. Four days after my twenty-first birthday, I left Mami's house, the rhyme I sang as a child forgotten: "*Martes, ni te cases, ni te embarques, ni de tu familia te apartes.*" On a misty Tuesday, I didn't marry, but I did travel, and I did leave my family. I stuffed in the mailbox a letter addressed to Mami in which I said goodbye, because I didn't have the courage to say goodbye in person.

I went to Florida, to begin my own journey from one city to another. Each time I packed my belongings, I left a little of myself in the rooms that sheltered me, never home, always just the places I lived. I congratulated myself on how easy it was to leave them, how well I packed everything I owned into a couple of boxes and a suitcase.

Years later, when I visited Macún, I went to the spot where my childhood began and ended. I stepped on what was left of our blue tiled floor and looked at the wild greenness around me, at what had been a yard for games, at the corner where an eggplant bush became a Christmas tree, at the spot where I cut my foot and blood seeped into the dust. It was no longer familiar, nor beautiful, nor did it give a clue of who I'd been there, or who I might become wherever I was going next. The *morivivi* weeds and the *culantro* choked the dirt yard, creepers had overgrown the cement floor, pinakoop climbed over what was left of the walls and turned them into soft green mounds that sheltered drab olive lizards and chameleons, *coquí* and hummingbirds. There was no sign we'd ever been there, except for the hillock of blue cement tile on which I stood. It gleamed in the afternoon sun, its color so intense that I wondered if I had stepped onto the wrong floor because I didn't remember our floor being that blue.

"Something could happen to you."

We came to Brooklyn in 1961, in search of medical care for my youngest brother, Raymond, whose toes were nearly severed by a bicycle chain when he was four. In Puerto Rico, doctors wanted to amputate the often red and swollen foot, because it wouldn't heal. In New York, Mami hoped, doctors could save it.

The day we arrived, a hot, humid afternoon had splintered into thunderstorms as the last rays of the sun dipped into the rest of the United States. I was thirteen and superstitious enough to believe thunder and lightning held significance beyond the meteorological. I stored the sights and sounds of that dreary night into memory as if their meaning would someday be revealed in a flash of insight to transform my life forever. When the insight came, nothing changed, for it wasn't the weather in Brooklyn that was important, but the fact that I was there to notice it.

One hand tightly grasped by Mami, the other by six-year-old Edna, we squeezed and pushed our way through the crowd of travelers. Five-year-old Raymond clung to Mami's other hand, his unbalanced gait drawing sympathetic smiles from people who moved aside to let us walk ahead of them.

At the end of the tunnel waited Tata, Mami's mother, in black lace and high heels, a pronged rhinestone pin on her left shoulder. When she hugged me, the pin pricked my cheek, pierced subtle flower-shaped indentations that I rubbed rhythmically as our taxi hurtled through drenched streets banked by high, angular buildings.

New York was darker than I expected, and, in spite of the cleansing rain, dirtier. Used to the sensual curves of rural Puerto Rico, my eyes had to adjust to the regular, aggressive two-dimensionality of Brooklyn. Raindrops pounded the hard streets, captured the dim silver glow of street lamps, bounced against sidewalks in glistening sparks, then disappeared, like tiny ephemeral jewels, into the darkness. Mami and Tata teased that I was disillusioned because the streets were not paved with gold. But I had no such vision of New York. I was disappointed by the darkness and fixed my hopes on the promise of light deep within the sparkling raindrops.

⌒⌐

Two days later, I leaned against the wall of our apartment building on McKibbin Street wondering where New York ended and the rest of the world began. It was hard to tell. There was no horizon in Brooklyn. Everywhere I looked, my eyes met a vertical maze of gray and brown straight-edged buildings with sharp corners and deep shadows. Every few blocks there was a cement playground surrounded by chain-link fence. And in between, weedy lots mounded with garbage and rusting cars.

A girl came out of the building next door, a jump rope in her hand. She appraised me shyly; I pretended to ignore her. She stepped on the rope, stretched the ends overhead as if to measure their length, and then began to skip, slowly, grunting each time she came down on the sidewalk. Swish splat grunt swish, she turned her back to me; swish splat grunt swish, she faced me again and smiled. I smiled back, and she hopped over.

"¿Tú eres hispana?" she asked, as she whirled the rope in lazy arcs.

"No, I'm Puerto Rican."

"Same thing. Puerto Rican, Hispanic. That's what we are here." She skipped a tight circle, stopped abruptly, and shoved the rope in my direction. "Want a turn?"

"Sure." I hopped on one leg, then the other. "So, if you're Puerto Rican, they call you Hispanic?"

"Yeah. Anybody who speaks Spanish."

I jumped a circle, as she had done, but faster. "You mean, if you speak Spanish, you're Hispanic?"

"Well, yeah. No . . . I mean your parents have to be Puerto Rican or Cuban or something."

I whirled the rope to the right, then the left, like a boxer. "Okay, your parents are Cuban, let's say, and you're born here, but you don't speak Spanish. Are you Hispanic?"

She bit her lower lip. "I guess so," she finally said. "It has to do with being from a Spanish country. I mean, you or your parents, like, even if you don't speak Spanish, you're Hispanic, you know?" She looked at me uncertainly. I nodded and returned her rope.

But I didn't know. I'd always been Puerto Rican, and it hadn't occurred to me that in Brooklyn I'd be someone else.

Later, I asked. "Are we Hispanics, Mami?"

"Yes, because we speak Spanish."

"But a girl said you don't have to speak the language to be Hispanic."

She scrunched her eyes. "What girl? Where did you meet a girl?"

"Outside. She lives in the next building."

"Who said you could go out to the sidewalk? This isn't Puerto Rico. *Algo te puede suceder.*"

"Something could happen to you" was a variety of dangers outside the locked doors of our apartment. I could be mugged. I could be dragged into any of the dark, abandoned buildings on the way to or from school and be raped and murdered. I could be accosted by gang members into whose turf I strayed. I could be seduced by men who preyed on unchaperoned girls too willing to talk to strangers. I listened to Mami's lecture with downcast eyes and the necessary, respectful expression of humility. But inside, I quaked. Two days in New York, and I'd already become someone else. It wasn't hard to imagine that greater dangers lay ahead.

Our apartment on McKibbin Street was more substantial than any of our houses in Puerto Rico. Its marble staircase, plaster walls, and tiled floors were bound to the earth, unlike the wood and zinc rooms on stilts where I'd grown up. Chubby angels with bare buttocks danced around plaster wreaths on the ceiling. There was a bathtub in the kitchen with hot and cold running water, and a toilet inside a closet with a sink and a medicine chest.

An alley between our bedroom window and the wall of the next building was so narrow that I stretched over to touch the bricks and left my mark on the greasy soot that covered them. Above, a sliver of sky forced vague yellow light into the ground below, filled with empty detergent boxes, tattered clothes, un-paired shoes, bottles, broken glass.

Mami had to go look for work, so Edna, Raymond, and I went downstairs to stay with Tata in her apartment. When we knocked on her door, she was just waking up. I sat at the small table near the cooking counter to read the newspapers that Don Julio, Tata's boyfriend, had brought the night before. Edna and Raymond stood in the middle of the room and stared at the small television on a low table. Tata switched it on, fiddled with the knobs and the antenna until the horizontal lines disappeared and black-and-white cartoon characters chased each other across a flat landscape. The kids sank to the floor cross-legged, their eyes on the screen. Against the wall, under the window, Tata's brother, Tío Chico, slept with his back to us. Every so often, a snore woke him, but he chewed his drool, mumbled, slept again.

While Tata went to wash up in the hall bathroom, I tuned in to the television. A dot bounced over the words of a song being performed by a train dancing along tracks, with dogs, cats, cows, and horses dangling from its windows and caboose. I was hypno-tized by the dot skipping over words that looked nothing like they sounded. "Shilbee cominrun demuntin wenshecoms, toot-toot" sang the locomotive, and the ball dipped and rose over "She'll be coming 'round the mountain when she comes," with no toots. The animals, dressed in cowboy hats, overalls, and bandannas, waved pickaxes and shovels in the air. The toot-toot was replaced by a bow-wow or a miaow-ow, or a moo-moo. It was joyous and silly, and made Edna and Raymond laugh. But it was hard for me to enjoy it as I focused on the words whizzing by, on the dot jumping rhythmically from one syllable to the next, with barely enough time to connect the letters to the sounds, with the added distraction of an occasional neigh, bark, or kid's giggle.

When Tata returned from the bathroom, she made coffee on the two-burner hot plate. Fragrant steam soon filled the small room, and as she strained the grounds through a well-worn flannel filter, Tío Chico rose as if the aroma were an alarm louder and more insistent than the singing animals on the television screen, the clanking of pots against the hot plate and counter, the screech of the chair legs as I positioned myself so that I could watch both Tata and the cartoons.

"Well, look who we have here," Tío Chico said, as he stretched until his long, bony fingers scraped the ceiling. He wore the same clothes as on the day before: a faded pair of dark pants and a short-sleeved undershirt, both wrinkled and giving off a pungent, sweaty smell. He stepped over Edna and Raymond, who barely moved to let him through. In two long-legged strides, he slipped out to the bathroom. As he shut the door, the walls closed in, as if his lanky body added dimension to the cramped room.

Tata hummed the cartoon music. Her big hands reached for a pan, poured milk, stirred briskly as it heated and frothed. I was mesmerized by her grace, by how she held her head, by the disheveled, ash-colored curls that framed her high cheekbones. She looked up with mischievous caramel eyes and grinned without breaking her rhythm.

Tío Chico returned showered and shaved, wearing a clean shirt and pants as wrinkled as the ones he'd taken off. He dropped the dirty clothes in a corner near Tata's bed and made up his cot.

Tata handed me a cup of sweetened *café con leche* and, with a head gesture, indicated that I should vacate the chair for Tío Chico.

"No, no, that's okay," he said, "I'll sit here."

He perched on the edge of the cot, elbows on knees, his fingers wrapped around the mug Tata gave him. Steam rose from inside his hands in a transparent spiral. Tata served Edna and Raymond, then sat with her coffee in one hand and a cigarette in the other, talking softly to Tío Chico, who also lit up. I brought my face to the steaming coffee to avoid the mentholated smoke that curled from their corner of the room to ours, settling like a soft, gray blanket that melted into our clothes and hair.

I couldn't speak English, so the school counselor put me in a class for students who'd scored low on intelligence tests, who were behavior problems, who were marking time until their sixteenth birthday, when they could drop out. The teacher, a pretty black woman only a few years older than her students, pointed to a seat in the middle of the room. I didn't dare look anyone in the eyes. Grunts and mutters followed me, and although I had no idea what they meant, they didn't sound friendly.

The desk surface was elaborately carved. There were many names, some followed by an apostrophe and a year. Several carefully rendered obscenities meant nothing to me, but I appreciated the workmanship of the shadowed letters, the fastidious edges around the *f* and *k*. I guessed a girl had written the cursive message whose *is* were dotted with hearts and daisies. Below it, several lines of timid, chicken-scratch writing alternated with an aggressive line of block letters.

I pressed my hands together under the desk to subdue their shaking, studied the straight lines and ragged curves chiseled into the desktop by those who had sat there before me. Eyes on the marred surface, I focused on the teacher's voice, on the unfamiliar waves of sound that crested over my head. I wanted to float up and out of that classroom, away from the hostile air that filled every corner of it, every crevice. But the more I tried to disappear, the more present I felt, until, exhausted, I gave in, floated with the words, certain that if I didn't, I would drown in them.

⌣⌒◯

On gym days, girls had to wear grass green, cotton, short-sleeved, bloomer-leg, one-piece outfits that buttoned down the front to an elastic waistband covered with a sash too short to tie into anything but a bulky knot. Grass green didn't look good on anyone, least of all adolescent girls whose faces broke out in red pimples. The gym suit had elastic around the bottom to prevent the sight of panties when we fell or sat. On those of us with skinny legs, the elastic wasn't snug enough, so the bloomers hung limply to our knees, where they flapped when we ran.

The uniform, being one piece, made it impossible to go to the bathroom in the three minutes between classes. Instead of wearing it all day, we could bring it to school and change before gym, but no one did, since boys periodically raided the locker room to see our underwear. With the gym suit on, proper hygiene during "the curse" was difficult, as we needed at least three hands, so most girls brought notes from their mothers. The problem was that if you didn't wear the uniform on gym days, everyone knew you were menstruating.

One girl bought two gym suits, chopped off the bottom of one, seamed around the selvage, and wore the top part under her blouse so that no one could tell if she had her period or not. I asked Mami to do that for me, but she said we didn't have money to waste on such foolishness.

Friday mornings we had Assembly. The first thing we did was to press our right hands to our breasts and sing "The Star-Spangled Banner." We were encouraged to sing as loudly as we could, and within a couple of weeks I had learned the entire song by heart.

Ojo sé. Can. Juice. ¿Y?
Bye de don surly lie.
Whassoprowow we hell
Add debt why lie lass gleam in.
Whosebrods tripe sand bye ¿Stars?
True de perro los ¡Ay!
Order am parts we wash,
Wha soga lang tree streem in.

I had no idea what the song said or meant, and no one bothered to teach me. It was one of the things I was supposed to know, and like the daily recitation of the pledge of allegiance, it had to be done with enthusiasm, or teachers gave out demerits. The pledge was printed in ornate letters on a poster under the flag in every classroom. "The Star-Spangled Banner," however, remained a mystery for years, its nonsense words the only song I could sing in English from beginning to end.

⌒

On a chill October afternoon, Mami, Don Julio, and I went to the airport to pick up the rest of my sisters and brothers, who'd stayed in Puerto Rico with our father until Mami could afford their plane fare. Delsa, Norma, Héctor, and Alicia were smaller than I remembered them, darker, more foreign. They huddled close to one another, holding hands. Their eyes darted from corner to corner of the enormous terminal, to the hundreds of people waving, hugging, kissing, to the luggage that banged into them. Birdlike, they lifted their heads, mouths open, toward the magnified, disembodied voices bleating orders from the ceilings. I wondered if I had looked that frightened and vulnerable only two months earlier.

We'd moved to a new, larger apartment on Varet Street. Tata and Tío Chico had been cooking all morning, and as we entered the apartment, the fragrance of roasting *achiote*, garlic, and oregano, the family milling around, laughing and talking, made it like Christmas.

We had many relatives in Brooklyn. Paco, Tío Chico's son, was short and muscular. His arms and face were always bruised, his eyes swollen and bloodshot, his nose bandaged, the result of his work as a wrestler. His professional name was El Santo. In the ring, he wore white tights and boots, a white leather belt, a white mask, a milky satin cape with a stand-up collar studded with rhinestones. He was one of the good guys, but although he usually won his fights, he always received a beating from the guys in black.

Paco's brother, Jalisco, worked in a factory. He was tall and lean like his father and groomed his mustache into a black, straight fuzz over his lips, like Jorge Negrete, the Mexican singer and movie star. Whenever Jalisco came over, I circled him like a febrile butterfly — offering drinks or food, or reminding him he'd promised to sing *"Cielito Lindo"* after supper. Mami never left me alone with him.

Tata's two sisters lived within a few blocks of our apartment. Tía Chía and her daughters — Margot, Gury, and La Muda — were close to my mother. They came dragging bags full of clothes and shoes they no longer wore. Gury, the youngest, was slender and soft-spoken. Her clothes fit me, although Mami said that the straight skirts, sheer blouses, and high heels Gury favored were not appropriate for a girl my age.

Her sister La Muda was deaf and mute. According to Mami, La Muda had been born with perfect hearing but as a toddler she got sick, and when she recovered, she was deaf.

"Then why don't they call her La Sorda . . ." I began, and Mami warned I was disrespectful.

La Muda read lips. If we spoke with our faces away from her, she shook our shoulders and made us repeat what we'd said while her eyes focused on our mouths. We quickly learned to interpret her language, a dance of gestures enhanced with hums, gurgles, and grunts that didn't seem to come from her throat but from a deeper source, inside her belly. Her hands were large, well manicured, bedecked with numerous gold and stone rings that shimmered as her fingers flew here and there.

La Muda liked us to read the paper to her. That is, Mami or Don Julio read it aloud, while we kids acted out the news. La Muda's eyes darted from Mami's lips to our portrayals of that day's murders, car crashes, and results at the track, enacted race by race around the kitchen table. Her laugh, frequent and contagious, was deep but flat, as if, unable to hear herself laugh, she couldn't get the tone.

Her boyfriend was someone we'd known in Puerto Rico. He was a thin, laconic, dark-haired man who dressed in a beige suit. When we first met him, my six sisters and brothers and I were afraid of him, but he took a deck of cards from his pocket, performed some tricks, and after that we called him Luigi, which sounded like the perfect name for a magician.

Tata's other sister, Titi Ana, had two daughters who were closer to my age than La Muda, Margot, or Gury. Alma was a year older, and Corazón a year younger. They spoke English to each other, and when they talked to us or to their mother, their Spanish was halting and accented. Mami said they were Americanized. The way she pronounced the word *Americanized*, it sounded like a terrible thing, to be avoided at all costs, another *algo* to be added to the list of "somethings" outside our door.

When they walked into the apartment, my sisters and brother submitted to hugs and kisses from people who were strangers to them but who introduced themselves as Cousin this or Auntie that. Delsa was on the verge of tears. Norma held on to Alicia as if afraid they'd get lost in the confusion. Héctor circulated among the men, followed by Raymond, who chattered about Paco's exploits in the ring or about Don Julio's generosity with pocket change.

Luigi, his usually solemn face lit by the hint of a smile, performed new tricks, and the kids relaxed somewhat, as if this reminder of our life in Puerto Rico were enough to dissolve their fears. Margot had brought a portable record player and records, which played full blast in the kitchen, while in the front room the television was tuned to the afternoon horror movie. The kids shuffled from room to room in a daze, overdosed on the Twinkies, Yodels, and potato chips Don Julio had brought for us.

The welcome party lasted into the night. Don Julio and Jalisco went to the *bodega* several times for more beer, and Tío Chico found a liquor store and came back with jugs of Gallo wine. Mami ran from the adults to the kids, reminding the men that there were children in the house, that they should stop drinking.

One by one the relatives left, and the kids once more surrendered to hugs and kisses. Our pockets jingled with pennies that the aunts, uncles, and cousins had handed out as if to pay for the party. Luigi escorted La Muda from the apartment. His pale fingers pressed against her waist, his too-big suit flapped around his scarecrow frame. As they walked out, the adults exchanged mysterious smiles.

Tío Chico and his sons were the last to leave. Tata and Don Julio went into her room and drew the curtain that separated their part of the apartment from ours. "It's time for bed," Mami reminded us. We got ready, Delsa and I on the top bunk, Norma and Alicia on the bottom, Héctor on the sofa, Raymond in the upholstered chairs pushed together, Edna and Mami in the double bed. She turned out the light, and the soft rustles of my sisters and brothers settling into their first night in Brooklyn filled me with a secret joy, which I never admitted but which soothed and reassured me in a way nothing had since we'd left Puerto Rico.

"I don't care what American girls do."

Like every other Puerto Rican mother I knew, Mami was strict. The reason she had brought me to New York with the younger kids was that I was *casi señorita*, and she didn't want to leave me in Puerto Rico during what she said was a critical stage in my life. Mami told her friend Minga that a girl my age should be watched by her mother and protected from men who were sure to take advantage of a child in a woman's body.

While my body wasn't exactly womanly, I knew what Mami meant. Years of eavesdropping on her conversations had taught me that men were not to be trusted. They deceived with *pocavergüenzas*, shameless acts that included drinking, gambling, and squandering money on women not their wives while their children went hungry. To cover up their *pocavergüenzas*, men lied. A man would call his wife *"mi amor,"* while looking over her shoulder at another woman passing by.

"A girl is smart to be suspicious of any man who talks sweet to her," Minga declared. "To her, his words are the most beautiful things she's heard. She has no idea he's said them a thousand times before . . . and will keep on saying them as long as there's some *pendeja* to listen."

According to Mami and her friends, women committed *pocavergüenzas* too. They flirted with men who were taken by more worthy women and lured those feckless men astray.

Having heard countless stories of deceitful men and wily

women, I decided never to become one of those calculating *putas*, but neither would I become a *pendeja*, who believed everything a man told her, or looked the other way while he betrayed her. There was a midpoint between a *puta* and a *pendeja* that I was trying to figure out, a safe space in which decent women lived and thrived and raised their families. Mami belonged there, as did her friends and female relatives. Her lectures, and the pointed conversations I was supposed to overhear, were meant to help me distinguish between a *puta* and a *pendeja*. But there was always a warning. One false move, and I ran the risk of becoming one or being perceived as the other.

I made a friend in school, Yolanda, a girl who spoke good English but spoke Spanish with me. Yolanda was the only Puerto Rican I'd met who was an only child. She was curious about what it was like to have six sisters and brothers, and I asked what she did all day with no one to play or fight with.

"Oh, you know, watch television, read, and I have my albums."

She collected pictures in three-ring binders, organized by type. "These are flowers," she said, pulling down a fat binder from a shelf over her bed. She opened it to a page cluttered with flowers from the Carnation milk can label. "And over here are lips." Pages and pages of lips, male and female, some with mustaches over them, others the disembodied smiles of movie stars. "This one is letters." Arranged alphabetically, hundreds of letters were pasted on the pages, uppercase letters sprinkled on the left side, lowercase on the right. Other albums contained product labels from cans, sanitary pad boxes, garment tags. Another held hair and beauty product advertisements cut out from newspapers and magazines. The fattest one held modes of transportation: cars, trains, cruise ships, ferries, bicycles built for two. Yolanda, I decided, spent too much time alone.

"Would you like to come to my house?" I offered. She had to ask her mother, but she was sure it was okay. The next day, she said her mother wouldn't let her. "I begged," Yolanda explained, her eyes misting, "but she's so strict with me." I was disappointed but understood, since Mami, too, was strict. But when I told Mami that Yolanda's mother wouldn't let her visit us, Mami was offended.

"What's wrong with that woman? Her place is good enough for you to visit, but ours is not good enough for her precious daughter?" After that, I wasn't allowed to go to Yolanda's apartment.

⟶⟶

One day Yolanda asked me to accompany her to the library. I couldn't because Mami forbade unplanned stops on the way home from school. "Ask her and we'll go tomorrow. If you bring proof of where you live, you can get a library card," Yolanda suggested, "and you can borrow books. For free," she added when I hesitated.

I'd passed the Bushwick Public Library many times, had wondered about its heavy entrance doors framed by columns, the wide windows that looked down on the neighborhood. Set back from the street behind a patch of dry grass, the red brick structure seemed out of place in a street of rundown apartment buildings and the tall, forbidding projects. Inside, the ceilings were high, with dangling fixtures over long, brown tables in the center of the room and near the windows. The stacks around the perimeter were crammed with books covered in plastic. I picked up a book from a high shelf, riffled the pages, put it back. I wandered up one aisle, down another. All the books were in English. Frustrated, I found Yolanda, whispered goodbye, and found my way to the front door.

On the way out, I passed the Children's Room, where a librarian read to a group of kids. She read slowly and with expression, and after each page, she turned the book toward us so that we could see the pictures. Each page had only a few words on it, and the illustrations made their meaning clear. If American children could learn English from these books, so could I.

After the reading, I searched the shelves for the illustrated books that contained the words for my new life in Brooklyn. I chose alphabet books, their colorful pages full of cars, dogs, houses, mailmen. I wouldn't admit to the librarian that these elementary books were for me. "For leetle seesters," I said, and she nodded, grinned, and stamped the date due in the back.

I stopped at the library every day after school and at home memorized the words that went with the pictures in the oversized pages. Some concepts were difficult. Snow was shown as huge, multifaceted flakes. Until I saw the real thing, I imagined snow as a curtain of fancy shapes, stiff and flat and possible to capture in my hand.

My sisters and brothers studied the books too, and we read the words aloud to one another, guessing at the pronunciation.

"Ehr-RAHS-ser," we said for *eraser*. "Keh-NEEF-eh," for *knife*. "Dees" for *this* and "dem" for *them* and "dunt" for *don't*.

In school, I listened for words that sounded like those I'd read the night before. But spoken English, unlike Spanish, wasn't pronounced as written. *Water* became "waddah," *work* was "woik," and wordsranintoeachother in a torrent of confusing sounds that bore no resemblance to the neatly organized letters on the pages of books. In class, I seldom raised my hand, because my accent sent snickers through the classroom the minute I opened my mouth.

Delsa, who had the same problem, suggested that we speak English at home. At first, we broke into giggles whenever we spoke English to each other. Our faces contorted into grimaces, our voices changed as our tongues flapped in our mouths trying to form the awkward sounds. But as the rest of the kids joined us and we practiced between ourselves, it became easier and we didn't laugh as hard. We invented words if we didn't know the translation for what we were trying to say, until we had our own language, neither English nor Spanish, but both in the same sentence, sometimes in the same word.

"Passing me esa sabanation," Héctor called to Edna, asking her to pass a blanket.

"Stop molestationing me," Edna snapped at Norma when she bothered her.

We watched television with the sound on, despite Tata's complaints that hearing so much English gave her a headache. Slowly, as our vocabularies grew, it became a bond between us, one that separated us from Tata and from Mami, who watched us perplexed, her expression changing from pride to envy to worry.

One day Mami told me I couldn't go to school because I had to go somewhere with her. "Don't start with your questions," she warned, as I opened my mouth.

We took two buses, walked several blocks to a tired brick building with wire screens on the windows. Inside, the waiting area was crowded with women on orange plastic chairs, each holding a sheaf of papers. A counter divided the room, and behind it, three rows of gray metal desks were littered with stacks of folders, brochures, printed forms, and other papers.

APPLICATION FOR PUBLIC ASSISTANCE, the top of the forms declared, DEPARTMENT OF PUBLIC WELFARE: AID TO FAMILIES WITH DEPENDENT CHILDREN (AFDC). "Here," Mami handed me a pen, "fill them out in your best handwriting."

"But what's it for?"

"So we can get help until I find another job." She spoke in a whisper, looking right and left for eavesdroppers.

I filled out the forms as best I could, leaving the spaces blank when I didn't understand the question.

As the morning wore on, more women arrived, some dragging children, others alone. It was easy to pick out those who'd been to the welfare office before. They sauntered in, scanned the room to assess how many had arrived before them, went up to the receptionist, took the forms, filled them out quickly — as if the questions and answers were memorized. The women new to welfare hesitated at the door, looked right and left until they spotted the reception desk, walked in as if prodded. They beseeched the receptionist with their eyes, tried to tell their story. She interrupted them with a wave of the hand; passed over forms; gave instructions to fill them out, have a seat, wait — always in the same words, as if she didn't want to bother thinking up new ways to say the same thing.

I hadn't brought a book, so I looked around. Mami elbowed me to stop staring. I immediately dropped my gaze to the floor. As I was about to complain that I was hungry, men and women straggled in through a back door and took seats at the desks behind the counter.

When it was our turn, the social worker led us to the far end of the office. He was a portly man with hair so black it must have been either dyed or a wig. He took the forms I'd filled out, scratched checks next to some of the squares, tapped the empty spaces. He spoke to Mami, who turned to me as if I knew what he'd said. He repeated his question in my direction, and I focused on the way his lips moved, his expression, the tone of voice, but had no idea what he was asking.

"I don't know," I said to Mami.

She clicked her tongue.

"Plis, no spik inglis," she smiled prettily at the social worker.

He asked his question again, pointed at the blank spaces.

"I think he wants the names and birth dates of the kids," I interpreted. Mami pulled our birth certificates from her purse, stretched each in front of him as he wrote down the information.

"Tell him," Mami said to me, "that I got *leyof.*"

"My mother *leyof,*" I translated.

"Tell him," she said, "that the factory closed. They moved to another state. I don't have any money for rent or food." She blushed, spoke quickly, softly. "I want to work, tell him that," she said in a louder voice. "*Cerraron la fábrica.*" she repeated.

"Fabric no," I said. "She work wants."

The man's eyes crinkled, his jowls shook as he nodded encouragement. But I had no more words for him. He wrote on the papers, looked at Mami. She turned to me.

"Tell him I don't want my children to suffer. Tell him I need help until the factory opens again or until I can find another job. Did you tell him I want to work?"

I nodded, but I wasn't certain that the social worker understood me. "My mother, she work want. Fabric close," I explained to the social worker, my hands moving in front of me like La Muda's. "She no can work fabric no. Babies suffer. She little help she no lay off no more." I was exhausted, my palms were sweaty, my head ached as I probed for words, my jaw tightened with the effort to pronounce them. I searched frantically for the right combination of words, the ones that said what Mami meant, to convince this man that she was not asking for aid because she was lazy but because circumstances forced her. Mami was a proud woman, and I knew how difficult it was for her to seek help from anyone, especially a stranger. I wanted to let him know that she must have been desperate to have come to this place.

I struggled through the rest of the interview, my meager English vocabulary strained to the limit. When it was over, the social worker stood up, shook Mami's hand, shook mine, and said what I understood to mean he'd get back to us.

We walked out of the office in silence, Mami's back so straight and stiff she might have been wearing a corset. I, on the other hand, tensed into myself, panicked that I'd failed as a translator, that we wouldn't get help, that because of me, we wouldn't have a place to live or food to eat.

"You did a good job," Mami reassured me in front of Tata and Don Julio that night. "You know a lot of English."

"It's easier for kids," Don Julio mumbled between sips of beer. "They pick up the language like that." He snapped his fingers.

I was grateful for Mami's faith in me but couldn't relax until we heard from the welfare office. A few days later our application was approved. By then I'd decided that even when it seemed that my head couldn't hold that many new words inside it, I had to learn English well enough never again to be caught between languages.

⤴⤳

I woke in the middle of the night with something crawling toward my ear. I batted it away, but it caught in the strands of hair near the lobe. I stumbled in the dark, frantically searching for whatever was caught in my hair. By the time I reached the switch by the door, I'd pinched a crackly, dry, many-legged cockroach between my thumb and index finger before it could climb inside my ear canal.

"Turn off the light," Delsa hissed from her end of the bed. I threw the roach down, whacked it with a shoe before it scuttled away.

"What are you doing?" Mami sat up on her bed.

"A roach almost crawled into my brain." I felt dirty, and my fingers itched as if the roach were still between them.

"I'll fumigate tomorrow," she grimaced, then settled back to sleep.

I shook the sheets to make sure no more roaches lurked in the folds.

"Stop that," Delsa pulled on her end of the covers. In the bottom bunk, Norma and Alicia moaned and turned over.

Where there was one roach, I knew, there were hundreds. I imagined hordes of dark brown cockroaches poised at the cracks of the baseboard, waiting for me to switch off the light so that they could begin their march across the room. I'd seen them skitter for cover when I came into the kitchen for a drink late at night. Roaches roamed over the counter, inside the cups and glasses, around the edges of the paring knife, in the space between the sugar bowl and its cover. Mami bought ever more powerful poisons to spray the corners of our apartments. The roach poison made us cough and irritated our eyes. For days after she sprayed, our clothes gave off the pungent chemical smell of Black Flag or Flit. But the roaches didn't die. They went away until the acrid poisonous gas dissipated, then returned, more brazen and in greater numbers.

Before we took a drink of water, we washed the already washed glass. Before cooking, we rinsed the scrubbed pots and utensils. Before serving, we ran every plate, bowl, cup, and spoon under water and dried it with a clean kitchen cloth. We kept food in tight-lidded containers, refrigerated what didn't fit in the cabinets, swept and mopped the kitchen floor every night before going to bed. But no matter how much we scrubbed and wiped and rinsed, the roaches always came back to parade across the floors, the counters, the dressers, the windowsills.

I lay in bed imagining an army of roaches crawling in orderly rows toward the bed I shared with Delsa. I pulled the sheets up and tried to cover my ears, but as I tugged my end, Delsa jerked hers down. I tried to cover my head with the pillow, but the bouncy foam balanced on my forehead, didn't conform to the shape I tried to impose on it, around the top of my skull, alongside my ears past the lobe. Images of roaches about to crawl inside me kept me awake. I was afraid to leave the bed. What if the legions of roaches I envisioned were marching around the floor? Before I could reach the light switch, I'd step on them in my bare feet. I squirmed, trying to wipe the images from my mind. I scraped the spot where I'd found the roach with a corner of the sheet, but no matter how much I rubbed, I still felt it. In fact, lots of crawly things crept over me, but as I reached to swat them, they moved to a different spot. I turned on my right side, then my left, because if I didn't stay in one spot for long, the roaches wouldn't have time to crawl inside the various orifices I imagined were their goal.

When the alarm rang, I slid out of bed, exhausted. I tiptoed, so that if there were roaches on the floor, I would step on as few of them as possible. The linoleum was bare, shiny clean, except for the yellowish ooze from the brown cockroach near the shoe I'd used in the middle of the night. There were no live cockroaches to be seen. But that was no comfort. I knew they hid in the crevices of the baseboard, inside the cracks along the door jamb, under the bed.

⌒

As fall became winter and the days cooled, we discovered that our apartment was unheated. Mami went to the *bodega* to call the landlord; sometimes the radiators clinked and clanged and got lukewarm, but not enough to reach the corners of the rooms. Tata lit the stove, and we spent most of our time at the formica table, in front of the open oven. Inevitably, one of us came down with a cold, and pretty soon, we were all up half the night wheezing and coughing.

Mami and Tata ran from one to the other with a bowl full of hot water into which they had melted a tablespoon of Vick's Vaporub. While Mami held the bowl under our noses, Tata tented a towel over our heads. Once each of us had inhaled as much steam as we could, Tata plastered leaves on our chests and backs with more Vick's Vaporub, then made us put on our warmest sweaters. The next day, Mami devised a concoction with Breacol cough syrup as a base, laced with her own formula of ingredients whose flavor didn't disappear despite the generous amounts of honey she poured into the bottle. The syrup was black, bitter, smelled like burnt cloves and camphor. She forced it on us, and within hours we no longer sniffled and our coughs were gone. From then on, as soon as one of us sneezed or showed a drippy nose, she brought out the sticky bottle, which was enough to cure us instantly. We called it *tutumá*, a mysterious name for that strange, powerful medicine that we didn't have to take to feel better.

Tata claimed that the first winter in New York was the hardest, because, coming from a warm climate, our blood was not thick enough. To thicken hers, she drank beer or wine daily, which also dulled the aches in her bones she swore didn't respond to anything else. To thicken ours, she cooked soups and stews dense with *ñames, yautías,* and other Puerto Rican vegetables.

"But," I argued one day, "if we eat the same food we ate in Puerto Rico, it won't thicken our blood. It didn't while we lived there."

"She has a point," Don Julio chortled.

"We'll just keep getting the same thin blood we've always had," I pressed.

"What they need," Don Julio suggested, "is American food."

Tata was unpersuaded. "American food is not nutritious."

"But look how big and healthy American kids are," Mami allowed. "Their food must be doing something for them."

"They look like boiled potatoes," Tata asserted.

"But their blood is thick," Delsa argued, "and they never get sick."

In spite of Tata's mistrust of American food, Mami was willing to try anything to thicken our blood. At our urging, she bought a few cans of products we'd seen advertised on television: Franco-American spaghetti, Chef Boyardee ravioli, Campbell's chicken noodle soup.

"Yecch, it's slimy," Tata stared suspiciously at the potful of canned ravioli Mami heated for us. "I don't know how you can eat it," she grimaced, as we scooped every bit of sauce out of our bowls.

Mami gave us canned American food every day for a week, but our colds didn't disappear with anything but a spoonful of *tutumá.* So she lost faith in American food and only fed it to us as a special treat, never as a substitute for the hearty Puerto Rican meals she and Tata continued to prepare. When Tata asked why she let us eat it, Mami explained: "They should learn to eat like Americans—in case someday they're invited to an American home, they don't act like *jíbaros* in front of their food."

That silenced Tata and gave me an idea. "Mami, all American girls wear makeup to school."

"I don't care what American girls do. You're Puerto Rican and too young to wear makeup."

It was good to be healthy, big, and strong like Dick, Jane, and Sally. It was good to learn English and to know how to act among Americans, but it was not good to behave like them. Mami made it clear that although we lived in the United States, we were to remain 100 percent Puerto Rican. The problem was that it was hard to tell where Puerto Rican ended and Americanized began. Was I Americanized if I preferred pizza to *pastelillos?* Was I Puerto Rican if my skirts covered my knees? If I cut out a picture of Paul Anka from a magazine and tacked it to the wall, was I less Puerto Rican than when I cut out pictures of Gilberto Monroig? Who could tell me?

Mami's cousins Alma and Corazón were born in Puerto Rico, but their mother, Titi Ana, brought them to Brooklyn as toddlers. They lived on the corner of Varet Street and Bushwick Avenue, at the top of a six-story building with bow windows in the front. The hallways and landings were paved with black-and-white mosaic tiles. Huge windows let light into the staircase, whose wide steps and banisters were cool, cool marble, worn in the center from years of up, down, up. There were four apartments on each story, two facing Varet Street, two in the back. As I climbed to the sixth floor, I stopped at each landing to catch my breath, and to listen to the sounds behind every door or to smell the delicious aromas of dinner being prepared. Behind one door someone watched a soap opera, muted voices punctuated by organ music. I smelled brewed coffee across the hall, and further up, someone cooked salted codfish with eggplant. On the next level, *sofrito* sizzled into hot oil, and across the hall, the beans needed water, because they smelled scorched. A *merengue* played full blast behind another door, while across from it, the two apartments in the back were silent, and no fragrance seeped into the landing. By the time I arrived at the top and knocked on Titi Ana's door, I was hungry and my ears rang.

Corazón opened the three locks and chain on their door to

let me in. She held a bottle of Coke in her hand. "Help yourself," she said, nodding toward the refrigerator. "Alma's in there," she pointed to a door off the kitchen, and disappeared into her room. There was always a six-pack of Coca-Cola in Titi Ana's refrigerator, ice cream in her freezer, Hostess cakes in the cabinet over the sink. I grabbed a soda and knocked on Alma's door.

She sat on her bed, reading a heavy book about men with big mustaches. "I have a test tomorrow," she said, looking up. "History."

Alma's room was familiar, not only because I'd spent so much time in it since I'd arrived in Brooklyn but because it looked like the rooms of all the girls I'd met whose parents had money to spend on things other than the bare necessities. Her bed was white, covered with a ruffled, flowery spread that matched the curtains and the skirt of her dressing table. The linoleum floor was also a flower print, giving the impression that Alma moved and slept in a bright, flat, eternal spring. A window looked out over the roofs of two-and three-story buildings.

"There's a new *Archie*," she pointed to the shelf where she stacked her comic books, the most recent ones on top.

Archie, Veronica, Betty, Reggie, and Jughead were the only American teenagers I'd come to know. There were no Americans in our Puerto Rican neighborhood, and the few that went to the same school as I did kept to themselves in tight, impenetrable groups of chattering, cardigan-wearing, ponytailed girls and pimply, long-legged boys. Like Archie and his friends, they were not Italian or Jewish, Negro or Puerto Rican. They had short, easy-to-remember names like Sue, Matt, Fred, Lynn. They were the presidents of clubs, the organizers of dances, the editors of the school paper and yearbook. They looked like the actors on television: white-skinned, dressed in clothes that never were wrinkled or dirty, hair always in place, an air of superiority setting them apart.

My neighbors, mostly dark-skinned or identified by country of origin, lived in rundown, vertical apartment buildings. From *Archie* I learned about another United States—the trim, horizontal suburbs of white Americans. Through him, I discovered that American teenagers' lives were very different from mine, their concerns as foreign to me as mine might be to them.

Archie and his friends lived in a world with no parents, made their own decisions about where to go and how to get there without consulting anyone but each other. My world was dominated by adults, their rules written in stone, in Spanish, in Puerto Rico. In my world, no allowance was made for the fact that we were now in the United States, that our language was becoming English, that we were foreigners awash in American culture.

Archie never ate at home. His meals, and those of his friends, were taken at Pop's soda shop, where their diet consisted of sandwiches, hamburgers, fries, ice cream sodas — food that could be eaten without utensils. In our apartment, Mami and Tata spent a lot of time in the kitchen, preparing thick *asopaos*, rice and beans, chicken fricassees, huge meals that required time to savor and a close connection to the cook, who lingered near us asking if it tasted good and checking that we ate enough.

Betty and Veronica talked and worried a lot about dating. At fourteen years of age, I was not allowed to go anywhere with a boy who wasn't my brother. We had no telephone, so unlike Betty and Veronica, I couldn't sit with shapely legs draped over the armrest of an upholstered chair chattering with invisible friends about boys. We had no upholstered chair. I had no friends.

Archie and his friends sometimes carried books, but they were never seen in class, or taking exams, or studying. Their existence revolved around their social life, while mine was defined by my obligations as a student and as the eldest sister. Neither Betty nor Veronica was called upon to be an example for younger siblings. They existed solely for themselves, their only responsibilities were to look beautiful and to keep their boyfriends happy.

From Titi Ana's kitchen, I plunged into Archie's bright, shadowless world, jealous of that simple life of fun and trivial problems so far removed from the realities of my own life. No one was ever born or died in Archie's world, no one shared a bed with a sister, or bathed in the kitchen, or mourned an absent father. I wanted to live in those uncrowded, horizontal landscapes painted in primary colors where *algo* never happened, where teenagers like me lived in blissful ignorance of violence and grime, where no one had seven sisters and brothers, where grandmothers didn't drink beer late into the night and mothers didn't need you to translate for them at the welfare office.

Mami surprised me one day in front of my school. I trembled as she frowned at my skirt, which was midcalf when I left in the morning but now hovered above my knees. She scrutinized the smudged lines around my eyes, the faint traces of rouge on my cheeks. Every morning on the way to school, Yolanda and I ducked into the doorway of an apartment building on Bushwick Avenue and rolled up our skirts to the length other girls wore theirs. We drew lines around our lids with an eyebrow pencil stolen from Yolanda's mother. In school, the girls who took pity on those of us with old-fashioned mothers often shared their lipsticks and rouge and helped us tease our hair into beehives sprayed stiff. On the way home, we unrolled our skirts to their natural length; removed traces of makeup with spit; brushed our hair back into limp, decent ponytails.

As soon as she saw my mother, Yolanda dropped her head so that Mami wouldn't see her face. Mami grabbed my arm, dragged me across the street before I could shake off her strong grip. I avoided the eyes of boys who laughed, slapped each other five, gave Mami the thumbs up and called "Go Mamma" as we passed. She silenced them with a withering look that wiped the smirks from their faces. "*Títeres*," she muttered, "so disrespectful to adults."

"Why did you have to spy on me," I screamed as we went up the stairs of our building. I expected a beating, the severity of which might be reduced if I showed the appropriate humility. But

I didn't care if Mami killed me once we got home. I'd been humiliated in front of the school, and I never wanted to go back there.

"I wasn't spying on you. I came to take you shopping," she said in a subdued voice, aware that the neighbors peeked under their chain stops to see what the yelling was about.

"You should have waited until I got home," I screeched, banging on the door, to which I had no key. Héctor opened it and held it as we stepped into the crowded room, and I slammed my books hard on the floor.

Mami grabbed my hair. "Who do you think you are?" she screamed, "talking back like that?" I raised my arms, tried to wrench loose, pulled my hair toward my scalp as she pulled in the opposite direction. "Don't think because we're here you can act like those fast American girls," Mami screamed, her face red, her eyes narrowed into slits, her lips taut. She pushed me away into the bottom bunk of the bed where Norma and Alicia sat, wide-eyed and scared. Tata appeared from the back of the apartment and stood between us. But Mami was done. I lay face down on the bed, stifled with rage, choked on the sobs that followed her beatings. I rubbed my burning scalp, wheezed without crying, beat the mattress with my forehead until Norma poked me with her toes. "Move," she said, "you're crushing our paper dolls." I raised my head to the bland stare of blonde, blue-eyed, red-lipped girls, their shapely bodies dressed in tight, short, revealing clothes. I swiped them off the bed, stepped on them as I stood up and climbed into the top bunk, Norma and Alicia's cries deafening mine.

～～～

That night, I lay next to Delsa and left myself and her, the apartment on Varet Street, Brooklyn, New York. I flew to the warm breeze of a Puerto Rican afternoon, the air scented with jasmine, the *coquí* singing in the grass. I placed myself at my father's side as he poured cement, his shovel working quickly in the gray mud, scraping the edges, mixing them into the gooey center. As he worked, he sang a Bobby Capó *chachachá*.

The wheelbarrow full of cement squeaked as Papi pushed it closer to the wall he built. His brown arms corded from the strain, the muscles on his back bulged down to his waist. I fell asleep telling him about my day, about the walk to school along the broad sidewalks, about the crowded classrooms, about the gangs kids joined to protect themselves from other gangs, about how in the United States we were not Puerto Rican, we were Hispanic. I told him Mami was disappointed in me, accused me of being Americanized when all I wanted was to be like other girls my age. I talked to him the way I used to when we lived together and he and Mami made up after every argument. And I asked him to come get us out of Brooklyn the way he used to rescue us from the places Mami took us to when they fought. One of these days he would show up at the door, the way he used to in Puerto Rico, to convince Mami that he'd changed, that he still loved her. He'd write her long, flowery poems about happy homes and the love a man feels for the mother of his children. He'd soften her up with gifts — a flower in a paper cup, a half-melted coconut ice. These had worked before, and they would work again. Mami would give in and agree to return to him, and we would go back to Puerto Rico, where we would never be cold, where our lives would resume in our language, in our country, where we could be a family again.

⟡

Papi wrote to say he'd married a woman none of us had ever heard of and had moved to a town none of us had ever visited.

I sat on the edge of Mami's bed reading the letter over and over, the tight, neat script, evenly spaced, wide-margined, so familiar and so painful.

I disliked his new wife instantly, swore never to visit them, never to accept her. My letters to him, until then newsy and full of fears and confusion, became short salutations, lists of grades achieved in school and the progress of Raymond's medical treatments, which were successfully saving his foot.

Mornings, on my way to JHS 49, I yearned for my life in Macún. I missed the dew-softened air, the crunchy gravel of the dirt road, the rooster's crow, the buzz of bees, the bright yellow sun of a Puerto Rican dawn. I resisted the square regularity of Brooklyn's streets, the sharp-cornered buildings that towered over me, the sidewalks spotted with crusted phlegm and sticky chewing gum. Every day we spent in Brooklyn was like a curtain dropping between me and my other life, the one where I knew who I was, where I didn't know I was poor, didn't know my parents didn't love each other, didn't know what it was to lose a father.

With Papi married, our ties to Puerto Rico unraveled. He was the strongest link we had to the island, since most of Mami's family was in Brooklyn and Papi's sisters and brothers had never been an important presence in our house.

When I tried to find out if Mami was as disappointed as I was, she brushed me off, saying that Papi had a right to his own life and that we should never blame or disrespect him. But I couldn't shake the feeling of being cast adrift. By not including us in his decision to marry, Papi had excluded us from the rest of his life.

"Are you going to be famous?"

We knew Mami was in love, because she hummed and sang *boleros* as she cleaned or ironed. She was in love, because once she found another job, she bought a new outfit, which she hadn't done since we'd arrived in Brooklyn. She was definitely in love, we knew it, because her brown eyes shone and her lips were quick to smile, and she beamed when she looked at us as if we were the most perfect children any mother could have. We were sure she was in love, because Tata argued with her over every tiny thing and stood at the window when Mami left the house to see which direction she took. Three or four times a week Mami went across the street after work, stayed for an hour or so, then came back cheerful. She never stayed past nine o'clock, but Tata made it sound as if Mami was all over town until dawn.

When we finally met Francisco, who lived across the street with his parents, we knew Mami was in love because she was calm around him, and the hunted expression cleared from her face. She was thirty, Francisco twenty-eight, and the two-year difference in their ages didn't seem as big a deal to us as it was to Tata.

On a bright, late winter day moist with melting snow, we emerged one by one from our building, each carrying a box or a suitcase. Passersby stared with bemused expressions. We were afraid to provoke Tata, so we tiptoed in and out of the old apartment with our belongings until we'd moved everything but the heaviest things to an apartment down the street. Paco and Jalisco came by at the end of the day to carry the furniture to our new place, and we settled into the two-room apartment before dark.

A few days after we moved, Francisco came for dinner. After-wards, he and Mami talked in the kitchen while we watched *Candid Camera* in the front room. He left early but came back the next day, and every day for a week, staying later each time — until one morning he was still there.

"What do we call him? " I asked Mami, when it was clear Francisco had moved in. "We can't call him Papi . . ."

She squinted her eyes in my direction, as she did whenever I was disrespectful. "No, he's not your father," she finally said, as she paired socks.

"And he's too young to be Don Francisco."

"Yes, he is." She found a pair of panties and smoothed them. I could tell she was embarrassed, that I should stop asking questions and leave her in peace.

"Then what do we call him?"

"Franky, that's what his family calls him," she said curtly, handing me the panties and a couple of folded shirts. "Put these in Edna's drawer." Her eyebrows met over her eyes, which meant she was not about to answer any more questions.

I put the clothes away, but I couldn't stop thinking about it. Franky didn't sound official enough, since he was our stepfather. Well, not quite. Because he wasn't married to Mami, he wasn't technically her husband. But she hadn't been married to Papi either, and he had been her husband. Or had he? Not officially. Papi was our father, it said so on our birth certificates. But what was he to her? And now that Francisco was part of our household, what was he to us?

I couldn't ask Mami. It was disrespectful to pry into her personal life. But I knew that women who were married looked down on those who weren't. "Oh, she's just living with him," they said, with a wave of the hand and a disgusted expression.

I also knew that marriage in a white gown and veil — with a

walk down the aisle of a church, a priest, bridesmaids in colorful dresses, and groomsmen in tuxedos — was Mami's dream for me and my sisters.

"What happiness," she declared with a wistful expression, "to see a daughter walk down the aisle in a long white dress and veil!"

Mami hadn't married in a church, but we were supposed to. We never went to church, but someday we would each stand in front of a priest and receive the vows she never had.

"I sacrifice myself for you," she told us over and over. A fancy church wedding for each of us was one of the rewards she expected for that sacrifice.

Soon after Mami's belly started growing with his child, Francisco was rushed to the emergency room with a stomachache. When Mami returned from the hospital she told us he had cancer.

"But don't worry," she said, "he'll be well soon."

Her face was tight, her lips pressed together, her eyes scared, and we knew she was just saying that to make us feel better.

We moved to an apartment down the street so that Tata could live with us. Don Julio brought Tata's cot and small dresser, her radio and clothes, a few pictures of herself as a young woman, her altar. Now that Francisco was sick, she didn't gripe about him being too young or about Mami setting a bad example by living with him. Instead, she cooked and watched us so that Mami could go to the hospital right after work to spend time with Francisco.

A few weeks later, the landlord told us to leave because too many people lived in the three rooms he'd rented to a woman and two kids. We moved for the fifth time in a year. In the new apartment on Ellery Street, the bathtub was again in the kitchen, covered with an enameled metal sheet to make a counter during the day, removed at night so we could bathe. When the temperature dropped, the radiators stayed metal cold, and wind whistled through cracks in the casings.

We all had to transfer to new schools. Junior High School 33, where I attended ninth grade, took up most of a city block. The cement playground and handball court were surrounded by hurricane fencing. Inside, the walls were the same amber-colored brick that covered the outside. The floors were shiny vinyl that squeaked when I wore sneakers, only allowed on gym days.

I scored well in a series of tests that Mr. Barone, the guidance counselor, gave me. I had no idea what the tests were for or why I had to take them, but Mr. Barone said they showed APTITUDE and POTENTIAL and that instead of going to the local vocational high school, I should apply to a school that would prepare me for college. While written English was getting easier for me to understand, spoken English still baffled me, so I agreed to an academic education not knowing what it meant and too embarrassed to ask. It was Mr. Barone's idea that I apply to Performing Arts High School in Manhattan.

"Why so far?" Mami asked. "Don't they have schools in Brooklyn?"

"It's a special school."

She frowned. "Special?"

"I have to apply . . ."

"A private school. We don't have the money . . ."

I explained that it was a public school for kids who wanted to be actors, dancers, or musicians.

She stared at me. "Do you want to be an actress?"

"I don't know. It's just a school."

"You'll do well there," Tata interrupted, "because you're so dramatic."

"There are no Puerto Rican actors on television," Delsa reminded everyone.

"What about Ricky Ricardo?" wondered Raymond.

"*Babalú!*" Edna beat an imaginary drum at her side and Alicia and Héctor joined her in a conga line, singing "*Babalú, Babalú Oyé!*"

"Stop that," Mami said, "the people downstairs will think we have savages up here."

"Ricky Ricardo is Cuban, and he's a singer, not an actor,"

Delsa continued once the kids settled. "And we know Negi can't sing."

"And if you could, Mami would never let you wear those skimpy costumes the vedettes wear," Norma warned. "Would you, Mami?"

"Stop this nonsense," Mami said, eyes back on her mending.

"You see!" Norma laughed.

Mami smiled but didn't say more.

I'd never considered acting as a profession, but once he suggested Performing Arts and I agreed to try out, Mr. Barone made a fuss over me, and that felt good. I didn't tell him that Mami might not let me go even if I were accepted. He helped me prepare for the required audition, chose a monologue, recruited Mr. Gatti, the English teacher, to coach me in the pronunciation of words that I memorized phonetically without knowing their meaning. Mrs. Johnson from Home Economics taught me how to enter a room like a lady and how to sit with my legs together.

I took every opportunity to show Mami I was preparing for my audition. I stood in front of her dresser mirror to practice my monologue, trying to overcome the lifelong habit of speaking with my hands, which Mrs. Johnson said was distracting. I felt like a paper doll, stiff and flat, a smile pasted on my face.

"You belong to a type that's very common in this country, Mrs. Phelps," I began. My sisters and brothers laughed at my attempts to be dramatic and repeated passages from my monologue, their faces twitching as they tried to be serious.

"Stop molestationing me," I yelled, and Mami or Tata shooed them into the next room, where I heard them laughing.

For weeks my sisters and brothers teased me about my lack of talent, while in school Mr. Barone, Mr. Gatti, and Mrs. Johnson helped me prepare. No one from JHS 33 had attended Performing Arts High School, and Mr. Barone made sure the whole school knew I was applying. Now, in addition to my family, everyone in ninth grade questioned my artistic ability.

"Hey, spick!" Lulu taunted as I walked into the girls' bathroom one day. "You think you're better than us? Well, you're just a spick, and don't you forget it." She shoved me into the stall, and for a moment I thought she'd punch my face, but she was happy to spit on it, laugh, and leave me sitting on the toilet, so scared I might have peed in my pants.

I wiped my face with toilet tissue, pulled down my panties and did pee, holding back the tears. She wouldn't see me cry. Neither would she see me fight, because I'd never win. Lulu and her friends were tough, a gang of girls who sat in the back of classrooms passing notes to each other, smoked in the stairwells, picked fights with anyone they didn't like. They knew I was afraid of them, and they made sure I stayed scared. They tripped me in gym class, pushed me in the stairs, took food from my lunch tray. Because of Lulu and her friends, I only went to the bathroom in school if I couldn't hold it in anymore. Because of them, I walked home the long way, to avoid the corner where they stood mornings and afternoons, smoking, laughing, threatening passersby.

For months, Lulu and her gang ignored me. I was one of the kids they bumped into in the hall during period changes. But the minute they heard that I was applying to Performing Arts, Lulu and her friends began a campaign to put me back in my place.

"There goes the actress," LuzMari jeered, as I passed her in the hall.

"She thinks she's white," Violeta mumbled when I was excused from social studies to work on my monologue with Mr. Gatti.

"What?" Denise asked, as I waited to climb the rope in gym, "Eli Whitney not good enough for you?" Almost everyone from JHS 33 ended up at the nearest vocational school, which trained secretaries and nurses, auto mechanics and refrigeration technicians.

"It's just a school," I defended myself, but it didn't matter. Lulu and her gang, to whom I'd been invisible, considered me a traitor because I accepted the teachers' guidance.

"They're jealous," my friend Natalia suggested, as we walked home from school one day. "They'll be pregnant and on welfare before we graduate from high school."

Natalia lived with her mother and sisters in a building down the block from ours. She was a native New Yorker, her English was perfect, and she spoke Spanish well enough so that I could speak a mixture of both without confusing her. Natalia's mother, like mine, worked in the garment factories of Manhattan, although mine sewed bras and girdles, while hers worked in sportswear.

On Saturdays we waved to each other as we helped our mothers lug shopping carts full of groceries up the steps. Weekday mornings, Natalia made breakfast for her two sisters and walked them to their school before she came to ours. Her mother picked the girls up in the afternoons, so Natalia and I went home together almost every day. When I first met her, I thought she was religious, because she never wore makeup, short skirts, or bright colors. Then I found out that she looked that way because her mother, like mine, was old-fashioned.

Because our mothers saw how strict they were with us, Natalia and I were allowed to be friends, as neither could be considered a bad influence on the other. We were both "good" girls who did as we were told, were expected to be an example to our siblings, and were supposed to take that responsibility seriously. Natalia was better at being a role model than I was, however. Goodness was in her nature, whereas I chafed at the idea that whatever I did was watched by six sisters and brothers who might then do the same. I worried that if I stumbled, Delsa, Norma, Héctor, Alicia, Edna, and Raymond were sure to fall behind me like a row of dominoes, never to rise again.

Natalia and I talked a lot about our future. She applied to the Bronx High School of Science, dreamed of becoming a doctor in one of the big hospitals, like Mount Sinai.

"I'll have an apartment on Park Avenue with a doorman and an elevator," she fantasized, hands pressed to her chest as if to contain the happiness it would bring her.

"When I become a famous actress, I'm going back to Puerto

Rico," I said, "to a farm in the country. And I'll have chickens and a rooster and maybe a dog."

"Why would you want to do that?"

"Because . . ." Could I tell her that I longed to return to Macún? That I missed the leisurely pace of rural Puerto Rico, the wild, green, gentle hills, the texture of the dirt road, from dust to gravel to sand to mud? I joked that the riches we hoped to make in our adult lives were meant to bring me back to where I'd started, while she dreamed of something completely different from what she'd known. She laughed politely, and I fretted that I had offended her by implying that my childhood was happier than hers.

———— ‿

"Are you going to be famous?" Raymond asked a few days before my audition.

"Leaf me a lone," I said, annoyed, and worried that maybe I was in over my head. I had memorized the monologue Mr. Barone had chosen and had practiced how to enter a room like a lady, how to sit without plopping on the chair, how to keep my hands still on my lap instead of using them to punctuate my speech. It already felt as if I were acting, and I hadn't even seen the school.

"Mami, the audition is next week, can you take me?" I showed her the paper on which Mr. Barone had written the school's address: 120 West 46th Street. She studied it as if there were more in it than the two numbers and two short words.

"When do you have to be there?" she asked after a long while, and I went limp with relief. I gave her the details, mentioned that Mrs. Johnson had suggested I didn't have to get dressed up, but that I should look nice. "I saw a dress that will look good on you," Mami offered, and I didn't argue that if she were to buy something new, I'd rather pick it out.

Several days later, she brought home a red plaid wool jumper and new shoes. "This is a garter belt," she told me, unwrapping a white cotton and lace undergarment with straps ending in rubber buttons snapped onto a metal loop. "It's what we're working on at the factory. I made this one myself."

I'd watched Mami pull on her stockings, smooth them with her fingers, snap them on. I'd seen her stand with her back to the mirror to check that the seams were straight, then gently tug them into place. Until now, I'd not been allowed to wear stockings, and I knew the garter belt and the flat package that held a pair of "Nude" seamless stockings were a concession from Mami, an acknowledgment that I was no longer a child, although neither of us was ready to call me a woman.

"Thank you, Mami," I gushed, hugging her.

"For special occasions," she said, as she kissed the top of my head. "They'll look good with your new dress and shoes."

Over the next week, Tata ladled out larger portions of our meals, as if to fatten me up for what was to come. Aware of the attention I was getting, my sisters and brothers followed me with big, puzzled eyes, searching for what other people saw that they couldn't.

I felt the same way they must have. So many adults fussing over me on the one hand, while on the other, Lulu and her flock stepped up their threats and taunts, as if to keep me from getting too confident. I sensed that getting into Performing Arts was important not only for me but also for Mr. Barone, who strutted around the school telling anyone who listened that I was going there, even though the audition was still days away, and I might not impress the school with my dramatic talent. And it was important for Mami, who boasted to the relatives that I was going to be an *artista*, which brought the same images to my mind as it did to Norma's: curvaceous women in skimpy costumes with feathers in their hair.

The day of the audition, Mami took me to Manhattan, the first time I'd been out of Brooklyn since our arrival in New York. The elevated train ran level with the upper windows of warehouses and apartment buildings a few feet from the tracks. I tried to peek at what lay beyond them, inside the apartments that seemed an arm's length away. But the train moved too fast for me to see more than blurred images of shapes that might or might not be people inside shadowy rooms.

The school was one block from the bright lights and commotion of Broadway. It was a cold, blustery day, and Mami and I walked arched inside our coats, our eyes teary from the frigid winds. The few blocks from the Times Square station to the school were packed with people oblivious to the cold, who admired huge billboards on the sides of buildings or stared into storefronts, most of which featured posters of women with their private parts covered by a black stripe narrow enough to show they were naked.

On the corner of 46th and Broadway, there was a Howard Johnson's, and we went inside to warm up. The tables along the windows were occupied by people who looked as if they hadn't moved from that spot in years. Mami and I sat at the counter, where we were waited on by a woman with frothy platinum hair, turquoise eye shadow, false eyelashes, hot pink lipstick, and a face as wrinkled as a raisin. She called us "honey" or "darling," and once she had served our coffee and pastry, she came over several times to see if there was anything else we needed and to refill our cups.

I was nervous, but that didn't stop me from eating my pineapple danish and half of Mami's and drinking two cups of strong coffee with cream and lots of sugar.

"She eats, for such a skinny thing," the waitress said to Mami, and she nodded and smiled as if she understood.

We walked the half block to the school, and as soon as I was called into the audition room, I was sorry there was so much food in my stomach. My innards churned and churled, and if the interview wasn't over soon, I might vomit in front of the three

ladies in whose hands lay my future as an *artista*. But I managed
to get through the monologue and a pantomime and to walk out
of the heavy red doors of the school before throwing up between
two parked cars as Mami held my hair back and fussed, "Are you
all right now? Are you okay?"

On the way home she asked what had happened in the audition, and I said, "Nothing. I answered some questions and did my
monologue."

I couldn't tell her that I'd been so nervous I'd forgotten everything learned from Mr. Barone, Mr. Gatti, and Mrs. Johnson. I
raced through the monologue, toppled a chair, answered questions
without understanding what I was asked. I wouldn't tell Mami
how badly I'd done after she'd spent money we couldn't waste on
a new outfit and shoes for me. I was ashamed to return to JHS 33
and tell Mr. Barone that I'd bungled the audition. Everyone would
laugh at me for presuming I could get into Performing Arts, then
fail to get in, in spite of all the help I'd been given. I imagined
myself in school with Lulu and Violeta, LuzMari and Denise,
who would never let me forget I thought I was too good for them.
Mornings, while I took the bus to Eli Whitney, Natalia would be
on the train to the Bronx High School of Science. I'd have nothing
to talk to her about, because she'd be busy preparing for college,
while I'd be sewing underwear in a factory alongside my mother.

As Mami and I rode back, the train charged out of the tun-
nels, clattered over the Williamsburg Bridge toward Brooklyn. The
skyline of Manhattan receded like an enormous wall between us
and the rest of the United States. My face away from Mami, I
cried. At first my tears came from the humiliation of what I was
sure was a terrible audition. But as we neared our stop in Brooklyn,
I cried because the weeks of anxious preparation for the audition
had left me longing for a life I was now certain I'd never get.

"But they're still illegitimate ..."

As Mami's belly grew larger, she had trouble moving around because her legs and back hurt. She quit her job, and I again accompanied her to the welfare office.

"I need assistance until the baby is born and his father is out of the hospital," she had me translate.

"And how long have you and Mr. Cortez been married?" the social worker asked.

"We're not married," Mami said. "We've lived together for the past ten months."

The social worker pressed her lips together. "Does your first husband provide child support?"

"No."

"How long since you've been divorced?"

"Tell her," Mami said, "that your father and I weren't married."

The social worker gripped her pen, and her slanted, left-handed writing crawled across lined paper like rows of barbed wire.

"Then the seven older children are also illegitimate," she said, and Mami blushed, although I'd not yet translated.

"Their father has recognized them all," she had me interpret, pulling our birth certificates from her purse.

"But they're still illegitimate," the social worker insisted, ignoring the documents.

"What does that have to do with it?" Mami asked in Spanish, and I translated, burning with shame because her voice rose and I could tell she was about to make a scene.

The social worker didn't respond, kept on writing on her clipboard. "That's all," she finally said. "We'll let you know."

When we came home, I looked it up. *Illegitimate* meant born of parents who were not married. But the way the social worker's lips puckered, *illegitimate* sounded much worse. It had a synonym, *bastard*, which I'd heard used as an insult. Without my knowing it, the social worker had offended me and Mami. I wished I'd noticed, so that I could have said something. But what was there to say? She was right. We were illegitimate. I worried then that Mami wouldn't get the help we needed from welfare because she and Papi were never married, but a few days later, the help came through.

The word, however, stayed in my conscience a long time.

A couple of months after his son was born, Francisco died. Mami's usually lively and curious eyes dulled, looked inward, where we couldn't reach her with hugs and kisses. On her dresser, she lit candles that burned day and night, their heat like Francisco's spirit hovering in watchful anticipation of whether, and how, and for how long we would mourn him.

I couldn't cry my disappointment that our family had fallen apart again. Papi had refused to follow Mami to New York, unwilling to help us cope with a cold, inhospitable city. Francisco had left us as quickly as he had come, taking with him the commitment he had made to love Mami forever, to be the man in our house, to make us a complete family with a mother, a father, and children. Every time I passed the altar, I stopped to look at the orange flames floating over melted wax. I placed my hand over them and felt the heat, the solid warmth like an embrace, a promise.

I tried to imagine Papi's life. He'd moved, and I wondered

what his new house was like. Was it in the country or in a town? Was his wife prettier than Mami? Was she as good a cook? Did her daughters sit near him as he read a poem he'd written, as I used to do? I wrote him subdued letters and didn't dare ask about his life, afraid he'd write about how happy he was.

If Papi had come with us, Mami would never have fallen in love with Francisco, he wouldn't have died, and we wouldn't be on welfare again. Yes, Mami and Papi fought, but they always made up. Just like me when I fought with my sisters and brothers; eventually, we made up and went on as before. If we could do it, why couldn't they?

I resented the men who stood on street corners, or who sat on stoops with their elbows on their knees, their hands around a can of beer or curled around a cigarette smoldering between their legs. They might be somebody's father, but they had nothing better to do than to stare at young girls and women passing by and mumble promises under their breath.

One morning, Mr. Barone bounded over as I entered the school. "Isn't it wonderful? Congratulations!"

My expression must have told him I had no idea what he was saying, so he stopped, caught his breath, and spoke slowly. "A letter came. You were accepted to Performing Arts."

"Oh my God!" I felt light enough to fly. Mr. Barone led me into the office, where the secretary, the other guidance counselors, and the principal shook my hand. "I can't believe it," I repeated over and over, "It can't be true."

"You worked hard," Mr. Barone said. "You deserve it."

On my way to homeroom, I ran into Natalia. "Guess what? I was accepted!"

She screeched, dropped her books, hugged me. "Oh, my God! I'm so proud of you!" She pulled away quickly, embarrassed at her enthusiasm. I bent down to help her collect her books.

"I can't wait to tell Mami," I said. "She needs good news."

"I wish I could see her face when she hears." Natalia stuffed some loose papers inside a notebook. She seemed about to hug me again but pulled her books into her chest. "I'm so happy for you," she said, and hurried down the hall.

I didn't realize I was smiling until Lulu passed me in front of the science labs, grabbed my arm, and asked, "What's so funny?"

"Nothing," I answered, suddenly serious, "nothing's funny." Lulu had lovely eyes — round, green, full-lashed. She blinked, seemed about to say something, but stopped when a teacher looked out.

"You girls better move on, the bell rang," she warned.

Lulu clicked her tongue at me, pushed me hard enough to let me know she could hurt me. "Wipe that shit-eating grin off your face," she growled, and went off in the opposite direction.

By the time I reached homeroom, Mr. Gatti was writing a question on the board for a pop quiz. He smiled and winked as I sat down. The telltale scratching of the speaker in front of the classroom let us know an announcement was coming. We dove for our books, intending to ignore the announcement for a few minutes of study.

"Ahem," the speaker started. "Girls and boys, ladies and gentlemen," Mr. Barone's crusty voice competed with the shrill feedback that accompanied the messages. "Ahem. I'm pleased to announce that one of our seniors, Esmeralda Santiago, has been accepted to Performing Arts High School."

I was embarrassed and pleased at the same time, didn't hear the rest of what he said. Mr. Gatti shook my hand. Andrea, the girl next to me, patted my shoulder. Someone applauded and the other students followed, except the too cool. I sat in awe for the rest of the period, aware that something good had at last happened to me, afraid that it was too good and that it would disappear before the day was over.

I ran home from school, burst in the door of our somber apartment, found Mami sorting papers on her bed.

"I got accepted, Mami. I got into Performing Arts." She looked puzzled. "The special school, remember? In Manhattan."

Her eyes widened. "¡Ay, *que bueno!*" she said, pulling me close for a hug. I held on to her. Mami's hugs were scarce these days, and I wanted to stay in her arms, to smell the flowery scent of her soap, so faint I buried my face into her neck to find it.

"What did Negi do?" Alicia appeared, and next to her, Edna and Raymond. As usual when one of us received Mami's attention, the others flocked to her, wondering how they could get some too.

Mami guided me to the other side of her papers. "Your sister was accepted into the school for *artistas* in Manhattan," she told them, and I was proud because I heard the pride in her voice.

"You're an artist?" Héctor asked from the other room.

"She's going to learn to be an artist, so that she can be rich and famous some day," Mami said with a smile.

I panicked. Is that what I was doing? "It's just a high school, Mami. So I can go to college."

"Didn't you say it was to study drama and dance?" she scowled.

"Well, yes . . ."

"Are you going to be on television with Ricky Ricardo?" Raymond asked.

"I don't know . . ."

"She's too ugly to be on TV," Héctor piped in from his corner.

Everyone laughed. Mami hugged me, kissed the top of my head. "I'm going to start dinner," she said. Performing Arts was never mentioned in that apartment again.

~~~~~

A week later, Natalia wasn't in school. She was absent several days in a row, so I went to look for her. Though we lived a few doors apart, we'd never visited each other, and it was strange to stand in an unfamiliar hallway knocking on a door I wasn't sure was hers. There was no answer. I knocked again, waited a while, pressed my ear to the door to listen for a radio or a television or a reason why no one heard my knock. All was silent, but the door across the hall opened a crack.

"Who's there?" asked a frail voice in Spanish, and when I turned, one eye and half a shrivelled old face peered under the chain stop.

"I'm looking for Natalia Pons. I think she lives here."

"They moved."

"But that's impossible. I just saw her, she didn't say anything."

"They're gone, that's all I know. Nobody has moved in yet, but someone will." She closed the door. Several bolts caught and the woman shuffled deep into her apartment.

I didn't believe her. Natalia hadn't told me she was moving. When I asked Mr. Barone why Natalia wasn't in school, he said the family had returned to Puerto Rico.

"But she never bean there," I said.

He shrugged his shoulders. "Her mother is sick."

Mami found out that Mrs. Pons had had an accident at work and that Natalia's uncle had come to take the girls back to Puerto Rico. It made no sense, but that's the way things happened in our neighborhood. People came and went with no warning, no farewells. My own family moved five times in one year, and there was never a goodbye or a backward glance. Each move was supposed to be for the better, and I wanted to believe that for Natalia, a move to Puerto Rico was good. But I also knew that Natalia's Spanish was really Spanglish, a mixture of English and Spanish that got the job done but was understood only by people who spoke both languages. What would happen to her in Puerto Rico? Would she still be able to study medicine? If she were accepted to the Bronx High School of Science, would she go?

I felt sorry for her, and for myself. The thing I wanted most, a return to Puerto Rico, came true for her. But her dream was the opposite of mine. She wanted to stay in New York, to be a success

American-style, surrounded by the things we thought would make us happy: the apartment on Park Avenue, the luxury car, the clothes and dinners out and nights at the theater. I curled into myself much the way Mami did, afraid to dream — no, afraid to speak my dreams aloud, because look at what had happened to Natalia's.

The candy store in front of JHS 33 was owned by an old couple. They lived behind the store, in a room on the other side of a door that was split in the middle, so that the owner's wife could talk to him as she sat at a round table before stacks of fabric scraps that she stitched into colorful quilts. The man's hands were mottled and swollen, his fingers round and unwrinkled, like hard sausages. Kids said that he was contagious, so we never touched him when he made change. He placed the coins inside a plastic bowl on the counter, and I picked mine up, threw them in my pocket, rubbed my hands against my skirt to get rid of his germs.

On the sidewalk in front of the candy store there was a metal bench for newspapers. The old man took the money for them through a small window in the storefront. Mornings, he sat by the window, watching the students go into school, vigilant of the rowdies who liked to run off with armloads of his newspapers.

If the gangs were acting up, I often ran into the store, browsed through a magazine, or took a long time to buy a candy bar — all the while peering over the counter to make sure the kids were gone. The man behind the counter knew that his store was a haven for those of us neither strong nor brave enough to stand up to the tough kids. If one of us came in and took a long time to choose a purchase, he leaned out the window over the newspaper bench and looked to the right and left along the sidewalk. With a gruff "What's taking so long?" he waved us over, growled the price of the item we held in hand, glowered if we put it back because we had no money. "Get out of here," he snarled, but we knew he was letting us know the coast was clear.

After Mr. Barone made his announcement about my acceptance to Performing Arts, Lulu's insults and threats became more frequent. Now that Natalia was gone and I walked alone, I left as soon as the bell rang, aware that Lulu and her gang were too cool to run out as if someone had chased them. But one afternoon after I crossed the street, relieved that once more I'd avoided her, Lulu stepped from the door of one of the abandoned buildings down the block from the candy store. Behind her were LuzMari and Denise. They surrounded me and pushed me into the cold, dark hallway, which smelled of urine and rotting wood. They punched and kicked me, their shrill voices a chorus of obscenities, their fists sharp and accurate, beating into my chest, my belly, my lower back. I fought back with kicks, scratches, and punches like the ones I used against my sisters and brothers whenever we tussled, only harder. The girls dug their nails into my arms and face, the back of my neck. I flailed against the six fists that pounded my ribs, the six legs that kicked my shins and crotch, the three toothy mouths that snarled and shrieked and spit, the six eyes that glinted in the musty darkness with fierce green hatred. I defended myself but, outnumbered, came out the loser, clothes torn and dirty, arms scratched, legs bruised, chest and back throbbing. As we fought, they screamed in English and I responded in Spanish, the obscenities I wasn't allowed to speak at home spewing from me like acid.

They left me sprawled against a pile of damp cardboard, screeched what must have been more threats, although I wasn't sure. I didn't know what they wanted from me, what I could do to make them ignore me as they used to. I didn't linger in the dark, smelly hallway. Creatures scurried in the depths of the abandoned building, I could hear them. I dusted myself off, found my belongings. When I stepped into the street, the candy store man stood on the sidewalk. He beckoned me in, handed me a frosty Yoo-hoo. From the back, his wife appeared with a damp rag and, mumbling in a language that was neither English nor Spanish, wiped the grime and tears from my face, her rheumy eyes searching for open wounds on the inside of my arms and on my cheeks.

"Those girls," the old man said, and slapped his swollen hands against the counter. He didn't look at me as his wife wiped alcohol on my bruises, making the welts and scratches on my arms and legs sting and burn. He stared through the window at the street in front of the school, his shoulders slumped, a sad expression on his face.

"Go home, tell mama," his wife said, guiding me out of the store. I thanked them, tried to make eye contact with both, but they looked past me and waved me out, unwilling to accept my gratitude. I dragged myself home, each step like needles into my ribs and hips. Mami was in the bathroom when I came in, so I slouched into the front room, changed into clothes that hid the bruises on my arms and legs, spent the rest of the night bent over a book so that she wouldn't see the scratches on my cheeks, the swollen lip. After dinner I took a long, hot bath, covered my sobs by splashing water and belting out Mexican *corridos* about traitorous lovers and revolution. If Mami noticed, she didn't say a thing, and neither did my sisters and brothers, whose own struggles with bullies had similar outcomes.

For the rest of the year I avoided the candy store, ashamed but not knowing why, the nameless owners' kindness like a weight, unrelieved by the fact that Lulu never bothered me again.

~

One day I came home from school and Mami's hair was in curlers. "Do you have much homework?" Mami asked as she set a cup of coffee in front of me.

"I have to study for final exams."

"We should buy you a graduation dress."

I'd given up on anyone noticing that in less than a month I'd be graduating from junior high school. My fifteenth birthday came and went during the sad times, and it seemed that the same would be true for the last day of school.

"Can we come?" Edna asked.

"No. You stay here with Tata, we won't be long." Before Francisco's death, Edna and Raymond would have argued, cried, offered to be the best children in the universe if Mami took them along. But now they just looked disappointed.

"I'll change." I ran into the front room where two bunk beds, Franky's crib, and Tata's cot were lined up in rows. The windows that looked out on the street were open. Delsa, Norma, and Alicia were on the sidewalk jumping double dutch.

Tata lay on her bed, cuddling Franky, and when I came in, she looked up with a smile. I grabbed a dress from one of the hooks Mami had screwed into the wall because the apartment had no closets. With two towels pinched under the mattress of the top bunk I created a private space in which to change out of my school clothes and put on the cotton dress.

Mami was in her room, which served as a passage between the front room and the kitchen. Her bed was pressed against the corner under a window that opened to a dark air vent. Four mismatched dressers, with a drawer for each of us and a couple for Mami, lined the walls. She stood in front of the one with a mirror above it combing out her curls.

"We'll be back in a couple of hours," she told Tata as we went out. Edna and Raymond watched us wistfully.

"Bring us candy," Raymond begged as Mami shut the door.

Delsa, Norma, and Alicia stopped jumping rope when we came down the front stoop. Before they could ask where we were going, Mami scanned the street.

"Where's your brother?"

"He went to the corner," Alicia answered.

"What corner, who said he could wander off like that?"

"Héctor always does that, Mami. He goes off whenever he wants. . . ." Norma nudged Delsa before she could say more. "He'll be back soon," Delsa continued in a subdued voice.

"Don't stay out here too long," Mami warned, and walked toward Broadway.

"Where are you going?" Alicia called.

"To buy me a graduation dress," I called back, pleased to see my sisters' envious expressions. I hurried after Mami, whose decisive steps had already brought her to the corner.

It was the beginning of the month, when the welfare and social security checks came in the mail. Broadway was crowded with harried shoppers going in and out of stores, or standing at the bus stops with bulging bags at their sides. Overhead, the elevated train rattled by every few minutes, screeched to a stop at the station on Flushing Avenue. The beams holding up the train tracks divided the street into four lanes, the center two, where traffic moved in both directions, and the outside lanes for local traffic, always congested with double-parked cars, slow buses, and delivery trucks.

I followed Mami into the check-cashing office, a storefront with a huge sign above the door and a group of men loitering on the sidewalk. This time of the month, they were always there, waiting for their women to hand them money from the checks they'd cashed. One kissed and hugged the woman when she gave him money. Another took it without looking at her, stashed the bills in a pocket, and walked away without so much as a thank you. A third started arguing with the woman the minute she came out. She said she needed the money to feed the kids and to pay the rent and electricity. But he wrested it from her, counted it, and took off, leaving her in tears and cursing him while passersby walked a wide circle around her.

Inside, there were two long lines in front of two men behind thick glass. The cashiers wore white shirts, black pants with suspenders, and skullcaps. They had ringlets on either side of their face, like the vendors at the *marketa* and at the used furniture stores on Graham Avenue.

We stood on line behind a skinny woman struggling with a child. The little girl screamed and kicked, scratched at the hand that held her tightly by the wrist. Those waiting stared at them, moved away without relinquishing their place on line. The woman yelled at the little girl to stop it, stop it, stop it, yanked her hand, smacked her, which made the child cry harder, fight more. The woman looked up at everyone staring, her eyes defying us to say something, and we shifted our gaze elsewhere. Inside their cages, the cashiers were the only ones who dared look back at her, their contempt directed at her, at the child, at all of us waiting on line.

When our turn came, Mami pulled a ballpoint pen from her purse and signed the welfare check in front of the cashier. She didn't look at the man insulated behind the plate glass, and he didn't look at her. Their transaction was silent, the air heavy with her shame and his disdain for people like us: female, dark-skinned, on welfare.

Before we stepped outside, Mami put her cash in her wallet, stashed it deep inside the purse she held tightly against her side, and led me out. The men glanced up expectantly and then turned from us, annoyed when neither of us was the woman they waited for.

"Which store are we going to?" I asked Mami as she led me past.

"That one." She glanced across the avenue, toward Dolores's Ladies Shoppé, where on the way home from school earlier that week, I had spotted the perfect thing in the window, a yellow sleeveless dress with a full skirt and a wide sash at the waist.

"Does my dress have to be black, or can I get a color?"

She looked at me quizzically as we crossed the street, didn't answer until we were on the other side. "You can wear any color you like."

My sigh of relief brought a smile to her lips, and she put her hand on my shoulder as we entered Dolores's Ladies Shoppé, where my dress waited, yellow as lemon peel, its bodice and skirt made of lace, the sash of nylon organza tied into a bow at the back.

"It makes you look jaundiced," Mami said when I tried it on.

I looked in the full-length mirror, at the golden glow on my brown arms and legs, at the light the dress reflected on my face. "I think it looks nice on me."

"Maybe she would like this baby blue one," Dolores rummaged through the clear plastic bags that encased every garment hanging along the walls of her cramped storefront.

"She doesn't like baby blue," Mami said, as she joined Dolores in her search through the plastic bags.

I narrowed my eyes to get a different view in the mirror, tried to see myself as a stranger might, and saw a young woman with dark brown hair teased into a flip, dark eyes with blue eye shadow on the lids and black liner all around ending in a tail at the corners. On my lips, pink frosted lipstick so pale that my lips looked white. On my feet, spiked heels with pointy toes. I looked like one of the Chiffons, the girl group that sang "He's So Fine." Opening my eyes fully, I saw the way I really looked, with shoulder-length hair in a loose ponytail, no makeup, brown loafers with knee socks.

"Here's one," Mami said. "It's more your color." She held up a navy blue dress with a square neckline, three-quarter sleeves, a dropped waist. It was like the dresses she always bought for me, simple and modest, not like the bold ones American girls wore.

I squinted into the mirror again. "I like this one." I sensed both of us brace for an argument. "It's my graduation, I should wear something dressy." I turned my back on her.

Mami stiffened, but she wouldn't make a scene before Dolores, who lingered near us holding two plastic bags with dresses as conservative and dull as the one Mami held. The yellow dress was luminous, made me feel special and pretty.

"You said I could wear any color," I reminded Mami, whose shapeless black dress hung from her shoulders unadorned, skimming her bust and hips without accentuating their fullness. Her black clothes, her belly still swollen from childbirth, her legs striped with varicose veins made her appear solid and heavy, earthbound.

The neckline of my yellow dress was cut above the gentle bumps of my growing breasts. The sash tied around a skinny waist, and the full skirt, made fuller by a built-in crinoline, appeared to lift me off my feet, off the dirty, scratchy rug in front of the narrow mirror in Dolores's Ladies Shoppé. Standing next to each other, Mami and I looked like darkest night next to brightest morning, each determined to get her way, knowing one would have to cede to the other, waiting until the last possible moment of uncertainty before she surrendered.

"Fine, take the yellow dress," she sighed, her voice brittle, exhausted, sad.

~⌒

"I don't know what's with you," Mami muttered as we walked back to Ellery Street. "You've changed."

I hugged the plastic bag with my yellow dress. "I'm getting older, Mami." I chuckled, to make light of it, so she wouldn't accuse me of talking back.

"Older, yes," she continued, unappeased. "And stubborn, and disrespectful." She looked at me from the corner of her eye. "Don't think just because you're going to that school for *blanquitos* I'm going to put up with any *pocavergüenzas* from you." She turned the corner, and I dawdled after, trapped between thoughts.

When Mami and I went to the welfare or unemployment office, a box in the forms asked us to identify our race: White, Black, Other. Technically, Mami was white. Her skin was creamy beige, lacked the warm brown tones her children with Papi had inherited. My memory of my paternal grandparents was that they were white, but Papi and some of his sisters and brothers were dark brown, evoking a not-too-distant African ancestor. Franky, Mami's son with Francisco, was lighter-skinned than the seven older brothers and sisters. He had his father's pale complexion, dark eyes and hair.

When I had to indicate my race, I always marked "Other,"

because neither black nor white was appropriate. Pretending to be white when I was clearly not was wrong. If I could "pass," which I couldn't, there was always the question Puerto Ricans asked when someone became too arrogant about the value of their white skin: "Y *tu abuela, ¿donde está?*" Asking "Where is your grandmother?" implied that in Puerto Rico no one really knew the total racial picture and claims of racial purity were suspect.

I was not oblivious to race in Puerto Rico. I'd noticed that white skin was coveted by those who didn't have it and that those who did looked down on those who didn't. Light-skinned babies in a family were doted on more than dark ones. "Good" hair was straight, not kinky, and much more desirable than the tightly coiled strands of "bad" hair, which at its tightest was called *pasitas*, raisins. Blue or green eyes proclaimed whiteness, even when surrounded by dark skin.

I was neither black nor white; I was *trigueña*, wheat-colored. I had "good" hair, and my features were neither African nor European but a combination of both. In Puerto Rican schools I had not stood out because of the color of my skin or my features. I never had either the darkest or the lightest skin in a room. But when we lived in the city, I was teased for being a *jíbara* from the country. When in the country, my city experience made me suspicious to others.

At junior high schools 49 and 33 in Brooklyn, I was a recently arrived Puerto Rican in a school where most students were Puerto Rican, Italian, or black. I stood apart with the other recent arrivals because of my struggle to speak English. The few Americans in our schools, who were all white-skinned, lived and moved in their own neighborhoods and groups, closed to the rest of us.

When Mami accused me of wanting to go to a school for *blanquitos*, she guessed that most of the people at Performing Arts would be white and, therefore, richer than we were. In Puerto Rico, as in the United States, whiteness meant economic advantage, and when Mami talked about *los blanquitos*, she referred to people of superior social status more than to skin color.

The implication that I was reaching higher than I ought to by going to Performing Arts stung, but I wasn't about to defend myself to Mami. Any response to her assessment of me and what I wanted to do with my life would have confirmed her conclusions that I'd changed since we came to the United States. I had become too independent, she claimed, too bent on my own way, too demanding. All the attention around my application to Performing Arts High School had gone to my head. I had become ambitious and hard to please, always wanting more than I had or was entitled to.

She was right. I had changed. Some nights I lay in bed next to my sister wondering if she was changing too, if the Delsa in Brooklyn was different from the Delsa in Puerto Rico. Other than her growing ease with English, Delsa was the same high-strung, responsible, hardworking girl she'd always been. *She* wasn't applying to a high school in Manhattan. She was going to Eli Whitney to study nursing, a real profession that would bring her a good salary and steady employment. If I thought about it, none of my sisters or brothers seemed to feel the dissatisfaction with their lives that I felt.

I wanted a different life from the one I had. I wanted my own bed in my own room. I wanted to be able to take a bath without having to shoo the whole family out of the kitchen. I wanted books without a date due. I wanted pretty clothes that I chose for myself. I wanted to wear makeup and do my hair and teeter on high heels. I wanted my own radio so that I could listen to La Lupe on the Spanish station or Cousin Brucie's Top 40 countdown on the American one. I wanted to be able to buy a Pepsi or a Baby Ruth any time I craved one. In Puerto Rico I hadn't wanted any of those things. In Puerto Rico, I didn't know they were within my reach. But in Brooklyn every day was filled with want, even though Mami made sure we had everything we needed. Yes, I had changed. And it wasn't for the better. Every time Mami said I had changed, it was because I'd done something wrong. I defied her, or was disrespectful, or didn't like the same things as before. When she said I had changed, she meant I was becoming Americanized, that I thought I deserved more and was better than everyone else, better than her. She looked at me resentfully, as if I had betrayed her, as if I could help who I was becoming, as if I knew.

"What's a Cleopatra dress?"

In the summer of 1963 we moved again, to an apartment above a drugstore on the third story of a building on busy Pitkin Avenue. Delsa and I shared a room that faced the street and, across the way, a Woolworth's and a Thom McAnn shoe store.

Unlike other places we'd lived in Brooklyn, no children played on Pitkin Avenue after school. It was a commercial block with stores crammed against each other, windows plastered with SALE signs and seasonal decorations displayed year after year by owners who watched their Puerto Rican and black customers with mistrust and resentment. Once the stores closed, the street fell asleep; traffic slowed; the buses that ran up and down Pitkin Avenue and Rockaway Boulevard chugged along, slow and easy, as if conserving energy for the frantic days.

Our welfare worker told Mami she was eligible for survivor benefits. Since Mami and Francisco hadn't been married, there was a lot of paperwork that I had to interpret and fill out. I was now better at telling Mami's story, at conveying her frustration at being *leyof* when she wanted to work, but it was a challenge to calm my nerves so that my English wouldn't flee the minute I had to speak. Many visits and interviews later, our claim was approved. Once confirmed, however, welfare reduced Mami's AFDC allotment, so the Social Security didn't help much.

After weeks of looking, Mami found a job in Manhattan. The sadness didn't leave her when she went to work. Her grief was like a transparent box that allowed her to sew bras in the factory, to talk to us, to cook and shop, but held her in, untouchable. Mornings, her muffled movements about the apartment woke me as she got ready for work. She woke up early, showered and put on a simple black shift or a black blouse and skirt. She brushed her black hair into a tight bun, scrubbed her face, powdered her nose and forehead. She never ate breakfast, not so much as a cup of coffee. She tiptoed down the wooden stairs, which creaked in spite of her efforts.

I stuck my head out of the window. The sidewalks were empty, the darkness broken by rings of light under the street lamps. Mami looked left, then right, before stepping onto the street. She stiffened her back, raised her chin, pulled her purse closer to her side, and walked to the corner, where she turned right toward the train station. Her shadowy figure pushed through the darkness without a backward or sideways glance, gaze fixed on a point somewhere in front of her. She looked so sad and alone that I worried she'd disappear into the city and never come back. As she turned the corner, her steps faded into the sounds of Brooklyn. I tried to still the fear that made my head pound with a thousand frightening scenarios. She constantly warned us of all the something that could happen to us. But what if *algo* happened to her? Was she as afraid for herself as she was for us?

Over the jagged horizon, the sun punctured through thin, wispy clouds that turned pink, then melted into yellow. A soft roar accompanied the dawn, a low growl that grew louder as the city awoke. Within minutes, people hurried up and down the street, across the avenues, into and out of stores, their staccato steps muted by the first horns, distant sirens, muffled radios.

School wouldn't start for weeks. The days dragged long and humid, each like the other except for weekends, when Mami was home and we did errands or visited relatives.

The highlight of the week was *la compra*, the Saturday grocery shopping. When we were on welfare, *la compra* took under an hour and was dragged home in one shopping cart filled with the staples of our diet: huge sacks of white rice, beans, cans of tomato sauce, onions, garlic, green peppers, fresh oregano, and *recao* for the *sofrito*. Mami also bought a couple of cans of Bustelo, the only Puerto Rican–style coffee we could find in New York, not as nutty-sweet as what we could get on the island; a five-pound bag of sugar; and evaporated or powdered milk for when there was no money to buy it fresh.

But when Mami worked, my sisters and brothers and I argued about who'd help her with *la compra*, because there would be cornflakes and fresh milk, Franco-American spaghetti, Chef Boy-ardee ravioli, and other canned American food. When Mami worked, there was Nestlé Quick, *queso del país* with guava paste, pork chops, hard salami on Ritz crackers, Cheez Whiz on Export sodas, beef stew with chunks of pumpkin and *yautías*, maybe a *pernil*. Mami was proud that even when things were bad, we never went hungry. "There's always bread and milk in the house," she said, "and there's always a cup of rice and a handful of beans."

But we didn't want rice and beans, milk and bread. We wanted Ring Dings and Yodels, pizza, Coca-Cola, Frosted Flakes, Jell-o, foods we never had in Puerto Rico and only got in Brooklyn when there was enough money or when the relatives gave us change for being well behaved during their visits. When we were on welfare, we talked about what we'd buy when we grew up and had jobs and could spend our money any way we liked.

"I'm going to buy the factory where they make Sno-Balls," Alicia said, and we tongued our lips, anticipating the sweet, coco-nutty, chocolatey, creamy-centered cakes sold in pairs that looked like flaky breasts under cellophane.

"I'll open a candy store so that I can eat Baby Ruths and Almond Joys any time I like," Raymond countered, and we agreed that a candy store with a variety of sweets was much better than a whole factory with only one kind.

When Mami worked and we helped her with *la compra*, we zigzagged up and down the market aisles looking for what new and tasty confection we might persuade her to buy. At home we savored every morsel, licked our fingers to get the last taste of sweet from the tips, drained the bottle of soda until there was no more of the fizzy, tickly liquid, until the hard, smooth glass pressed firmly against our tongues.

～◯

Now that Tata lived with us again, Tío Chico found a room in the Bowery. We'd heard that's where bums lived, but Mami insisted Tío Chico wasn't a bum. "He drinks too much sometimes," she said, "but he works and takes care of himself."

No, Tío Chico didn't smell like the bums we passed on the side streets branching from Pitkin Avenue. He was clean, even if his clothes were rumpled, the collars of his shirts frayed, the soles of his shoes worn. He shaved at least every other day. When he didn't, black and white stubble grew around and inside the deep creases that ran from his nostrils to the corners of his lips. He had brown eyes like Tata's and a well-formed nose, long but not grotesque, well shaped. And he had beautiful, long-fingered, graceful hands.

Once he touched my left breast with those long fingers, gripped the nipple and pinched it. He'd been watching me comb my hair, and when Tata called him to the kitchen, I didn't move when he went past me, and he reached across and squeezed my breast. "Don't tell anyone," he muttered into my ear. On the way back, he dropped a dollar in front of me.

I could have told Mami what he'd done, could have used the dollar as evidence, but I didn't. I spent it on an ice cream sundae and told myself he was drunk. From then on, I avoided him whenever he came around, disappeared into another room, hid in the bathroom, or sat as far away from him as possible when he came to visit. His caramel, red-streaked eyes followed me when I walked around the apartment. I avoided his gaze, aware that we shared a shameful secret, weighing whether the blame should fall heavier on him who touched me, or on me who let him do it.

Now that Mami was working again, she had a telephone installed. "With you going to the city every day," she reasoned, "we need a phone so you can call if you get lost or *algo*."

Evenings we sat around the kitchen table discussing the "*algos*" that could happen. They appeared in daily newspaper reports of the crimes committed in the city, illustrated with grainy black-and-white photographs that electrified the imagination. We reenacted the more colorful events of the day, adding details not reported, but which we were sure existed. The day a suspected drug dealer was found hanged in his jail cell, Héctor unhooked his belt, tied it loosely around his neck, held it up, stuck his tongue out, crossed his eyes, and made hacking noises as his body shook in paroxysms that made us laugh until our eyes teared. When we enjoyed ourselves too much at the expense of the dead, maimed, or victimized, Mami stopped our parodies. "That poor man's mother," she'd sigh. Or, "How she must have suffered before he killed her." Her comments shamed us for a moment, but they didn't stop us from doing the same thing again the next day.

When crime threatened near, however, when Don Julio was mugged, or when our neighbor Minga was pushed into traffic and her handbag snatched, we didn't laugh. We huddled closer to Mami and to each other in speechless fear, visualizing the dangers outside our door, certain that the only safe place in the world was the four walls that enclosed us, small and vulnerable, in our mother's shadow.

Performing Arts High School was organized by departments: Dance, Drama, and Music. It was possible to tell students' majors by looking at them. The dancers had muscular calves and barely touched the floor when they walked, their feet turned out from their hips like the hands of a clock at twenty past eight. The musicians carried black cases in a variety of shapes, drummed their fingers during academics, listened intently to the silliest prattle. The drama students were the worst listeners but the best talkers. I had the impression, when talking to other drama students, that during their brief silences they were just waiting their turn to hear themselves speak.

We were assigned homerooms, each divided roughly equally among music, dance, and drama students. Our day was split between our majors and academic classes. We had to maintain a high average in both, or we'd be asked to transfer elsewhere. Mrs. Schein, my homeroom teacher, congratulated us for our success in a process she said was highly competitive. "You demonstrate artistic as well as academic potential. By admitting you to Performing Arts High School, we're showing our faith in you as artists and as scholars."

I was flattered and inspired by her words, most of which I understood because she spoke in a deep, modulated voice, every word enunciated clearly.

"There is a dress code," she informed us. Boys were not allowed to wear jeans to school, and girls could not wear pants.

"What if it's a really cold day?" asked a girl with ratted hair and more makeup than the teacher.

"You may wear pants under your skirts, but in school you must take them off and wear a skirt or dress." Muted protests followed, but faded as Mrs. Schein continued. "You may not leave the school wearing theatrical makeup. It's unprofessional."

Professionalism was an important concept at Performing Arts. Most of the teachers were working actors, dancers, and musicians. They took themselves seriously as artists and expected us to do the same. "You have a gift," they each said at different times, "and it is our job to help you develop your talents, but it is also our responsibility to prepare you for the real world."

None of us, they stressed, should expect to become overnight successes. It would take an average of ten years after we graduated from high school for our talents to be fully developed and recognized in "the business," and at least that long before we could make a living from our art.

The ten-year wait depressed me. How could I tell Mami that I faced three years of high school and ten years of struggle before I could support myself? I expected that, upon graduation from Performing Arts, I'd get a job as an actress and earn enough to help Mami. But according to the teachers, graduating from Performing Arts was only the beginning.

"The only people who make it," they never let us forget, "are those committed to their art, willing to sacrifice for the privilege of performing for an audience. You can expect to be 'starving artists' for a while before you're discovered."

When I told her what the teachers said, Mami was horrified. "I'm not working this hard to send you to a fancy school so you can starve," she warned. We both envisioned legions of actors, dancers, and musicians filling out forms at the welfare office as we'd done so often.

"I don't care what *monerías* they teach you at that school," Mami made clear. "As soon as you graduate, you better get a job."

⌒⌒

We drama students were required to study dance so that we could develop a sense of how our bodies moved in space and prepare ourselves should we ever, in spite of our dramatic aspirations, get work in a musical. Although the school had high-ceilinged, wood-floored, well-lit, mirrored dance studios, they were reserved for dance majors. Actors danced in the lunchroom. The benches on the tables collapsed into the tops, and these were then pushed to one end of the room and stacked, leaving the tiled floor free. If we danced after the lunch period, we sometimes had to sweep crumbs off the floor.

It was a good thing that the lunchroom had no mirrors, for most of us weren't used to the outfits required for dance classes.

Girls wore black footless tights, a black scoop-necked leotard, and a dance skirt that had to cover us to midthigh. We danced barefoot, as did the boys, who wore black tights and a white T-shirt. The first day, we skulked into the lunchroom, the boys with hands crossed in front of the bulge enhanced by the required "dance belt," we girls hunched over our breasts, hugging ourselves.

Our dance teacher, Miss Lang, led us through what was for many our first formal dance class. Gawky and uncoordinated, we giggled as she demonstrated how to leap across the floor, toes pointed, head up, back straight. "Right foot out, left arm up," she sang, as she beat a rhythm on her hand drum that most of us defied with ungainly hops and turns. At the first class, it was clear that we needed to develop muscles we didn't know existed before we could execute graceful leaps or pirouettes that wouldn't land us sprawled on our behinds. The following week, and for many weeks thereafter, Miss Lang's dance class took place mostly on the floor, where she coached us through rigorous stretches that left us pained and sweaty. Students grumbled that we were actors, not dancers, and that we shouldn't have to take that stupid class, but I loved dance. I loved the open space before me in the lunchroom/studio. I loved the weightless feeling as I leaped across the floor. I welcomed the dull aches after class, the stretched muscles that vibrated for hours, the rush of blood to my face, arms, and legs. It was the only time I was warm, the only time in the Brooklyn winters when my body moved the way I remembered it moving in Puerto Rico — free, open to possibilities, unafraid.

〜

Most of my classmates were New Yorkers born and raised who spoke with the distinctive accent of the neighborhood where they'd grown up. Our teachers claimed they could tell what borough we came from simply by listening to us speak. In Brooklyn, for example, "I am" sounded like "Oyem," "here" sounded like "heah," "bathroom" was "batrum," and "in there" was "innair." I spoke

Brooklyn English with a Puerto Rican accent, a variation in a place where the goal was to get us to speak eastern standard speech.

Accent eradication was important, we were told, to widen the range of parts we could play. An actor must be versatile enough to change the way he or she spoke to fit the character being played. Standard speech laid the foundation for other accents, including, if necessary, the one we had when we first walked through the doors of Performing Arts High School.

My voice and diction teacher was King Wehrle from Kansas.

"You need a name that stands out," he told us when asked whether he was born King. "I changed mine when I came to New York."

He listed famous actors who had traded in their unimpressive names for the ones everyone remembered: Archibald Leish/Cary Grant; Eunice Quedens/Eve Arden; Betty Joan Perske/Lauren Bacall; Frances Gumm/Judy Garland.

"Do you believe a guy named Marion Morrison could get a part as a cowboy in the movies?" Mr. Wehrle asked. "No. He had to become John Wayne!"

When considering a change, Mr. Wehrle suggested we pick names with few letters, easy to fit on a marquee, easy to remember, and American, not foreign. "Anne Bancroft," he said, "not Anna Maria Italiano. Tony Curtis, not Bernard Schwartz. Kirk Douglas," he intoned in his most distinguished announcer's voice, "not Issur Danielovich."

So, in addition to having to wait ten years after graduation to make a living in my art, I also had to find a new name, since Esmeralda Santiago was clearly too long to fit on a marquee, hard to remember, and definitely foreign.

~○

If I looked at Performing Arts strictly along racial lines, Mami was right; it was a school where almost all the students and teachers were white. In my tenth-grade class there were 126 students: four-teen black, three Puerto Rican, and two Asian. Two of the twenty-four teachers in the arts majors and two of the twenty-three academic subject teachers were black.

But as I walked the wide halls of Performing Arts High School, what I saw was not a school for *blanquitos*. Although it was true that those of us with dark skins were in the minority, the hierarchies set up along racial lines that I'd come to accept in junior high school weren't as marked. At Performing Arts, status was determined by talent. The elite of the school were the students who played the lead roles in scenes, or solo instruments in chamber concerts, or danced a solo or virtuoso pas de deux. The rest of us, whose talent had yet to develop, watched the stars of the school with a mixture of awe and envy. *They* wouldn't have to wait ten years to "make it" in "the business."

I recognized and accepted the hierarchy based on talent. It was fair, unlike those set up along racial lines. But there was another distinction among the students — more subtle, though not invisible. I was keenly aware of being a poor kid in a school where many were rich. In Brooklyn, most of my classmates came from my neighborhood and lived in similar circumstances, but Performing Arts drew from all over the city. As I talked to other students, the meagerness of my resources was made real. I knew my family was "disadvantaged"; it said so on the welfare applications. But it was at Performing Arts that I saw first hand what being "advantaged" meant.

It meant trips to Europe during vacations, extra classes on weekends with dance masters or voice coaches, plastic surgery to reduce large noses or refine broad ones. It meant tennis lessons and swim meets, choir practice, clubs, academic tutoring, dates. It meant money for lunch at the deli across the street or down the block. It meant taxis home.

Being disadvantaged meant I found my dance tights and leotard in a bin in the guidance office. It meant washing them and setting them to dry on the barely warm radiators of our apartment and wearing them damp when there was no money to pay the heating bills. It meant a pass so that I could get a free bowl of soup and half a sandwich for lunch. It meant that, if invited to a party given by a classmate, I said no, because there was no money to buy presents for rich people. It meant never inviting anyone over, because I didn't want them to see the wet diapers hanging on ropes strung from one end of the apartment to the other. Or the profusion of beds that left no space for a proper living room.

Advantaged meant being able to complain about having too many things to do, all of them fun, being unable to decide whether to sleep over at Joanie's or to take an extra dance class at Madame's. It meant that papers handed in to the teacher were typed on crisp white pages, not handwritten with a cheap ballpoint pen on blue-lined notebook paper from Woolworth's. The advantage was not talent, nor skin color, it was money, and those of us who were disadvantaged had little or none.

I wasn't the only poor kid at Performing Arts — or in my class. There were many of us. We found each other and hovered on the fringes of the lucky few whose Monday reports of fun-filled weekends intensified our sense that our talent had to take us a long way, a very long way indeed, from where we were.

〜

We learned to act by working on improvisations and scenes from well-known plays. For improvisations, the teacher set up situations, then let us work them in front of the whole class or in small groups. At any time, the dynamics could change; the teacher might send in another actor with different motivations or a conflicting situation right in the middle of our improvisation. Or a loud noise might intrude, or the situation might change naturally as the scene evolved. Besides developing our ability to think fast and concentrate, improvisations helped us work through the nuts and bolts of a scene by allowing us to discover a character's motivations and subtexts to the dialogue.

For scene work we were paired with partners. Teachers assigned plays and scenes appropriate to our talent and personalities, but they avoided typecasting, which was no challenge to the actor. For each scene we prepared "sides," half-page scripts with one side for our lines and cues written in block letters and the facing page for notes about meaningful subtext, stage directions, or motivation.

We didn't have sets. Wooden boxes with splintery corners created the illusion of a southern kitchen or a Roman Senate, depending on whether we were playing a scene from *Member of the Wedding* or *Julius Caesar.* The rehearsal space was the Basement, actually the ground floor of the school, with lockers at one end and entrance doors and stairways leading up on the other. We staked out areas of the Basement, hoarded boxes to create our set, and worked independently, while the teacher roamed from one group to another watching, questioning motivation, suggesting other ways to block the scene. At the end of class, we might be asked to perform our work-in-progress in front of the group. One-piece school desks/chairs were arranged in a semicircle so that everyone had a front row seat. Sometimes we were asked to perform in gibberish, to demonstrate that acting was more than parroting words from a page, that it conveyed a human experience independent of language.

My first scene was in act 1, scene 1 of George Bernard Shaw's *Caesar and Cleopatra.* I was paired with Roman-nosed Harvey, who was cast as Julius Caesar to my Cleopatra.

I was thrilled. That summer I'd read mostly biographies. Cleopatra was one of my favorite historical figures, and I'd acquired a lot of information about who she was, what her motivations might have been, what she looked like. As actors, we researched the characters we played, the fictional as well as the historical ones, on the theory that the more we knew about them, the better we could bring them to life on the stage.

I loved the preparation to act. I loved reading the entire play, even if I performed only a short scene from it. I loved figuring out the character beyond what the playwright had written. I loved designing a costume and scrounging at home for materials from which to make it, since the school didn't provide wardrobe except for the performances at the end of the year.

I found a yellow tablecloth Mami had bought at the thrift shop. "Can I use this?"

"For what?"

"To make a Cleopatra dress."

"What's a Cleopatra dress?" She pursed her lips, a sign she thought I was asking for a fashion I wasn't allowed to wear.

"Cleopatra was an Egyptian queen," I explained. "She lived thousands of years ago, and she wore tight dresses."

"Why do you have to dress like her?" She took the tablecloth from my hand and examined it.

"It's homework. I have to dress like the people in the plays."

"In a tablecloth?"

"I told you, I'm making a dress out of it."

"It's got an *achiote* stain," she pointed out.

"That's why you might not want it anymore."

"I'll make it for you," she offered, still suspicious. I envisioned Mami's idea of a Cleopatra dress, nothing like what I imagined.

"We're supposed to make it ourselves," I lied.

"All right," she conceded, "but let me see it before you finish, in case you need any help." She wanted to make sure it wouldn't be too revealing.

I cut and sewed a tubelike dress so tight it required that I walk sideways, like an Egyptian hieroglyphic figure.

"*Ay, mi Dios,*" Mami gasped when she saw it.

"You look like a banana," Edna volunteered.

"Shut up," I screamed.

"Shut up yourself."

"You're not wearing that in public," Mami said.

"It's only in school, Mami, for a scene in a play. I'll show you a picture." I minced to the bedroom, followed by my sisters' and brothers' giggles. To pick up the costume book I'd left on the floor,

I had to bend slowly from the knees. I took tiny steps back and opened the book. "Look, these people are Egyptian. See how they wear their clothes close to their bodies?"

Edna, Delsa, and Norma looked over Mami's shoulder at the picture, then at my dress.

"They didn't walk very far, did they?" laughed Norma. I sent her a hateful look, and she stuck out her tongue.

Mami studied the illustration, which showed the dresses to be transparent, which the damask wasn't. "I'm supposed to make it look like what they really wore." I tried not to sound desperate. "I'll only wear it in the classroom, in front of other students and the teacher."

"What are *they* wearing?"

I ignored her sarcasm. "My partner made a costume from a sheet, and another girl made hers from a drape." If I kept to the materials, maybe Mami wouldn't focus on the fit. "We'll be graded," I lied, "on how much our costumes look like the real thing."

"At least you can't see through it," Edna offered.

"Not that she has anything to show," Delsa snorted and slapped Norma five.

"You'll have to let it out," Mami said. "The seams are straining."

"Okay." I wouldn't do a thing to the dress. There wasn't enough fabric to let out, and Mami would never see me in it, as I'd wear it only in school, as Cleopatra. I looked in the small oval mirror over the dresser in the room I shared with Delsa. She was right, there wasn't much for me to show. Still, I didn't look like a banana. Bananas don't have breasts, and I did, even if my *nalgas* were flat and I had no hips. I raised my hands in a posture like the hieroglyph pictures I'd seen, and thought I looked pretty close to what Cleopatra might have looked like. At fifteen, Cleopatra was soon to be queen of Egypt, while I had to argue with my mother over every little thing. I wondered what it was like not to have a mother, and a chill raced up from my toes to my head. I had to walk to the door and peek out to make sure Mami was still there before I could be warm again.

⌒──◦

The drama department taught the Method developed by Stanislavsky in his book *An Actor Prepares*. Method actors explored their deepest selves for the emotional truth that informed the moment lived on stage.

I refused to venture into my deepest self, to reveal my feelings, to examine my true emotions publicly. If I did, everyone would know I was illegitimate, that I shared a bed with my sister, that we were on welfare. The result was that I was accused by my peers of "indicating," the worst sin a Method actor can commit on stage. To "indicate" meant to pretend to be in the moment by going through the motions, rather than to actually live it.

It was humiliating not to be a good enough actress to fool my teachers and fellow students, but I simply couldn't abandon myself to the craft. I didn't have the skills to act while acting. Because the minute I left the dark, crowded apartment where I lived, I was in performance, pretending to be someone I wasn't. I resisted the Method's insistence on truth as I used it to create a simulated reality. One in which I spoke fluent English, felt at home in the harsh streets of New York, absorbed urban American culture without question as I silently grieved the dissolution of the other me, the Spanish-speaking, Puerto Rican girl most at home in a dusty, tropical dirt road. I created a character that evolved as the extended improvisation of my life unfolded, a protagonist as cheerful and carefree as my comic book friends Betty and Veronica, Archie, Reggie, and Jughead.

"Don't you want to sound Puerto Rican?"

One day I returned from the library to find a woman and a girl about my age surrounded by my sisters and brothers, sipping coffee and chewing cake around the kitchen table.

"Guess who this is?" Mami grinned.

The girl eyed me from under mascaraed lashes; and the woman, petite, corseted and skillfully made up, sized me up and found me deficient. I had no idea who they were and didn't care. "Friends from the factory?" I suggested, and Mami laughed.

"This is your sister Margie."

My mouth dropped in surprise, and I quickly closed it, because they laughed. Margie; her mother, Provi; my sisters and brothers, who were bunched on the side of the table closest to Margie, all seemed to think it was hilarious that I didn't recognize someone I didn't remember meeting.

"She's got the most expressive face," Provi giggled, and my cheeks burned. Mami crinkled her eyes at me and tipped her head toward Margie and Provi. I touched each one's shoulders with my fingertips, leaving lots of space between us, and kissed them lightly on the right cheek.

Provi had been my father's "wife" before he met my mother. I'd expected Margie to look like our father, with his high forehead, prominent cheekbones, broad nose, full lips. I'd expected his coloring, but she was lighter and looked more like my sister Norma, with the same tightly curled auburn hair, slanted brown eyes, regal bearing.

75

Mami served me coffee and cake. "Provi brought it from a bakery near her apartment in Manhattan." It sounded like a warning, but when I looked up, Mami's back was to me as she refilled her coffee cup.

Margie was uncomfortable at our table, her back to the wall, as my sisters and brothers jostled and pushed one another to stand the closest to her. Héctor brought out his entire bottle cap collection, and Edna drew flowers and birds and offered them for Margie's approval. Every once in a while, Margie smiled at me, and I wished we could go somewhere to talk. But there was no other place, no living room, no yard, no room that wasn't filled with beds or people. I was embarrassed and tried to read Mami's feelings. But she was serene, didn't seem to notice that Provi's eyes darted from the sink stacked with clean but battered pots and pans to the next room, where a rope was strung from the window to the door jamb. Under it, water dripped onto the dull linoleum from the diapers hung up to dry. Every once in a while, Delsa grabbed the mop, soaked up the puddles, then pushed her way back to Margie's side.

I was annoyed at Mami's composure. She should have been as ashamed as I felt. As soon as the thought surfaced, I banished it. Mami worked hard for us, and while I had less than I wanted, as the eldest I got more than my younger sisters and brothers. When they complained that Mami favored me, I argued that she didn't; but inside I knew she did, as did Tata. I settled back on my chair, seething, alternating shame with guilt, envious of Margie's fashionable clothes; her rolled, teased, sprayed hair; her meticulous makeup; the charm bracelet that tinkled on her right wrist, the Timex on her left. At the same time I longed to talk to her, to find out if she was in touch with Papi, if it hurt her when he remarried, if she remembered our grandmother, whom, Provi said, I resembled.

Mami spoke with pride about how much English we'd learned in a scant two years, about the school I attended, about how sweet-natured baby Franky was, about her job as a Merrow sewing machine operator in a Maidenform factory. The two of them talked as if they were long-lost friends, when in fact for years Mami had referred to Provi as "that woman" and Provi must have had a few names for Mami when she wasn't sitting at our kitchen table drinking coffee and delicately chewing the too-sweet cake she'd brought.

Provi boasted about their apartment in Manhattan, where, she pointed out, Margie had her own room. About how Margie was one of the top students in her school, about how they'd lived in the United States so long, they were forgetting their Spanish while still learning English.

"And then what do we do?" she cackled. "We'll be mute, with nothing to say!" Mami and I exchanged a look, remembering our far-from-speechless La Muda.

I interpreted Provi's friendliness as an act. Used to the drama student's obsession with finding subtext in dialogue, I listened to Provi chatter but heard the unspoken "You weren't woman enough to hold on to Pablo," while Mami's unsaid "I had him for fourteen years, four times longer than you did" heated the air.

I imagined Provi was glad Mami was widowed, saw Francisco's death as a punishment for the wrong I guessed Mami had done her. Mami, younger and prettier, was, I suspected, the reason Papi had left Provi.

I sulked at my end of the table, listened to our mothers babble, aware they were still competing for my father, who wasn't there, who was married to another woman neither one of them had met. I heard nothing but criticism in Provi's remarks, only defenses in Mami's. I pitied Margie, whose shoulders slumped into the chair, as if she too was embarrassed by her mother's behavior. I resisted Provi's tight smiles and Margie's frequent attempts to make eye contact. Every second of their visit was a test we had to pass to rise to another level, but I wasn't sure what that level was, where it lay, if it existed. Margie had come too late, but I didn't know what she was late for, or whether and why I'd been waiting for her.

As Mami closed the door after them, she breathed a deep sigh. My sisters and brothers scattered to other parts of the apartment. Tata, who stayed in her room during the entire visit, stumbled into the kitchen and began chopping onions for that night's supper.

"Isn't Margie pretty?" Mami asked, not expecting an answer. Tata grumbled about "that woman." I was about to make a sarcastic remark but decided against it.

"She has nice hair," I allowed. "I like the way she lines her eyes, with the little tail at the corner," I added, to say something nice, and Mami fixed her gaze on me, as if seeing what wasn't obvious before.

"You have better hair," she said, running her fingers through it. "It's wavy, not so curly as hers. You can do more with it." She took my face in her hands, tipped it to the light. "As for her makeup, that line wouldn't look good on you. Your eyes are a completely different shape." She pushed my face to the left, to the right. "Maybe if the tail were shorter. . . . Why don't you try it?"

I dashed to the dresser where she kept the cosmetics she hadn't worn since Francisco's death. Breathless, I opened the zippered pouch. Inside, there was a mirrored plastic compact with a thin circle of pressed powder around the metal bottom, the once fluffy cotton pad flat and frayed around the edges. A smaller, round cardboard box held her powdered rouge, which leaked a fine red dust over two lipsticks and a stubby eyebrow pencil. I uncapped the point, whittled the wood with a Gem blade, and drew a curve on the back of my hand. When I tried it on my lid, the hard point slipped and left a faint ashen stripe, which I wiped with spit and toilet tissue. When I finally got it to sketch a dark line on my upper lid, I extended it to a jaunty angle, like a smile.

"What do you think?" I tried to still the thumps inside my chest that betrayed my excitement. Mami leaned against the counter, squinting as if evaluating an expensive purchase.

"It looks nice," she said. "But next time, make the tails shorter."

"Okay." Next time, she'd said. Next time! I ran back to the bathroom, erased the ends of the lines so that they didn't extend beyond the lids.

"Like this?"

"Perfect," she smiled. "That looks nice."

Tata watched from her post by the stove. "She's growing up," she said softly, and I pleaded for silence with my eyes. She turned with a grin. Mami smiled and went back to washing the rice.

In my room I stared at my reflection, fingered the thick dark lines around my eyes that made me look older, sophisticated. Delsa was in bed, wrapped in a blanket, her black curls peeking through the top.

"Quit it," she mumbled, though I hadn't made a sound. I left the room, curled up against the wall on Norma and Alicia's bed, and watched television. My eyes felt heavy, as if the black line added weight to them. During a commercial, Alicia stared hard at me, then trotted to the kitchen yelling. "Mami, Negi is wearing makeup."

"Shut up," I rushed after her and held her back.

"What's all the shouting?" Mami called.

"Negi's wearing makeup," Alicia repeated, fighting me.

"Leave your sister alone," Mami yelled, and I wasn't sure if she meant me or Alicia. "Next time I go to the drugstore," she said over her shoulder as she headed back, "I'll buy you your own pencil."

I let go of Alicia, who looked from me to Mami with a puzzled expression. She was nine, I was fifteen, and although Mami took my side in many arguments with my sisters and brothers, we both knew that something important had happened. I had stopped being a little girl because Mami wouldn't be outmothered by Provi.

⌒

It was always still dark when I left the apartment at five-thirty in the morning, my books and dance clothes in La Muda's old black leather bag. The fifteen-minute walk to the elevated train station was a gauntlet of shadows under burned-out street lamps that lengthened the distance between abandoned buildings and parked cars. I walked in the middle of the sidewalk, eyes fixed straight ahead but alert, expecting danger from any direction at any moment. Once, a rat scurried in front of me. I didn't know what to do, afraid to walk, afraid to stand in the same spot. After a few seconds, I ran past the pile of garbage into which the rat had disappeared and added "bite from a rabid rat" to the list of *"algos"* that could happen away from home.

Even at six in the morning the trains were packed, and I often stood most of the way into Manhattan. That morning, I was lucky. When the train came, I spotted a space in the two-seater bench across from the conductor's booth. I took it, careful not to disturb the woman who slept on the seat closest to the door, her gloved hands pressed against a handbag on her lap. The passengers already on the train were black and Puerto Rican, but as we moved from East New York to Brownsville into Crown Heights, Prospect Heights, and Brooklyn Heights, the people waiting at the platforms were white and older than the passengers already on board. They pushed into the subway car as everyone squeezed together to make room.

A man elbowed his way toward the hang-strap above where I sat against the wall. He set his briefcase on the floor between his legs, grabbed the hang-strap with his left hand, unbuttoned and pulled open his coat, his right hand in the pocket. I kept my eyes on my book, only dimly aware of the movement in front of me, until I realized he was leaning in so close that he blocked the light. When I looked up to ask him to move, I saw that his zipper was open and his penis dangled outside his pants, not two feet from my face. I quickly looked down at my book, too embarrassed to say or do anything. His coat formed a curtain on one side, and the wall trapped me on the other. I pretended to read while I tried to figure out what to do. I could get up and move, but my bag was under my feet, and if I bent down to reach it, I'd be dangerously close to his wan, wrinkled penis. I considered but didn't have the nerve to look him in the eye and tell him to put it back where it belonged. As we reached a station and the train slowed, he dropped his arm from the hang-strap, covered himself, and waited until the train was moving, then raised his arm so that his penis was again in my face. I felt him stare while I struggled with what to do. I could grab the penis and pull hard. I could bite it. Without touching it, I could slam the pages of my biology text around it. But I sat stony-faced and silent, pretending to read, angry that I was being such a *pendeja*, wondering what I'd done to provoke him.

Theatrical makeup was taught in a room across from the auditorium's backstage entrance. The teacher, Mrs. Bank, a no-nonsense woman with a reputation for being exacting and difficult to please, was nevertheless beloved by those students who managed to impress her with their talent. I wasn't among her favorites. I had too little range as an actress to meet her high standards.

During the first class, she gave us a list of supplies, and I had to convince Mami the expense was necessary, that makeup was a real course in which I'd be graded. She frowned at the brushes and pencils, sponges, puffs, powders, and creams that cost more than what she put on her face. But she never said I couldn't have it.

Mrs. Bank moved us quickly through the rudiments of stage makeup. We began with techniques to enhance our natural features. Boys as well as girls were taught to apply foundation, lip liner, cheek color, and mascara. We were encouraged to study our faces, to learn their contours, to examine the shapes that made up our appearance, to look at ourselves not as who we were, but as who we could become.

To this end, we were taught to alter our features. Through skillful use of highlights and shadows, we learned to narrow a broad nose and to flatten a pointy one. Eyes could be made larger, lips fuller, flat cheekbones rounded, high foreheads lowered.

I loved the class because I could apply as much makeup as I wanted and Mami couldn't complain, since I told her it was my homework to practice. I spent hours in front of the mirror making myself up to look innocent, sultry, elegant, Chinese. One of the assignments was to bring in a picture of an animal and to recreate the animal's features on our own face. At home, I made myself up as a tiger, a camel, an orangutan, then chased my sisters and brothers around the apartment, making the appropriate animal sounds, until Mami or Tata put an end to my grunts and their screams.

One of the last assignments of the semester was to make ourselves up as old people.

"Follow the natural contours of your face," Mrs. Bank instructed. "Darken the creases from your nostrils to your lips. Highlight along the edges to deepen them."

Most of us were fifteen or sixteen years old, and finding wrinkles on our faces was difficult, not because they weren't there but because we didn't want them to be.

"If you pucker your lips like this, then draw lines where the puckers are, you'll get some interesting wrinkles."

We followed her instructions, giggling as our faces aged under puffs and brushes.

"Most people have lines around their eyes," she pointed out. "Don't forget your neck and hands, they age too."

We drew liver spots on the backs of our hands. We powdered our hair to make it white. Jay applied a wart to his cheek. Elaine practiced a quiver in her voice to go with her frail, old-lady face.

At the end of the class, when Mrs. Bank asked us to evaluate the work we'd done, I looked closely at my wrinkled cheeks, at the curious eyes inside deep circles, and burst into tears.

"What's the matter?" Mrs. Bank, asked, alarmed.

"I'm an old lady," I whined in what I thought was a playful manner, to cover up my embarrassment.

Mrs. Bank smiled. "Not quite, not yet. Lucky for you, it disappears with Albolene cream."

"That's good," I giggled listlessly, "I'm too young to be old."

She moved on. I faced the mirror again and saw my grandmother, Abuela, whom I hadn't seen in three years. But if I turned to the left, there was Tata, the grandmother I lived with. It was frightening to see them both stare at me from my own face. Abuela's sad eyes, Tata's sensual mouth, Abuela's small nose, Tata's intelligent gaze. But I wouldn't admit that to Mrs. Bank or to the other students who laughed at my fear of growing old. Let them think what they will. They will never know, they can't ever understand, who I really am.

I had a secret life, one not shared with my sister, with whom I shared a bed. Or with my classmates, with whom I shared dreams of fame and fortune. Not with my mother, whose dreams were on hold since Francisco's death. My secret life was in my head, lived at night before I fell asleep, when I became someone else.

In my secret life I wasn't Esmeralda Santiago, not Negi, not a scared Puerto Rican girl, but a confident, powerful woman whose name changed as I tried to form the perfect me. Esme, I was once. Emmé, another time. Emeraude, my French class name. I tried Shirley, Sheila, Lenore, but names not based on my own didn't sound quite right. So I was Emma, Ralda, or just plain E.

In these dreams I had no family—no mother or father, no sisters or brothers, no grandmothers, no wrestling cousins, no drunk uncles, no deaf mutes. I was alone, sprung from an unnameable darkness, with no attachments, no loyalties, no responsibilities. I was educated, successful, professional. Whatever I did, I did well, with no false steps, no errors, no embarrassing mistakes that caused others to judge or to laugh at me.

I was the pilot of my own plane and flew around the world,

and everywhere I went people were happy to see me and no one asked where I was from. I was a movie star, and my character never died. I was a scientist, surrounded by test tubes and beakers, bunsen burners hissing blue flames as I received the Nobel Prize.

In my secret life I drove a convertible, and my house at the end of a long, sinuous driveway overlooked miles of green, rolling hills where it never snowed. I lived alone in my hilltop house, surrounded by books that I didn't have to return to the library. And every room was tidy, though I never cleaned.

In my secret life I wasn't Puerto Rican. I wasn't American. I wasn't anything. I spoke every language in the world, so I was never confused about what people said and could be understood by everyone. My skin was no particular color, so I didn't stand out as black, white, or brown.

I lived this secret life every night as I dozed into sleep, and every morning I resisted opening my eyes to the narrow bed in the narrow room I shared with Delsa, my chest tight with surprise and disappointment that it was all a dream.

⌒⌒⌒

"Eee, eee, eee, eee." I enunciated the vowels as Dr. Dycke, the head of the drama department, instructed. "Ay, ay, ay, ay. Eee, eee, eee, eee."

Raymond peeked around the door jamb. "What you doin'?"

"Practicing. Eee, ay, eee, ay, eee."

"Why?"

"So I can learn to speak English without an accent."

"Oh." He went away.

"Eee, eee, ay, ay, eee, eee, ay, ay."

A few minutes later Edna appeared at the door. "What you doin'?"

"Practicing. Eee. Eee. Eee."

"Practicing what?"

"Ask Raymond!" I closed the door on her face. "Ay. Ay. Ay.

Oo. Oo. Oo." The door opened. "Gettata here!" I screamed, then, "Oh, it's you."

"I have to find something," Delsa pointed at the dresser.

I backed up to let her through. "Eeu. Oo. Eeu. Oo. Ay."

"What *are* you doing?" She pulled a clean shirt from the drawer.

"That's it," I pushed her into the front room. "Everybody here!" I shouted. "Héctor! Norma! Mami! Tata!"

"What do you want?" Norma called from the back of the apartment.

Mami appeared from the kitchen. "What's all the yelling?"

"I want everyone here, so I can say this once."

"Say what?" Raymond asked.

"Norma! Héctor! Alicia! Get over here!"

"Quiet," Mami snapped. "Franky's sleeping."

"Hold on. I'm not as fast as I used to be." Tata shuffled toward the front room.

As everyone settled on the beds, the floor, the sofa, I began. "I have a class called voice and diction where I'm learning to talk without an accent."

"Why? Don't you want to sound Puerto Rican?" Héctor smirked.

"Let her speak," Tata said.

"It's part of my schoolwork," I pierced Héctor with a look.

"It sounded like you were imitating animals," Edna scoffed, and everyone laughed.

"Ha, ha, very funny." Unsmiling, I waited for them to settle. "I have to practice, and I can't have you interrupt me every five seconds to ask what I'm doing. So if you hear any weird sounds coming from the room, I'm doing my homework. Okay?"

"Is this what the yelling was about?" Mami asked.

"Yes. The kids were bothering me." I glared at Edna, Raymond, and Delsa. They looked at Mami, who stared at me hard. For a minute, she seemed about to scold me for making a big fuss out of nothing. But she turned to the kids.

"Let your sister be when she's doing her homework," she warned.

"It sounds like a zoo in there," Norma protested.

"Go to the other side of the apartment when she's practicing."

I backed into the bedroom, followed by Norma's "But it's not fair."

It wasn't. Since I'd started Performing Arts High School, Mami favored me. If I was reading and complained that the television was too loud, she made the kids turn it down. If I wanted to go to bed early, everyone was moved to the kitchen, where they could make a racket and I wouldn't hear. If I brought home a list of school supplies, Mami didn't say we had no money. She gave me enough to buy them or she'd get them for me without complaints about the cost. I knew how hard she worked to support us, so I didn't abuse her. But I felt guilty that so much of what little we had was spent on me. And I dreaded the price.

"I live for my children," Mami asserted. I was certain that no matter how hard I worked, I'd never be able to repay all she'd given up so that I could have what I needed.

Mami had dropped out of elementary school and didn't let us forget what a mistake she had made by not pursuing an education. While she never complained that we were a burden, her voice quivered when she told us it was hard to be both mother and father to eight children. Although she never talked about them, she must have had dreams once, but I was born, and every year after that, when one of my sisters or brothers was born, those dreams ebbed further and further as she focused on making sure we had dreams of our own.

"What do you want to be when you grow up?" she'd ask.

"A doctor," Delsa answered. She had high marks in school, better than mine, especially in math and science. And it was more likely that she'd be a doctor than that I'd ever be a good actress.

"A race car driver," Héctor announced, his eyes bright, his hands around an invisible steering wheel. At eleven years old, Héctor already worked at the pizzeria next door. Every few days he brought home a couple of pizzas with plenty of sausages and pepperoni that Gino, the owner, gave him for us.

"Your son is a good worker," Gino told Mami, "You raised him right." Mami beamed at the compliment, and Héctor worked harder, and at the end of the week he gave Mami most of what he'd earned.

"And you, Raymond," Mami urged, "what do you want to be when you grow up?"

"A policeman," responded Raymond. "And I'll give you a ticket if you drive fast on my street," he warned Héctor. Raymond's foot, after three years of treatments, had healed, his limp gone. It was easy to imagine him in uniform, strutting down a street, looking for bad guys.

"I'll have my own beauty parlor," Alicia declared. At nine, Alicia already knew how to form her thick, black, wavy hair into many styles by skillful use of brush, comb, and bobby pins. "And I'll give you a permanent for free!"

Edna, who spent hours drawing curvaceous women in bizarre outfits added, "I'm going to have a dress store. And you can get all the clothes you want. For free!"

"Wow! I'm going to be a rich old woman," Mami laughed, and we giggled at the image of Mami being old. It was impossible to imagine she'd ever look any different than she looked then, her black hair tousled, the curls hugging her freckled cheeks.

When we talked like this, Don Julio and Tata watched with bemused expressions, as if they could see into the future and knew what our lives would really be like. They, unlike Mami, were old, and even through the haze of cigarettes that surrounded them and the slurred speech after too much beer or wine, they seemed wise in a way Mami didn't.

"Don't count your chickens . . ." Tata began, and she didn't have to finish to confirm what I'd already learned was true: that to announce what was to be was to jinx it.

Mami, Tata, and Don Julio often told me how smart I was, but I interpreted their compliments as wishful thinking. My grades were average to low, and I'd failed geometry, which meant summer school and no job. I'd learned English quickly, but that was no surprise, since at Performing Arts we analyzed, memorized, and recited some of the best works written in the English language. My sisters and brothers hadn't the benefit of Performing Arts and could speak the language as well as I did, though with a Brooklyn accent.

Mami was proud that I went into the city every day by myself, returned when expected, was watchful that *"algo"* wouldn't happen. But I never admitted how scared I was early in the morning walking down our dark streets to the subway. I didn't mention that men exposed themselves, that sometimes they took advantage of a crowded subway to press themselves against me, or to let their hands wander to parts of my body no one should touch unless I asked them to. I didn't report the time I was chased from the subway station to the door of the school by a woman waving an umbrella who screamed "Dirty spick, dirty fucking spick, get off my street." I never told Mami that I was ashamed of where we lived, that in the *Daily News* and the *Herald American* government officials called our neighborhood "the ghetto," our apartment building "a tenement." I swallowed the humiliation when those same newspapers, if they carried a story with the term "Puerto Rican" in it, were usually describing a criminal. I didn't tell Mami that although she had high expectations for us, outside our door the expectations were lower, that the rest of New York viewed us as dirty spicks, potential muggers, drug dealers, prostitutes.

Mami was happy that I, at sixteen years of age, and now *"casi mujer,"* almost a woman, showed no interest in boys.

"She's too smart to get involved with those good-for-nothings around here," she asserted, when she knew I was listening.

And I didn't argue, although quality was not the issue. There were no boys my age in our neighborhood. And in school, some of the boys were homosexual, while those who weren't had no interest in girls like me. I was poor, talented enough not to embarrass myself on a stage, but only good enough to play Cleopatra and other exotic characters. When the subject of dating came up in social studies class, I admitted that my mother didn't allow me to date unless chaperoned. That ensured no boy in the entire grade would ask. What was the point? If I asked Mami to let me date, I'd get a lecture about how boys only want one thing, and I wasn't willing to give it to anyone. All I had to do was look around me to know what happened to a girl who let a man take the place of an education.

In the cramped, noisy apartment where my mother struggled to keep us safe, where my grandmother tried to obliterate her pain with alcohol, where my sisters and brothers planned and invented their future, I improvised. When it hurt, I cried silent tears. And when good things came my way, I accepted them gratefully but quietly, afraid that enjoying them too much would make them vanish like a drop of water into a desert.

"I don't care if the whole world is going."

Mami emerged from mourning gradually. She curled her hair one day, or topped her black skirt with a gray blouse instead of a black one the next. Little by little, she abandoned drab clothes for dark blues and browns; then, a few at a time, she dug out the flower prints and bold patterns she favored. The high heels reappeared, along with bright lipsticks, jangly earrings, necklaces, nail polish. Her smiles returned. Small, shy smiles at first, then full ones, her whole face brightening, as if she were trying on her old self a little at a time, to see if it fit.

We adjusted our mourning to her reactions. We played the radio softly, and if she didn't say anything, we raised the volume. We danced around the apartment or sang in the shower, quiet *boleros*, and when she didn't object, *merengues* or Mexican *rancheras*. Visits from relatives became more frequent and lasted longer. La Muda came with Luigi, who looked sadder every day, even though he and La Muda now lived together in an apartment in her mother's building. Luigi said he didn't like New York. He couldn't find work and complained that the cold winters gave him arthritis. And it was true. His bony fingers, which once flipped through a deck of cards with lightning speed, were now clumsy, hindered by bumps and bulges around the knuckles. He no longer performed his magic but sat quietly when he came to visit, hands folded on his lap.

Tío Chico disappeared for weeks at a time, then showed up

in the middle of the day, sometimes sober, but most often drunk. Tata cleaned him up, cooked rich *asopaos* and strong coffee to help him get over his hangovers. He spent a few days with us, sleeping mostly, and then he fixed a meaty *sancocho* or rooster stew with red wine and lots of cilantro. He was a wonderful cook, and he, Tata and Mami each cooked a different dish for Sunday supper and then pretended to argue over whose food was better. Our downstairs neighbor, who was critical of the noise we made when we first moved in, now came up daily to sit with Mami or Tata and often stayed to dinner. Her oldest son, Jimmy, was a little younger than me. He had a long, pimply face, close-cropped hair, a wispy mustache, and big ears. My sisters and brothers teased that Jimmy liked me, and when he came over, I stayed in my room so that the kids would leave me alone. Whenever he heard steps coming down the stairs, Jimmy peeked to see if it was me and then said he was going out too and walked with me to the bus stop where I caught a ride to summer school. Almost every day when I came back, he was on the corner of Rockaway Avenue, waiting to walk me home.

"Mami, can I go to Alma and Corazón's after school?" I asked one day. She said yes, and after that I visited my cousins daily to avoid Jimmy's hopeful face at the bus stop after I'd spent the morning in summer school struggling with triangle congruent theorems.

Weekends, Mami took us to the beach at Coney Island. Carrying blankets; coolers packed with ice, drinks, and food; a stack of towels; a couple of plastic buckets and spades, we trooped into a subway already filled with people similarly burdened. Once, the picnic started there when a child complained she was hungry, and in no time, everyone was dipping into the fried chicken and the potato salad and passing it around to total strangers who were equally eager to share their coleslaw and sliced ham and cheese sandwiches.

The long street leading to the beach was lined with kiosks selling hot dogs and hamburgers, sodas, ice cream, newspapers and magazines, sun tan lotion, stuffed animals. There was a wide boardwalk with games and more food stands, and, best of all, an amusement park with thrilling rides and a world-famous roller coaster.

But we weren't allowed to buy anything at the kiosks, because it was too expensive, nor could we go on the boardwalk, where *"algo"* could happen, or to the amusement park from which terrified screams came every few minutes as the roller coaster climbed and dipped on its rickety tracks. Holding hands, we fought the crowds toward the beach and, once there, pushed our way to a patch of sand big enough to settle our stuff and stretch a couple of blankets for one adult and seven children. Tata, who never came with us, kept Franky at home.

None of us could swim, so we looked for a spot near the lifeguard, although we wondered how he could tell anyone was drowning among the thousands of people screaming and jumping in and out of the water because it was fun to scream when you jump in and out of the water.

In order for the younger kids to play in the waves, someone watched them, while one of us sat on our blanket to make sure no one stole the cooler full of food, Mami's wallet, and our street clothes. I usually volunteered for this, as I found the beach, with its interminable, crashing waves, terrifying. The only time I'd been in that cold ocean, jumping waves with Delsa and Norma, a giant swell had thrust me under a ton of water and dragged me away. I was rescued not by the muscular lifeguard, who never saw me drowning, but by my mother and a bystander, who hauled me out sputtering and coughing, near death from humiliation.

One time after a day at the beach, we persuaded Mami to take us to the amusement park. We packed our stuff, took turns carrying the cooler and blankets, and wandered from one ride to the next, deciding which one we'd choose if we could only go on one, when Mami realized *algo had* happened: Edna was missing. We retraced our steps, called her name, searched in ever-tighter circles toward the spot where one of us always waited surrounded by our things. Mami was hysterical, calling for a police officer, but there was none to be seen. Finally, one appeared, and in between sobs we explained that Edna was lost, described her, and waited for him to find her. He told us to stay where we were, disappeared for a few moments, then came back saying he had "called it in," an action that didn't satisfy Mami, who wailed that he was doing nothing while her child was in mortal danger. A few people gathered around. We explained what was wrong, told them what Edna was wearing, when she was last seen. Several men and boys went to search for her while their wives and girlfriends stayed with us, rubbing Mami's shoulder and telling her everything would be fine.

Then the crowd parted. An enormous chestnut horse, mounted by a burly policeman galloped toward us. Sitting in front of the policeman, her face ecstatic, was Edna. The officer handed her down to Mami, who hugged her, kissed her, thanked the police officers, the bystanders, God, and the Virgins for saving her little girl, while we pestered Edna about what it was like to ride a horse.

"It was fun," she said, "but his hair tickled my legs."

Back home, we joked and laughed about Edna's adventure, but for the next few nights, I fantasized about being rescued by a good-looking man in uniform atop a horse. I imagined the wind fanning my hair, his arm around my waist, and the way the horse's coat tickled my bare legs. I seized the image of the policeman and his horse as if it were a gift and ignored Mami's litany of the *algos* that could have happened if Edna hadn't been found on time.

Mami was definitely out of mourning when she wanted to go dancing.

"A group from the factory is going," she told Tata.

"Hummph," Tata responded, an unspoken "I don't care if the whole world is going, you're not."

"Tito Puente is playing." Mami added casually. Tata dragged on her cigarette.

From where I sat reading, I watched Mami sorting socks

and underwear from the clean-laundry basket. Every so often, her eyelids flicked up to gauge Tata's mood. It was funny to see her behave the way I did when I wanted something: the not-so-subtle hints, the "all my friends are doing it" justification, the mention of a celebrity. Tata was as unimpressed with Mami's technique as Mami was with mine.

After a few minutes, she started again. "The girls need to be exposed to those situations, so they know how to behave in them."

Tata turned her head slowly toward Mami, fixed her with a withering stare. "You want to expose them to a nightclub so that they know how to behave in one?" Tata asked, each word enunciated with such clarity, she could have been one of Dr. Dycke's star voice and diction students, had Dr. Dycke spoken Spanish.

"Negi is studying to be an *artista*, she should meet other *artistas*," Mami said, inspecting a pair of socks.

"Those places aren't for decent women," Tata concluded after a while, and that seemed the end of it, because Mami got up, gathered the balled socks into the basket, and went to distribute them in the appropriate drawers.

She didn't give up. For days Mami badgered Tata until she agreed to watch the kids. Tata lived with us and rarely left the apartment, so it wasn't as if she had any plans on Saturday nights. But Mami didn't assume that Tata was our babysitter just because she was there, and she never left the building without telling Tata where she was going and when she'd be back.

Saturday night as we got ready, my sisters and brothers came in and out of the room as Mami and I dressed, giving unrequested opinions about what to do with our hair, makeup, and clothes. They were as excited as we were, as if seeing Mami so happy, dressed up for the first time in two years, were something to celebrate. When it was time to leave, Don Julio insisted on walking us to the station. He watched us go up the stairs to the train platform and waited until we were out of sight before heading back to Pitkin Avenue.

The club was on the Upper West Side. It looked like our neighborhood, with businesses on the street level and apartments on the higher floors of four- and five-story buildings, only there were more people on the street. When we climbed up from the subway, we heard the music coming from blacked-out windows above a restaurant. Men loitered in front of the door leading to the club, their clean, pressed shirts tucked into belted pants with stiff seams. They eyed us, mumbled compliments. Mami grabbed my hand, pulled me close, practically dragged me inside, up steep stairs toward the deafening music. Our hands were stamped by a large woman in a tight, short, low-cut dress that displayed more flesh than I had in my entire body. When we entered the club, Mami craned her neck this way and that, a panicked expression on her face, as if, now that we'd come so far, she wasn't sure if this was such a great idea. She held my hand very tight, my fingers cramped, and towed me as she wove in and out of the crowd looking for her friends. When she spotted them, her grip eased, and I jiggled my fingers to get the feeling back.

I'd never been in such a large room with so many people, so many perfumes and after-shave colognes mingling with the pungent odor of cigarette smoke, hair spray, rum, and sweat. The women were dressed in glittery outfits, the men had slick and shiny hair, jewelry sparkled in the dark. The hot, steamy air of too many bodies too close together was dizzying.

The dance floor was in the middle of the room. It was packed with men and women whose hips seemed detached from their torsos, whose arms undulated in, out, around each other like serpents in a pit. Mami introduced me to her friends, but the music was so loud that I couldn't catch anyone's name. It appeared that the woman in the green sequined dress was with the man in the beige *guayabera*, and the woman in the pink taffeta was with the dark man wearing a baby blue suit.

The minute we sat, two men extended their hands in front of us. I looked at Mami to make sure it was okay to accept, and she nodded as she got up with her partner, a short, round man with a horseshoe of hair around a shiny pate. My partner was younger, skinny, smelled of cigarettes and sweet cologne.

I'd never seen Mami dance, had no idea where she learned

to do it, but she was good. Lips parted in a half-smile, eyes ablaze, cheeks flushed, she twirled and whirled as her partner guided her here, then there, pulled her in close and spun her in a tight circle. It was distracting to see her smile at unknown men who held her hand, pressed their fingers against her back, guided her by the elbow to our table.

If seeing Mami dance was new, experiencing strange men so close was newer. Even though I was already sixteen and *casi mujer*, I'd never had a boyfriend, had never been kissed by anyone not related. I didn't think I was ugly, but no one had called me pretty. At home, my sisters Delsa and Norma were frequently told they were lovely, while I was called "intelligent."

But on the dance floor, every woman who can dance is beautiful, and every man with loose hips and grace is dashing, regardless of facial features or body types. When my partner took me out and led me through the complex paces of a *salsa* number, I felt beautiful for the first time in my life. It was not what I wore, nor how much makeup I'd managed to get away with. The feeling came from the heat generated by the dance itself, had nothing to do with the way I looked but everything to do with the way I moved. I became the complex rhythms, aware only of the joy of moving freely, gracefully, in and out of the arms of a man I'd never seen, to music I'd never heard.

I danced with many men: short, tall, skinny, fat, old, young, dark, light. And so did Mami. Sometimes a man who took me out asked her to dance the next number. Or they danced with her, then asked me, and through hand gestures and exaggerated lip movements reminiscent of La Muda, complimented me on having such a pretty mother and her on having a daughter who danced so well.

The band played long, loud sets. I was surprised that it really was Tito Puente. I'd thought Mami had made that up to impress Tata, who was a fan. When Tito Puente's musicians took a break, another band came on and played slower numbers, as if to give the dancers a rest with a few *boleros* before the *salsa* started again.

The dance lasted into the small hours, and when we came out, I was practically deaf and so thirsty my tongue stuck to the roof of my mouth. Mami's friends invited us to an all-night diner down the street, and we took over two booths overlooking Broadway and ate fried eggs, pancakes with syrup, sausages, and many cups of coffee. From time to time Mami watched me to see if I showed any signs of exhaustion, but I was exhilarated, and only worried that we'd look like *jíbaras* on the subway at six in the morning in our party clothes.

We said goodbye to her friends, who informed us there was another dance the following week somewhere else. "We'll see," Mami said.

We arrived home as everyone was waking up with their questions about whether we'd had a good time and whether I'd found a boyfriend. We drank some coffee with the kids and with Tata, who glowered at our disheveled hair, streaked makeup, sweaty clothes.

"Yes, we had a good time," Mami allowed. "I think next time Delsa and Norma should come, don't you think?"

I agreed they'd enjoy it but hoped she would take me too, since I was the eldest. She smiled and dragged herself to sleep, while I sat up with Delsa and Norma, giving them minute descriptions of everything I'd seen and done the previous night. We agreed that if Mami was going to take us dancing, we should practice at home, and I promised to teach them the new steps I'd learned from my partners. When I finally got to bed, I lay awake a long time, revisiting every moment of the evening, while my body jerked in uncontrollable spasms of unreleased energy. I fell asleep lulled by the sounds of a remembered *bolero*, certain I'd never been happier than I was that night.

⌒⌒◯

Now we went dancing almost every Saturday. Although Delsa and Norma were only fourteen and thirteen years old, it wasn't unusual for there to be younger kids at the clubs. People brought their entire families: mothers, fathers, grandparents, children so young they toddled around, shook their diapered bottoms during the *merengues* while everyone clapped and encouraged them along.

Admission was half price for children under eighteen, free for those under twelve, which was how Mami was able to afford to bring us three oldest girls and, sometimes, Héctor. Drinks were sold à la carte, or one could buy a *servicio*, which consisted of a bottle of rum, two bottles of Coke, a bucket of ice, plastic cups, and sliced lemons. There were long tables arranged around the dance floor, eight folding chairs per table, a stack of cocktail napkins, and two aluminum ashtrays on each. Some places sold Puerto Rican fried food like *alcapurrías* and *pastelillos*, or bags of potato or corn chips. But most served only drinks. The only way to guarantee we could get a table was to order a *servicio*, so if we came alone, we always bought it, drank the Cokes, and brought the rum home for Tata and Don Julio.

We only went to clubs with live music, usually in the Upper West Side or El Barrio, but we never ventured into the Bronx or Queens, because Mami didn't know her way around those boroughs. At some dances we met people we'd seen at other clubs, and sometimes, if we had a particularly good partner, Delsa, Norma, or I told him where we'd be the next week. We didn't think of them as boyfriends. The only time we saw them was at the clubs, and the relationship was monitored by Mami, who, with a glance or a movement of her lips, made it clear we were getting too chummy with whomever we were dancing with and to ease up or she'd take us home.

Although Tío Chico had touched my breast once, and though I'd seen several penises dangling helplessly from the opened zippers of flashers, or triumphantly erect from a brazen truck driver's lap, I'd never come so close to men as I did on the dance floor. Some danced so close that they got an erection. When faced with this situation, we were to give them the benefit of the doubt. If they pulled away sheepishly, it was an accident.

If they pressed tighter, they were being fresh. We called them *rompemedias*, stocking rippers, because they danced so close, the friction made our nylons run. A man who got fresh risked being abandoned on the dance floor. A man on the dance floor alone was noticed by everyone and was sure to have trouble finding other partners. So most men were polite, maintaining a respectful distance while still managing to dance a *bolero* with enough heat to make a *puta* blush.

There were also the *pulpos*, octopuses, whose hands, instead of guiding us in intricate dance combinations, crawled over our backs, down to the buttocks, up under our arms, near our breasts, while their legs tried to insinuate themselves between ours. These men too were to be avoided.

Every once in a while, I didn't withdraw when a man got excited. We'd be dancing a slow number, and when I felt him growing, I pressed closer, to test his reaction. If he aggressively thrust himself toward me, or if, octopuslike, his hands and legs strayed where they shouldn't, I drew away, because it didn't feel as if I was giving him something, but as if he thought he was entitled to it. I liked the man who gasped in surprise, who tenderly pulled me closer, moved his hips in discreet slow circles around and against mine without missing a beat. I savored the power of being able to excite a man, to feel his hot breath against my ear, slow at first, then sharper, hotter, our bodies pressed into a sinuous whole that moved rhythmically across the crowded, steamy floor. I lost all sense of time, embraced and embracing, beautiful, graceful, trembling with sensations possible only this way, in this place.

When the *bolero* was over, my partner wanted to stay for the next dance. But I insisted he bring me back to my table. I didn't trust the feelings that made me dance that way, was embarrassed I let it go so far. I refused to look him in the eyes, afraid of what I'd see there. If he asked me to dance again, I refused, or told him I'd only dance fast numbers. I never acknowledged any part in what we'd done.

Later, shame was replaced with the thrill of his body against mine, his face an anonymous blur, until all that was left was the tingle on my skin, the heat between my legs, the slow, billowing rhythm of the *bolero*.

Sometimes, in spite of Mami's efforts to keep us safe from a violent world, *algo* happened. We mourned President Kennedy's assassination with the rest of the country and bawled when John-John saluted the coffin as it went past. The radio and television brought us news of how at least thirty neighbors heard Kitty Genovese screaming as she was being stabbed to death and no one came to help. For weeks afterward, Mami was in a state if we so much as went downstairs to the pizza shop. But she wasn't the only one who worried. When she got off the train from work, Don Julio or Héctor was waiting at the bottom of the steps to walk her home.

The scariest thing to happen during that summer of 1964 was when whole neighborhoods like ours turned against themselves. We read about it in the papers, heard about it on the radio, saw the fuzzy, black-and-white images of people who looked like us running down streets that looked like ours, setting fires, beating each other, being chased by police — some of them on horses like the one that rescued Edna. The officers, all white men, dragged the dark-skinned rioters off the sidewalks littered with broken glass and garbage. They beat them with nightsticks, pushed them into police cars, then drove away followed by a crowd screaming and cursing, their faces twisted into grimaces.

Mami refused to go to work after news of a riot, and I didn't go to summer school. Our apartment was stifling, but we weren't allowed out. Don Julio, whose grown daughters lived in another part of Brooklyn, brought news of buildings set on fire, of crowds breaking store windows and taking whatever they could carry.

"I saw a man run off with a color television," he said. "And a woman and three kids dragged a sofa out of a furniture store and then went in and got a table and chairs."

We thought it was funny, but Mami didn't. *"Desordenados,"* she muttered. "If I catch one of you kids doing a thing like that . . ."

One hot night, we had just gone to bed when we heard screams, breaking glass, alarms going off.

"Get away from there! Turn out the lights!" Mami screeched when she saw us leaning out of the windows to see what was going on. A couple of blocks away a mob ran toward Rockaway Avenue, armed with bats and tire irons, banging everything in sight. She pushed us into the middle room, checked that the doors were locked, picked up the phone.

"Should we call the police?" I asked, ready to translate for her. "No," she whispered, "I just want to make sure it's working."

We huddled in the dark, listened for steps running up the stairs, or for the crack of splintering wood, or for an explosion, anything to indicate that the violence had reached our door. When we heard police sirens, Héctor crept over to the window, peeked out, crept back.

"They stopped them down the street. Nothing's going on out there."

After a while, Mami went to see. I followed, even though she whispered that we should stay where we were. The street was deserted. A block away, a couple of police cars were parked in the middle of the avenue, their lights flashing, their radios droning chatter. In the other direction there were more police cars, but no people. The sidewalks were littered with trash from upturned garbage cans and shimmering fragments of glass. Mami closed the windows, drew the curtains.

"Everyone back to bed," she ordered.

It was impossible to sleep. For hours the shrill store alarms kept us awake. Also the waiting. I was sure if I fell asleep I'd wake up in the middle of a fire or of a mob looting the drugstore on the street floor. But daylight came and nothing more had happened. The merchants whose windows were broken placed plywood over them, scrawled notes, or spray-painted "OPEN FOR BUSINESS" or "CLOSED UNTIL FURTHER NOTICE," depending on the damage.

When we shopped, they watched us with distrustful eyes, as if we'd been part of the violence, and we stared back, resentful that no one was immune from their suspicions and anger.

"As soon as I save enough for two months' rent and a security deposit," Mami sighed, "we're moving."

⟨⟩

The night before the summer school geometry Regents exam, Ray Barretto was playing at a club in El Barrio.

"You stay home and study," Mami said.

"I don't need to. I have good marks in every exam I've taken."

"But if you fail this one, you have to repeat the course again."

"I won't fail. I know the stuff now."

"Fine, then, if you're sure."

"I'm sure."

I danced until my feet hurt. I danced until my throat was hoarse from yelling to be heard above the music. I danced until my eyes smarted from the smoke in the room, and from the melted makeup that dripped into them. I danced until my eardrums throbbed like Ray Barretto's congas. When the music stopped, we followed the crowd outside and found ourselves in the middle of a riot.

Exhausted and still dressed in our party clothes, high heels, and inexpensive but showy jewelry, we pressed together against the wall of a building and watched a crowd of men run past with bats, sticks, the covers of garbage cans. The entrance to the subway was half a block away in the opposite direction, and when the crowd thinned, we ran toward it and made it down the stairs as another angry group turned the corner. People who were at the dance were down in the subway station, and there was talk that the mob would come after us. The men in their *guayaberas* and pastel suits formed a line in front of the women and children, who converged at the far end of the platform, anxiously searching the dark tunnel for signs of a train. Above us, alarms shrieked, people screamed and cursed, cars screeched to a stop, glass shattered, and heavy objects thudded to the ground. After a long time, sirens wailed. When the train finally came, we ran into it, pushed into the farthest corners, and didn't feel safe until the doors closed. As soon as the train moved, everyone relaxed, laughed at the foolishness of running from a crowd with no interest in us. But it was lame laughter; our fear was real; and although Mami, Delsa, Norma, and I made jokes and laughed along with everyone else, we didn't mention what had happened at home. It was too close an escape to joke about.

Three hours after we came home from our night of Ray Barretto and its aftermath, I chewed on a pencil trying to remember what postulates were and why x equaled z. But it was no use. The formulas, theorems, and hypotheses had fled. I failed the Regents exam for a second time, which meant I'd have to repeat geometry for the third time in two years.

Once school started, our dancing weekends came to an end. There was a lot of work and expense in getting seven children ready for school. We wore one another's clothes and received hand-me-downs from relatives, but Mami always bought each of us a new outfit and shoes for the first day of school. The girls got new book bags and new hairstyles. The boys got cropped haircuts, new pants, white shirts, and ties for Assembly. But clothes weren't the only expense. Pencils and pens had to be purchased, as did ruled pages, binders, construction paper, crayons, adhesive tape, glue. Teachers sent home lists of other supplies: gym suits and sneakers, maps, protractors, rulers, sketchbooks, dictionaries. Then there was carfare for me and Delsa, who had started high school, and a small allowance for us to buy a soda or a cup of coffee. As the weather cooled, we needed coats, gloves, boots, hats.

Sometimes, even with a full-time job and whatever overtime

she was able to put in, Mami wasn't able to cover all the back-to-school costs. Besides giving up our dancing weekends, we gave up the telephone, canned food, sweets. When we still fell behind, we went to welfare to request an emergency allowance for winter clothes, electricity, or to meet a couple of months' rent until things went back to normal. Mami had to take a day off work, lose that day's wages, then be told that welfare didn't help unless she had no job. Once, a welfare worker asked me why I didn't help my mother.

"I'm in high school," I responded, taken aback.

"You can work part-time."

"I don't have time. The school is an hour and a half from our apartment. . . ."

"What's going on?" Mami asked, when she noticed the welfare worker had lost interest in her to argue with me.

"He says I should get a job."

"She job school," Mami informed the welfare worker. Every once in a while she spoke a few phrases in English that were very effective. When she did, and if the person she was speaking to understood, she beamed with pride but didn't push her luck by trying any more.

On the way home, I told Mami that maybe I should get a job after school.

"I don't want you out on the street after dark."

"But Héctor has a job . . ."

"He's *casi un hombre*. It's different."

Héctor was twelve, long and scrawny and not "almost a man" from what I could see. But he was male and I was female, and that was the difference. As much as we could have used whatever money I might be able to bring in, it wasn't worth the risk of my being away from home after dark. *Algo* could happen.

"She's not exactly Method."

I wanted to play Scout in *To Kill a Mockingbird*, Eliza in *Pygmalion*, Laura in *The Glass Menagerie*, Sophocles' Antigone. But again I was cast as Cleopatra, this time with William as Julius Caesar.

Harvey, my first Caesar, played the character as a soldier, all macho bluster and strut. William played Caesar as an emperor used to being obeyed. I dug out the yellow tablecloth costume, tried to find a different approach to the same part. My first Cleopatra was kittenish and flirtatious; this one I decided to play as a cunning queen meeting an equally duplicitous opponent.

It was hard to get into character. The few times I tried to get away with what I wasn't supposed to, I was caught, so cunning didn't come easily.

"That's where acting comes in," Laura Figueroa affirmed when I explained my dilemma. She was one of the best actresses in the class, capable of any role, any accent, classic to contemporary. Her specialty, however, was old ladies. Not that she preferred playing them, but every time we were cast, I was Cleopatra and she was old. "Maybe you can model her character on someone you know." I shook my head. "Well, then, a combination of people."

"I wish I'd seen Elizabeth Taylor's Cleopatra."

"It might help, but she's not exactly Method."

At Performing Arts, we scorned movie actors. They "indicated," and their acting relied on minute facial and eye gestures that were often no more than mannerisms. They seldom worked with their voices and seemed more worried about how they looked than creating a character.

It was crucial in our development as actors, we were told, to learn the difference between self-consciousness and self-awareness. A self-conscious actor was too earnest, too vigilant of his or her performance. Self-aware ones trusted that the weeks or months of preparation for a role helped them become the character, while maintaining a level of alertness that allowed them to react to the other actors and to the situation. A performance, we were told, was a living thing that changed and developed every time the actor stepped on stage.

I understood the concepts, observed and stored moments and situations in my "sense memory" for later, when I'd need to draw upon them. But I was convinced that my life didn't provide enough variety to make me a good actress. How could it, when every move I made was monitored by Mami? But whenever I so much as considered going against her wishes, a little voice went off in my head to remind me that between her and the rest of the world was nothing but hostile eyes and low expectations. Were I to fall, only my mother would be there to pick me up. Yes, there were seven sisters and brothers, but they were younger and more helpless. Yes, there was Tata, but she was often drunk. The other relatives were there, but they had children of their own, lives of their own, problems of their own. There was my father, far away in Puerto Rico, with his new wife and his new kids and his new life. If I didn't have Mami, I'd be alone. And at seventeen, I didn't want to be alone. Not yet.

My drama teacher, Mrs. Provet, called me to the office one day and asked if I'd be interested in a job on weekends, working as an usher in a theater.

"I can't work at night."

"It's on Sunday afternoons."

I accepted, happy that I'd finally make some money, eager for any exposure to the theater, even as an usher. I'd see actors at work, study their technique, and maybe get some pointers.

The job didn't require an interview. I was to report to the theater at noon on the following Sunday.

The address was in lower Manhattan. I came out of the subway station in front of a row of shabby two- and three-story buildings, not a theater marquee in sight. I looked at the directions and read the address again, walked up and down the block until I found a tattered awning over a dark doorway that led to a set of stairs. I was nervous, reluctant to go up, uncertain of where I was. The *algos* that could happen in dim halls of unfamiliar buildings repeated in my brain, but I silenced them, took a breath, and rose. At the top of the stairs were three doors and a ticket window. I knocked on the door marked "Office" and was greeted by a bearded gentleman dressed in black.

"I'm from Performing Arts," I introduced myself. "The usher."

"Oh, yes," he said, "Come with me." He led me down the hall. "I'm Mr. Rosenberg," he said, as he opened the middle set of doors. "I'll be selling tickets, and you'll be right here." He noticed me hesitate, looked in, and saw that the room was dark. "Uh, sorry," he said, flipping a switch, and we were in the back of a small theater.

"The numbers are on the armrests. See? You show people to their seats and make sure they get a program."

He rummaged behind a curtain against the back wall and pulled out a box full of printed pages in a script I couldn't read, but which I knew to be Hebrew. The stark black characters were similar to those in storefronts all over New York, and I'd learned that כָּשֵׁר meant that the establishment served kosher food, although I wasn't sure what kosher food was.

"Fold them in half like this," he demonstrated. "The play begins in an hour. You can watch from any seat that's free in the back." He pulled out a flashlight from behind the curtain and handed it to me. "If people come late, wait until a change of scene to bring them to their seats. At the end, make sure they don't forget their belongings."

I sat on one of the hard wooden chairs that flipped up and folded the programs. When I was done, I walked down the stepped aisles to the foot of the stage. It wasn't raised high, only about knee height on me. The set was a kitchen in an apartment. A door stage right led to stairs going down offstage, and a window stage left led to a fire escape. A table covered in a checkered cloth, three chairs, a stove, curtains on the windows, and some dishes completed the set. A bare light bulb lit the stage, and I felt a sudden thrill. This was a real stage, in a real theater, and I was about to see a live performance by real actors.

In a few minutes, there was a shuffle of feet up the stairs. Mr. Rosenberg opened the doors, and I ran to my post at the back of the theater, took a bunch of programs in my hand, and handed them out as people showed me their tickets. They were mostly elderly, very orderly and polite, and seemed grateful to be shown to their seats, though it was clear that many of them were familiar with the layout and knew where they were going. Everyone was as dressed up as Mami and my sisters and I were when we went dancing. The women wore wigs, jewelry, furs. The men wore suits and hats, which they perched on their knees the minute they sat down. There was a strong scent of mothballs, cigars, and perfume.

When the lights went down, I stood in the back of the theater. The actors entered, dressed in the clothes I associated with the owners of secondhand stores and delis on Graham Avenue. They spoke Yiddish, a language that sounded familiar because I'd heard it in the *marketa*, at the check-cashing place, on the streets of Williamsburg.

Even though I didn't understand a word, I was caught up in the action on the stage. The drama revolved around a family whose son had strayed from the traditions they had brought from their home country to the United States. He'd fallen in love with an American girl, and his family refused to meet her.

At the end of act 1, I applauded vigorously, along with the rest of the audience. A woman in front turned and smiled in my direction. When she passed me on the way out during the intermission, she asked if I understood any of it.

"I don't know the language, but I can follow the action. The actors are very good."

"Wonderful!" she said, and patted my hand.

When the second act began, a new character was introduced, and I was surprised to see Mr. Rosenberg on the stage. He played a grandfather or other older relative and made several impassioned speeches. At the end of act 2, he delivered a long monologue that brought the audience to its feet and had everyone, including me, in tears.

In act 3 the young man decided not to marry the American girl, and the play ended with the entire family on the stage around lighted candles singing a solemn, beautiful hymn. By this time I was sobbing, and the lady who had talked to me earlier came over with a Kleenex.

"Yiddish theater," she said, opening her arms in a dramatic gesture. "The best!" I thanked her, nodded agreement, and tried my best to clear the theater, but I was so distraught that I just sat in the back row crying and feeling stupid because I couldn't stop.

Mr. Rosenberg came out stage right, hopped down to the floor, made his way to me.

"I'm so sorry," I said, "I don't know what happened. It was so beautiful. Your performance. The song at the end. And the candles. I have no idea what you said. . . ." I blubbered on and on, wiped my face with the Kleenex, which by now was shreds in my fingers.

"It's all right," he said. "It's flattering," he added with a smile. He offered to introduce me to the actors and took me backstage to the cubicle dressing rooms. I shook each actor's hand, told them how much I enjoyed the play. They looked at me curiously, and the woman who played Mamma touched my cheek. I was almost brought to tears again, but Mr. Rosenberg led me out.

"Come back in two hours," he said.

I ushered another show that day, and still the play moved me beyond words. For four Sundays in a row, I watched those actors perform the same play once in matinee and once in the early evening. No performance was the same twice. Their voices, their gestures, the level of concentration changed the dynamics each time they spoke their lines, making the play completely different and new.

Until then, a theatrical experience was a concept taught at Performing Arts, not one I'd had. But now I understood why my teachers at Performing Arts loved the theater so much, why they claimed the sacrifices were worth making.

After the sixth Sunday Mr. Rosenberg said he didn't need me anymore. "We're rehearsing for a couple of months," he said, "then we open another play." I was disappointed, told him to call the school when he needed me. A couple of months later, he did.

"Bring a handkerchief," he said, before he said goodbye. I did.

<hr />

Mami was told about a dance in the Armory on Park Avenue. "It's been a while," she reasoned, "and it *is* almost Christmas."

I saved my ushering money for a dress and was allowed to shop alone.

"But don't come home with anything *estrámbolico*," Mami said.

"I don't want to look like a clown . . . maybe black."

"Ay, no! Don't get black." Mami had recently rid herself of mourning clothes. She was afraid that if she kept them, they'd bring bad luck. When I suggested she burn them, she flinched, and I understood that fire implied bad things for poor, dead,

Francisco. If she gave the clothes to someone not in mourning, they'd bring the recipient bad luck. So she stuffed them in a plastic bag, tied the bag with several knots so that the bad luck in them wouldn't escape, and put them out with the garbage.

"Red, then, since it's Christmas."

"Heaven forbid!" Tata said. Red clothes, she claimed, brought on heavy periods and, on a woman of childbearing age, miscarriages.

"I'm not planning to get pregnant any time soon," I reminded her.

"Still," she warned.

"Get something with all the colors in the rainbow," Edna suggested.

"Never mind, I'll figure it out," I replied. I used the excuse of looking for my dress to shop in Manhattan.

"Why can't you shop around here?" Mami asked, "or on Flatbush Avenue. They have lots of nice things."

But I didn't want to shop in Brooklyn. At Performing Arts, I'd learned that Brooklyn was not New York City. It was referred to as an "outer borough" by the mayor himself. Manhattan was the financial, theatrical, and artistic center of the United States. I wanted to be in it, to move from the margins into the center. I wanted to climb to the top of the Empire State Building, to gaze over the city and beyond it to the vast horizon that I knew existed but couldn't see from the ground in Brooklyn.

The dance at the Armory was the best we'd been to. Three bands played nonstop, and there were more Puerto Ricans than I'd ever seen in one enormous room. After the dance, Mami, Delsa, Norma, and I walked down Park Avenue looking for a place to eat, but there was none. The street, divided by an island of low bushes and scrawny trees, was mostly residential, and its businesses opened only during the day. Hungry as we were, we liked walking on Park Avenue and, still giddy from the dance, laughed and joked and pretended to be rich ladies out for a stroll in the neighborhood. We left the Armory behind, but still we walked, our coats off our shoulders as if they were furs, our high heels clicking, our hands dangling limply from our wrists, toward an invisible *caballero.*

Lights flashed behind us. A police car pulled up ahead, and an officer climbed out and straddled the middle of the sidewalk like the sheriff in cowboy movies about to challenge the bank robber to a shoot-out.

"Good morning, ladies," he said. "May I direct you where you're going?" His fake-polite voice came out of a smirk, and his eyes, invisible under his cap, were like hands, roaming every inch of our bodies.

Mami placed herself between us and the cop, but she needed one of us to translate. Her face went from joy to panic in seconds, to the hard, serious expression she put on when she was afraid but had to be strong for the sake of the children. "Tell him we're just looking for a place to eat," she said to me, Delsa, or Norma, whoever spoke up. I jumped in front of her, smiled my most enchanting smile, and became Cleopatra, queen of the Nile.

"We were at a dance at the Armory, officer," I enunciated clearly. "It's such a nice evening, we decided to walk home."

"You live around here?" He tried to stare me down, but I held my noble bearing, though my knees shook.

"Yes, that way." I pointed with my whole arm, my whole body, to a faraway place, my palace, toward Brooklyn. Mami, Delsa, and Norma looked at me as if I had sprung horns and a tail. They pulled up and buttoned their coats, stood humbly before the police, hoping we hadn't done anything illegal and that I wasn't making it worse, while I prayed he wouldn't ask for an address.

"You were making a lot of noise," His voice lost its edge. "This is a residential neighborhood." Now he stated the obvious, somewhat sheepishly, I thought.

"What?" Mami yelled in English, as if to speak louder were to be better understood. "What the matter?" She sounded scared, definitely not like someone who lived on Park Avenue.

"We've been denounced for making too much noise," I said in Spanish, my voice low and even.

"What, you can't talk and laugh on Park Avenue?" Delsa snapped in Spanish, and I shot her a shut-up look. I turned to the officer.

"We'll keep it down." I, cunning Cleopatra, flapped my eye-lids, smiled haughtily. "So sorry we disturbed the neighbors. Come on, girls." I waved them toward me and started to walk past him. "Thank you," I said, as the officer backed up to let us pass. Cleopatra, queen of the Nile, and her faithful retainers, who followed, puzzled, not certain we'd been dismissed by the law. I kept walking until I heard the patrol car door shut and saw it pull ahead and past us, down Park Avenue. The minute he was out of sight, we cracked up.

"How did you dare?" Mami laughed.

"I don't know. I didn't think . . . I just did it." We turned the corner away from Park Avenue, in case the police officer came around to see if we went into a building in the neighborhood.

"Wow, Negi, those acting classes are sure paying off," Norma said. "You made him believe we live on Park Avenue!"

I was elated. I'd just performed before the most critical and demanding audience I'd ever encounter — to rave reviews.

We went dancing again, not as often as in the summer, twice a month or so. At one of the clubs, Mami met, danced with, and fell in love with Don Carlos. He was gangly, with chocolate skin, a shy smile, a soft voice. He wore a dark suit with a white shirt and thin tie, and horn-rimmed rectangular glasses with green lenses. I thought he was blind. Why else would anyone wear dark glasses in an already dimly lit nightclub?

He danced with me, Delsa, and Norma, kept more than the required distance, stared over our heads the whole time, as if displaying any interest in us beyond the proper courtesy were forbidden. Afterwards, he took us to a diner, asked us about school, what we wanted to be when we grew up, the expected questions adults trying to ingratiate themselves with young people always asked. Delsa, Norma, and I asked him what he did (accounting), where he worked (Xerox), if he was married (divorced), how many children he had (three), and whether he was ever sick (rarely), while Mami kicked us under the table for our impertinence. But this was the only man Mami had shown any interest in since Francisco's death.

Mami must have told him which dances we'd be attending, because after the first meeting, every time we walked into a club, there he was. Delsa, Norma, and I soon figured out what was going on, especially since Mami didn't dance with anyone else. He sat at our table, and even though the music was deafening, he and Mami carried on animated conversations through the whole evening, even when they danced.

Delsa, Norma, and I teased Mami that she had a boyfriend, and she blushed, then asked us not to tell Tata. We liked sharing a secret with her, knowing something about her life that no one else knew. But we didn't like it when Don Carlos sat at our table. Men thought he was our father and didn't ask us to dance.

"He sits there with his dark glasses on, like a gangster or something, and scares the guys away," we complained to Mami.

The next time, he wore regular lenses on his glasses, thick as windowpane, through which he squinted as if they were the wrong prescription. It didn't help. Men now thought he was scrutinizing every move they made.

After weeks of courtship, Mami invited Don Carlos for Sunday dinner. When Mami told her a man was coming to visit, Tata's eyes narrowed, her lips puckered, and she walked away from Mami without a word.

"Good for you," Don Julio said. "You're still a young woman. You should have a husband."

"He's just a friend," Mami said, but her face turned red.

Sunday came and the house was spotless. The clothes-drying ropes strung across the rooms were down, the diapers folded and put away, the floors scrubbed, every bed made up with chenille bedspreads, the pillows discreet mounds at the heads. Mami was afraid Tata would be in a bad mood and embarrass her in front of Don Carlos, but Tata dressed early, took her place alongside Mami at the stove, and helped cook—at one point telling her she'd take over so that Mami could get ready.

Don Carlos showed up hours after we expected him, carrying a box of Italian cookies for us and a bottle of wine for Tata. He didn't bring anything for Mami, who was cold and polite to him, her face a hard mask. He wore his dark glasses again, didn't take them off the whole time he was with us. He never apologized for being late, made no excuses, sat at the kitchen table talking and drinking with Tata and Don Julio while my sisters and brothers paraded in and out checking him out, then running to the back rooms to compare notes. When he was about to leave, he asked Mami to walk with him to the front door, two floors below. He shook hands with everybody, even the kids, then followed Mami down the stairs. The minute he left, we started talking about him.

"He's an intelligent, well-educated person," was Don Julio's assessment.

"He makes a lot of money," Delsa informed every one. "When we go dancing, he pays, and then he takes us to breakfast and pays for that too."

"He treats Mami with respect," noted Norma.

"Oh, yeah? He showed up three hours late," Héctor recalled.

"Maybe he had to work," Alicia defended him.

"On Sunday?" I asked.

"He sure is tall," observed Raymond.

"But he's so skinny!" added Edna.

"All I can say," Tata finally spoke up, "is that I don't trust a man who won't look me in the eye."

Oh-oh, I said to myself.

As with Francisco, Tata and Mami argued over whether it was appropriate for Mami to bring a man into our family. Tata accused Mami of setting a bad example for us, and Mami insisted that at thirty-three she was still a young woman and deserved a life. If Tata didn't like it, she could move out. Don Julio took Mami's side, and Tata, outnumbered, accepted the inevitable. One evening Don Carlos came for dinner, and the next morning he was still there.

My junior year at Performing Arts turned out to be my best. My average was excellent, aided by near perfect grades in geometry, which, after three attempts, I'd mastered. My cunning Cleopatra was a success, and in spring semester, when we did character work, I was cast as one of the evil stepsisters in scenes from *Cinderella*. We were encouraged to use an animal as the physical model for the character, and I chose a camel, for its haughty look and ungainly walk.

I was a hall monitor, charged with checking that students wandering around during classes had a pass signed by a teacher. My favorite hall to monitor was on the dance department floor. I sat where I could watch a ballet class in session, could see the dancers hurl themselves through space, their controlled abandon making my own muscles ache for movement. I was envious of the training that made them so graceful and strong, the intricate steps they performed as the teacher called each movement in French.

The training for actors at Performing Arts was modern dance, its language English, its purpose to keep us from embarrassing ourselves if we had to perform musical theater. But I'd come to love dance class more than acting. While I knew I wasn't a great actress, I could see I was one of the better dancers in the drama department. I practiced all the time. The semester we'd studied jazz and learned isolations, I'd begun to practice minute movements of my torso, hips, and back while waiting for the train, or while sitting in history class. At home, I couldn't sit still in front of the television while we watched *Candid Camera* or *The Jackie Gleason Show*. One eye on the screen, I stretched, did splits, counted out hundreds of pliés in first, second, third, fourth, and fifth positions while my sisters and brothers complained that my movements distracted them. To pick up something from the floor, I bent over from the hips, back straight, to stretch my thigh and calf muscles. I used the kitchen counter for a barre, leaped from one room to the other, held my leg up to my cheeks like the can-can dancers on *The Ed Sullivan Show*.

I knew I'd never be a ballerina; that wasn't my intention. At Performing Arts we learned that if actors had to wait ten years to make a living at their art, dancers were lucky if they could get that many years out of theirs. For me, dance was not to be shared but to bring me to a place nothing else did. I danced for myself, even when being led across a shiny floor by a skillful partner. It didn't matter if no one saw me dance. It only mattered that I could.

At the Yiddish theater, I ushered two shows every Sunday, for which I was paid at the end of the day in wrinkled bills. The company worked in repertory, alternating comedies with tragedies. When they were in rehearsals, I was laid off. When there was a performance, an actor staffed the ticket window, making me wonder if Mr. Rosenberg only chose plays in which one of the characters always made his first entrance in the second act.

I came to know the regular audience members by name. Mr. and Mrs. Karinsky took the same two seats in row C, center. Mrs. Shapiro and her sister Miss Levine liked front row, center, because Miss Levine was hard of hearing. Mrs. Mlynarski always brought a coffee cake for the actors, which she handed to me with ceremony, and which I was supposed to take backstage immediately while she stood at the door, a huge, immovable bulk, blocking anyone from entering until I returned and conveyed profuse thanks from the cast. Almost all the regulars knew where their seats were, and I wondered why Mr. Rosenberg paid me to usher, until the day Mr. Aronson had a fit of loud, hacking coughs. I came down the aisle with the flashlight to help him out of the theater and into the hallway, followed by a distraught and embarrassed Mrs. Aronson and another man who told me to get a glass of water.

"Don't worry," the man said as he bent over Mr. Aronson, who was turning blue, "I'm a doctor."

I couldn't find a glass anywhere, so I ran to the deli down the street and told the counterman that there was an emergency at the theater and could I please, please, please have a glass of water. When I returned, the play was in intermission and Mr. Aronson was sitting on the floor with the doctor on his knees at his side. He'd regained some color, and his coughs had subsided. He drank the water in little sips as the audience watched and hovered and commented on what was happening.

"You're looking better, Morey," Miss Levine said.

"It's his gallbladder," Mr. Klein diagnosed.

"Move away, he needs fresh air," Mrs. Mlynarski ordered everyone.

As the lights for the second act flashed, his wife and the doctor helped Mr. Aronson down the stairs and out of the building.

When everyone was seated and the play resumed, I broke into a sweat and shivers, imagining that one of the elderly people might some day have a heart attack or stroke during a performance, and there wouldn't be a doctor to help. Later, when Mr. Rosenberg was paying me and I expressed my fears, he reassured me.

"Don't worry," he said, waving his hand, "there's always a doctor in *this* house." He laughed, but I didn't get the joke.

Mami decided we needed an apartment that would allow everyone more privacy. She found one on the second floor of a two-story house, on a tree-lined street of identical houses, the stoop separated from the sidewalk by a cement yard behind a wrought-iron fence. She and Don Carlos took the bedroom in the back, Tata and we kids scattered our belongings in three rooms, one of which, the living room, faced the sunny street. The other rooms didn't offer much light, because their windows faced an air vent. When I was arranging my things in the middle room with Delsa and Norma, I noticed that a hallway off the kitchen was wide enough to hold a fold-out cot.

"Mami, can I take this room?"

"This isn't a room, it's a hall."

"If I close these doors," I shut the ones to the outside hall and to her room, "it still leaves me with a door to the kitchen, and I can put a cot in here, and a table, and have my own room."

Mami stepped into the room I'd created. "It's so dark."

"It's got a light. See?" I pulled the chain of an overhead bulb. "The room is useless. We don't need another entrance."

"Umm," Mami considered for a few minutes, then agreed. At the secondhand store we found a gold metal and glass vanity table with an oval mirror and matching chair covered in white vinyl. I dragged the folding cot into the hallway, where it hugged the walls tight enough so that the only way I could get into bed was by climbing over the foot toward the head against the door to Mami's room. The vanity table fit against the other entrance door. I screwed hooks into the wall for my clothes and stuffed my underwear into a basket that went under the bed. It was like living in a long box, but it was private, my own room, where I could keep my things and where I slept alone, even if every time I turned over I hit a wall with a leg or a foot.

"It sounds like you're fighting in there," Tata complained one morning when I emerged from my room, elbows and knees bruised. "And you don't get any fresh air. You'll get sick."

"Maybe that room isn't such a good idea," Mami warned.

"I had a nightmare," I lied, "and there's plenty of air."

That night I began to train myself to sleep on my back, perfectly still: Cleopatra, surrounded by her belongings, in her sarcophagus.

As soon as school was out, I answered a classified ad for a summer job at a photographic developing company. I was interviewed by Mr. Murphy, a high-strung man who asked questions but never let me finish the answer.

He reviewed the job application. "You go to Performing Arts, right?"

"Yes, sir," I said, unable to hide the pride in my voice.

"What'd they teach you there?" He had an exquisite Brooklyn accent.

I turned on my standard speech. "I'm in the drama department, so we study acting, voice, and. . . ."

"What? You wanna be a movie star?"

"It's an academic school, too."

"Oh, yeah? Did you see *West Side Story*? You look like that girl there, what's her name, Mareer. You could play her."

"I can't sing. . . ."

"Not too many parts for Puerto Ricans," he broke in again.

"We're trained to play anything. . . ."

"What's this? Yiddish theater? D'you talk Yiddish?"

"I was an usher. . . ."

"What? They fire you 'cause you couldn't talk it?"

"No. They don't perform in the summer. . . ."

"That was some movie," he mused, and it took me a while to realize we were back to *West Side Story*. "What's her name won an academy award, didn't she?"

"Rita Moreno. She's Puerto Rican."

"Can you start on Monday?"

"Sure!"

"Eight in the morning. I'll have a card for you by the clock where you punch in." He stood up and led me to the door, "Yeah, Reeter, that's her name." He showed me out.

I was happy I had found a job but annoyed that it should have been because the boss loved *West Side Story*. I despised that movie, and it didn't help that every time I told someone I was a drama student, they expected me to lift my skirts and break into "I feel pretty, oh so pretty . . ."

Although I hadn't seen a stage performance of *West Side Story*, I'd read that the original María was played by an American actress, Carol Lawrence, while Anita was played by Chita Rivera. In the movie, Natalie Wood played Maria, and Rita Moreno was Anita. It was subtle, but it wasn't lost on me that the only virgin in the entire movie — sweet, innocent Maria — was always played by an American, while the sexy spitfire was Puerto Rican. And that wasn't all.

The Jets had a nice, clean, warm place to hang out, reminiscent of the malt shop where Archie hung out with Betty, Veronica, and Jughead. It was owned by a kindly old man who put up with all sorts of *pocavergüenzas*, including the near rape of Anita. The Sharks had a rooftop, and what did they do there? They argued over whether "America" was better than Puerto Rico.

"It's just a movie," Laura Figueroa reminded me once, when I was on a rant about *West Side Story*.

"It's not *just* a movie," I argued, "it's the *only* movie about Puerto Ricans anyone has seen. And what's the message? White Puerto Rican girls dangle from fire escapes singing sweet tunes to Italian guys, while dark-skinned Puerto Rican girls sleep with their boyfriends. Dark too, I might add."

"You're reading too much into it," she insisted.

When we read *Romeo and Juliet* in English class and Mrs. Simmons said *West Side Story* was based on the Shakespeare play,

I was disappointed. I thought the Bard could have done better. The death scene at the end of the play and the movie was the dumbest thing I'd seen. During the discussion, my classmates tried to help me see it differently.

"But don't you understand?" Brenda said. "They died for love."

"What kind of stupid reason is that?" I wondered.

"They couldn't live without each other," Ardyce explained.

"Oh, please! That's the most ridiculous reason over which to commit suicide."

"Obviously, you've never been in love," Myra sniffed.

"If I had, I'd still never kill myself over a guy."

"Even if he looked like Richard Beymer?" Roger asked.

"Especially if he looked like Richard Beymer."

"Cleopatra killed herself over Marc Antony," Jay reminded me.

"Not exactly. She thought Antony was dead and she'd lost her most important ally. With him gone, the Romans would strip her of her dignity." No one could invoke Cleopatra around me and hope I didn't have my facts straight.

Mrs. Simmons held up her hand to stop the discussion. "*Romeo and Juliet* is one of the great love stories of all time," she concluded, "but apparently, it's not for everybody." The bell rang. "Next week, we begin *Hamlet.*" She smiled in my direction. "I think you'll like that one better," she said as I left the classroom.

~～⌒⌒

My summer job consisted of stuffing negatives and pictures into envelopes, then mailing them to the people who'd sent in their film for processing. The film was developed next door, but fumes seeped through the wall into the room where I worked, which was dark and windowless. Two other women worked at desks doing the same thing I did, and one of them, Sheila, a black woman not much older than I was, was charged with teaching me how to do the job. The other, an older Asian woman, mumbled to herself the whole time she worked and rarely looked up from her stacks of envelopes, negatives, and prints.

"That's what happens when you work here too long," Sheila said, tipping her head in Mimi's direction. "You go cuckoo. All those chemicals." She laughed, and I figured she must have been kidding.

"How long have you worked here?"

"Me? Oh, about seven months. I've got two kids to support, you know. I'm not like you, stayin' in school and all that." Sheila worked three days a week; the other two she was enrolled at a training program for nursing assistants. "I had to get my GED," she said, "then they made me take biology and chemistry and all that shit I slept through the first time. Do you have to study that in your school?"

"Yes."

"You like it, don't you?"

"I don't mind it."

"I wish I'd stayed in school. Now I got two kids to support. Don't you go thinking it's good to quit school."

"My mother wouldn't let me."

"I'm with her." She shuffled through some photographs. "Look at this fool in this picture here! What does he have on his head?"

"It looks like a bunch of bananas."

"You see the foolest people in this job. Check this one out . . . she thinks she looks good."

For hours, I stuffed people's memories into envelopes, to the sound of Sheila's chatter and Mimi's mumbles. Every evening as I stepped onto the sidewalk, I breathed the air of Brooklyn, fresh and clean compared to that in the building where I spent eight hours a day. I went home, changed, and closeted myself in my room to read, or to write rambling entries in a journal La Muda had given me for my seventeenth birthday.

I was paid every Friday. At home, I gave Mami a portion of

my salary and paid my sisters or brothers to do the chores assigned to me that I didn't want to do. The rest was spent on clothes for the coming school year, but my biggest expense was for books that I didn't have to return to the library.

My first purchase was Dr. Norman Vincent Peale's *The Power of Positive Thinking.* I liked his theory that negative thoughts result in negative actions. Mami, my sisters and brothers, friends in school had accused me more than once of having a morbid, negative streak. I hoped Dr. Peale's book would help me to think positively when life turned grim, which I was certain it would.

As Dr. Peale suggested, I made a list of the good things in my life:

1. I'd passed my third geometry Regents with a 96.
2. I had a job.
3. Mami had a job, was in love and happy again.
4. Delsa, Norma, and Héctor also had jobs.
5. With five people working at home, we now had more money than we'd ever had.
6. I had my own room.
7. Raymond's foot had completely healed, and the doctors said he didn't have to come for checkups any more.

Dr. Peale suggested ten things, but I could only come up with seven, which I interpreted to mean that I desperately needed the book.

To help me get into a positive mood, I memorized songs about the good life. At the library, I listened to scratchy recordings of Broadway musicals and learned to belt out "Everything's Coming Up Roses" like Ethel Merman. I sang "Luck Be a Lady Tonight" from *Guys and Dolls* as I showered every morning. But the song that I hummed in moments of doubt came from the despised *West Side Story.* I found it insulting that the only positive thing in Maria's life was Tony under her fire escape. But I loved his song, and promised myself that there would be something good every day, and that the minute it showed, I would know it. While in *West Side Story* good things were around the corner only for the non–Puerto Ricans, I made myself believe that a miracle was due, that it would come true, and that it was coming to me. So I slowed when I turned the corner and imagined what a miracle might look like whistling down the river.

～～～～

Since Don Carlos had come into our lives, we didn't go dancing as much, because the only time Mami saw him was on weekends.

"Isn't it strange?" Tata asked Mami, "that he doesn't live here?"

"It's because of his work," Mami explained. "It's too far for him from here to his job in the city."

"You and Negi go into the city every day," Tata pointed out.

"It's different. He has two jobs. One in the daytime and another one at night."

Whether Tata put doubts in her mind or not, by the middle of the summer, when Mami showed signs that she was pregnant, she began to question Don Carlos about his whereabouts during the week. From my room next to theirs I heard them argue. Or rather, I heard Mami. Don Carlos responded in a low voice, as if he didn't want anyone but Mami to hear his defenses. Sometimes, he didn't answer her at all, which infuriated her, so that she hurled accusations that he stubbornly refused to respond to. He just picked up his briefcase and left. When Mami cooled off, he returned, and things were fine for a while.

He told us he had three children. We pestered him about meeting them, but he always postponed the visit with one excuse or another. He said he worked as an accountant during the day and in the evening kept books and did taxes for private clients. During his courtship of Mami, he made a show of paying for our tickets and breakfasts after the clubs. But once he moved in, he had trouble opening his wallet. He didn't offer to help with *la compra*, didn't hand out spare change or offer to pay the phone bill when Mami couldn't keep up the payments and it was cut off.

"*Tacaño*," was Tata's assessment, as she tapped her elbow with her fist. None of our relatives was rich, but neither were they stingy. They were generous with what they had, and Don Carlos's unwillingness to part with his money was interpreted as a weakness of character, a sure sign that there were other, more unpleasant traits in him that we had yet to discover.

"Stop thinking and dance."

At Performing Arts, we read Shakespeare in English classes, but the drama department didn't cast us in scenes from his plays until we were ready. Now that we were seniors, with two full years of voice and diction and acting classes behind us, we'd finally get to perform some of the Bard's greatest scenes. I'd already expressed my dislike of *Romeo and Juliet*, so it was no surprise that I wasn't cast as a Capulet. I was to be — what else — Cleopatra, in iambic pentameter.

I was paired with Northern Calloway (no relation to Cab, he said), one of the stars of the drama department, equally at home in tragedy, comedy, or musical theater. I liked him, but his openness and subversive humor sometimes turned me off. When we were assigned act 1, scene 2 of Shakespeare's *Antony and Cleopatra*, I worried that we wouldn't work well together, but he was more disciplined than I'd expected. He helped me find aspects of Cleopatra's character that I'd underplayed or ignored. He advised that I give up the yellow tablecloth costume, because I'd developed mannerisms based on the limited range of motion the dress allowed.

I bought a pair of filmy nylon curtains, and made a transparent dress. After almost three years of seeing me concoct costumes out of sheets, drapes, and scraps of material, Mami no longer asked to inspect everything I made. But when she saw the sheer fabric, she warned me: "I hope you're planning to wear a slip under that."

I explained that the queen of the Nile didn't wear slips but agreed that, for the sake of decency, I'd wear the costume over tights and leotards.

～～ᴐ

I was in the hall reading the drama department bulletin board, where newspaper clippings of famous alumni were posted along with the year they'd graduated noted in a corner. At Performing Arts, one didn't just stand around. Every opportunity to exercise body or craft was to be taken advantage of, so as I read, I executed pliés in second position.

I felt someone standing behind me, and when I turned, I was face to face with a man with a large head topped by wild black hair, a big nose, piercing black eyes under shapely brows, and well-formed lips that didn't smile. I knew him to be one of the teachers in the dance department.

"You must be an Indian classical dancer," he declared in a deep voice with a hint of a foreign accent.

"No, sir. I'm a Puerto Rican actress."

He seemed annoyed at being corrected. "I didn't say you are, I said you must be. Come see me."

I was intrigued, imagining Indians in feathered headdresses and moccasins performing *en pointe* around a campfire. During a free period, I ran up to the dance office, but there was no one there. I tried a couple more times that week but never found him.

One day, Miss Cahan, a dance teacher in the drama department, stopped me in the hall and asked if I could try out for a play. "It's for a children's theater company."

She told me the audition was later that week, gave me the address. "Other students are auditioning," she added. "Don't be late."

The address was on Madison Avenue. A doorman had me wait as he called up my name and, after a few minutes, told me to go up to the fifth floor. The elevator operator, a short, swarthy man in a natty uniform that made him look like Napoleon stranded in the wrong century, didn't look at me as we rose, pointed to the left when we reached a dim, carpeted hallway, waited until I pressed a button under the peephole of the apartment door. When the door opened, the elevator closed. Miss Cahan, dressed in tights, leotards, and a long dance skirt, greeted me and led me inside an enormous room with broad windows at the far end.

I was seventeen years old and had never been in an American home. Here I was, inside an apartment on the Upper East Side — thick carpets at my feet, dark brooding paintings on the walls, yards of fabric around the windows, two sofas, upholstered chairs, side tables with china and crystal figurines. I ached with envy.

Miss Cahan introduced me to Mrs. Kormendi, the writer and director of the play. Another Performing Arts student was in the room — Claire, whom I knew to be a superior actress. Her shoes were off, and she sat cross-legged on the floor at Mrs. Kormendi's left. The simple shirt and pants she wore, the casual "Hi" with which she acknowledged me, led me to believe that she lived in the apartment.

"Why don't you take your shoes off and put them under that bench." Miss Cahan pointed to a plush, upholstered piece of furniture I would have never called a bench, although I didn't know what else to call it. I wore a skirt, as always, because Mami didn't think decent girls wore pants unless they were on a horse.

"Maybe you should remove your stockings too," Miss Cahan said, "so you don't slip."

"Okay." I turned my back and discreetly unhooked the stockings from the garter belt and rolled them down, wondering why I needed to get undressed to audition for a children's play. Miss Cahan read my mind.

"I should have told you we were going to dance," she explained, "so you could come prepared."

"Oh!" I walked over, my toes digging into the plush carpet as I used to dig them into the soft, warm mud of Puerto Rico, then sat with legs folded under me on the floor, although there were about ten sumptuous chairs I longed to drop into.

Mrs. Kormendi explained that the play was based on an Indian legend. "India Indian," she specified, "not American." They were casting someone to play the goddess Lakshmi, who in the play was a statue that became a swan. I didn't ask how. There was quite a bit of dancing, the reason Miss Cahan was helping with the audition.

"All right, then," Miss Cahan said. "Let's try some things."

Mrs. Kormendi sat on the sofa with a clipboard on her lap and took notes while Miss Cahan led me and Claire through a series of steps unlike anything we'd ever done in dance class. They were stylized, dramatic postures that required we move in a wide, second-position plié, our torsos rigid, our arms and hands in gestures that demanded coordination and strength in muscles I had never used. I couldn't follow the choreography and stopped several times, embarrassed and frustrated, as Miss Cahan and Claire moved across the floor with ease.

Miss Cahan adjusted my stance. "Stop thinking," she said, "and dance. Don't worry about remembering the steps. Your muscles will remember."

That was a new concept. I worked hard in dance, pushed myself to leap higher, stretch farther. I never just let it happen. But I trusted Miss Cahan, who as a professional knew more about it than I did. I stopped thinking. Next thing I knew, the audition was over and Mrs. Kormendi promised to get back to us.

Claire and I rode the elevator down. While she and I were classmates, we didn't have much to say to one another. She was one of the smart, talented, popular girls who were cast in the best roles: Antigone or her sister Ismene, Juliet, Emily in *Our Town*, Frankie in *Member of the Wedding*. We parted in front of the building, but as I walked to the subway station on my way back to Brooklyn, I knew the part was mine. Claire might be an angelic ingenue, but I'd perfected exotic characters. Cleopatra, queen of the Nile, I was sure, was about to become Lakshmi, swan goddess.

A few days later, Miss Cahan asked me to stay after class and told me that Mrs. Kormendi wanted me in her play. I couldn't wait to get home and tell Mami that one full year before graduation, I already had a part in a play. Only nine more years of sacrifice, and I'd be a star.

⟳

The first rehearsal for Mrs. Kormendi's play was on a Saturday morning, at a studio on Madison Avenue not far from her apartment. A ballet class was in session when I arrived. I watched from the open door, but the teacher, a tight-faced woman with a sour expression, came over and slammed the door in my face. I was so embarrassed that tears came to my eyes, but I swallowed them when I heard steps down the hall. Mrs. Kormendi appeared as the ballet class ended and the hall filled with long-legged, haughty ballerinas.

Mrs. Kormendi kissed the sour-faced *madame* on both cheeks, and they talked as the room cleared. The dance teacher looked scornfully in my direction, and I heard Mrs. Kormendi say my name. I stripped to my tights and leotards but didn't dare warm up at the barre while *madame* was in the room. Her eyes followed me, and I expected her to apologize for her rudeness, but she didn't.

Within a few minutes the rest of the cast appeared, boys and girls no older than twelve years of age. They too stripped to their tights and leotards but weren't afraid to use the barre. By now the instructor had left, so I joined the kids, most of whom had obviously studied ballet before they could stand up. They went through exercises and stretches that I tried to copy, but I couldn't keep up with them.

When everyone arrived, Mrs. Kormendi handed out copies of the play, and we read through it. "Memorize your lines," Mrs. Kormendi instructed, "next week we begin blocking." Those of us who were dancing were to arrive at the next rehearsal two hours before the rest of the cast, because the choreographer had to work with us.

The following Saturday, as I came up to the studio, I heard strange music, rhythmic stomping, bells jingling furiously from behind the open door. In spite of having the door slammed in my face once already, I couldn't contain my curiosity. In the room was the dance teacher who'd confused me for an Indian. He wore a sheet wrapped around his waist and legs and a long white shirt with embroidered designs down the front and on the sleeves. On his legs, he wore bells. His movements were fierce, low across the floor in a deep plié, his big toes curled up from the ground. He jumped, his arms and legs jabbed the air, his eyes rolled in his head, his mouth twisted into an evil grin, his head snapped back and forth on his neck, and then he landed in the same deep plié with toes pointed up. I'd never seen anything so savage or so beautiful. It couldn't be dance, but it couldn't be anything else. When he stopped, Mrs. Kormendi's voice called from inside, where she sat on the only chair in the studio, clipboard on lap. She waved me over to her side.

"You know Matteo, don't you?" she whispered.

"I've seen him around school." The other person in the room was Northern, my Antony, who smiled cheerily at my surprise to see him.

Mrs. Kormendi and I watched Matteo teach Northern the stylized gestures and facial expressions he'd just performed. When the rest of the actors arrived, Matteo taught us our first class in Indian classical dance, which had nothing to do with feathered headdresses and moccasins. It was an ancient dance form, actually six ancient dance forms, each associated with a different part of India, and each having distinctive music, choreography, postures, costumes. The dance he was teaching Northern was based on Kathakali, the dance theater of Kerala, while the rest of us were to learn Bharata Natyam, associated with southern India. Matteo demonstrated some of the ways the two dance types differed in style and in the kind of stories the dancers told with their bodies.

He explained that historically, Kathakali was performed by men, Bharata Natyam by women. He spoke with reverence of choreography passed down generation to generation by dancers who were often ostracized for their dedication to their art. He showed pictures of sculptures based on the movements he was about to teach us.

He put us through a class more demanding than any I'd ever taken. It wasn't just the physicality of the dance that was so challenging. It was that what we were learning was more than theater and more than dance. It was a complete art form that combined theater, dance, music, and spectacle. It had its own unique language; every gesture had a name, every emotion a gesture. When I looked in the wall-size mirror of the studio, I saw what Matteo must have seen the day I was doing pliés in front of the Performing Arts bulletin board. I didn't look like a Puerto Rican actress from Brooklyn. I looked like an Indian classical dancer.

Matteo taught at a studio on the Upper West Side. He charged more money per class than I made from ushering. I called Mr. Murphy at the photographic developing company, and he offered me work on weekends and whenever I could come in. The problem was that between school, rehearsals, and the work it took to pay for classes, I didn't have time to go to Matteo's studio. And he didn't appreciate dancers who weren't committed to the art. I took classes with him a few times, but mostly I paid attention to what he taught during rehearsals, came even when my character wasn't involved, and soon learned the dances in the play, including the attendant's story dance and Northern's ferocious devil dance.

As rehearsals evolved, I abandoned my fantasy of being whisked on wires above the stage like Mary Martin in *Peter Pan*. Lakshmi spent the entire first scene standing on one leg inside a temple while the princess cried and prayed, in despair from being in love with the prince but betrothed to a rajah who was really a devil. At the beginning of scene 2, a sitar thrummed, my cue to begin the transformation from stone to swan. My fingers trembled, my eyes flicked from side to side, my arms softened and fluttered. Flying was simulated by *mudras*, hand gestures that were slow and tentative at the beginning, then fully realized into the sinuous movements of a creature discovering she's no longer hard stone but a soft, graceful bird. In performance, when my fingers came to life, the audience gasped, and by the end of the dance, they were on their feet, clapping.

La Muda came to the last show. My dance, so much like her wordless language, was the best I'd ever achieved. As I transmuted from silent stone to effusive goddess, I *was* La Muda, trapped in silence but avid to communicate, speaking with my body because voice failed me. When I danced, I had no tongue, but I was capable of anything. I was a swan, I was a goddess, I vanquished devils.

When Mami was five months pregnant, she found out why Don Carlos didn't have money to spare and didn't come home every night. He'd told us he was divorced, but the truth was that when he wasn't with us he was with his wife in the Bronx. Mami found out when the wife called and cursed her, her ancestors, and every future generation into eternity. When Mami confronted Don Carlos, he admitted that he wasn't technically divorced but insisted that it was only because the paperwork hadn't come through. Neither Mami, Tata, Don Julio, nor any of us believed him. In my eyes, the courteous and soft-spoken Don Carlos became just another *sinvergüenza* who promised more than he had any intention of delivering.

Respectful attention gave way to a mouthy, aggressive insolence that Mami punished. Her threats, slaps, and insistence that we owed Don Carlos proper courtesy and deference because he was an adult and the father of our soon-to-be sister or brother didn't change our behavior. Instead, a bitter grudge sprouted where there had once been affection, and although eventually Don Carlos did divorce, did introduce his children to us, and did loosen his wallet, for me at least the damage was done. I'd never forgive him for reopening the still tender wounds caused by Papi's surrender of us to an American fate and Francisco's death.

But what scared me most about Don Carlos's betrayal was that Mami was not immune to the seductive power of a man with a sweet tongue and a soft touch. "Men only want one thing," she'd said so many times that I couldn't look at a man without hearing it. If *she* could fall under the spell, how could I, younger and less experienced, hope to avoid the same destiny?

Mami worked until a few months before she was due, and then we humbled ourselves at the welfare office. After we explained the situation, the social worker came to the apartment unannounced to make sure Don Carlos wasn't hiding behind the shower curtain or in the closets.

Because we hadn't been warned, the apartment was the familiar chaotic mess I found comfortable but embarrassing, because I knew people shouldn't live like that. The beds were not neat, because they served as seats when we watched television or did our homework. The dishes hadn't been washed, because it was my turn and I always waited until the last minute if I couldn't bribe one of my siblings to do them. Mami hadn't been to the laundromat, so there was a pile of soiled clothes spilling out of the hamper. The bathroom was adorned with drying bras, panties, and stockings, as well as with a few hand-washed shirts and blouses on hangers. Franky's nose was snotty, and no one had helped him clean it. Mami's back ached and she'd been in bed all day, one of the reasons the apartment was such a mess. Tata's bones hurt, so she'd begun to drink early and now sat in the kitchen smoking, her caramel eyes on the doughy social worker who went from room to room opening cabinets and drawers.

While the social worker was there, we were subdued, afraid to look at her, as if we'd done *algo* and she'd caught us. Mami trailed her, with me and Delsa to interpret. The kids sat on their beds pretending to read because, while I translated for Mami in the kitchen, Delsa ran back to warn them to behave. Don Julio was due any minute, and we worried that the social worker would think he lived with us, which he didn't. Even so, it felt as if he shouldn't visit, as if we shouldn't know any men.

The social worker was thorough. She wrote cryptic shorthand symbols in a pad, pushed her glasses up, opened the refrigerator, made a note, checked inside the oven. When she asked questions, we weren't sure if she was making conversation or if she was trying to trap us into admitting there was a man under the bed or behind a door, even though we knew there wasn't one.

Once the social worker left, the apartment looked smaller and meaner than before she came. There was a dead roach in the corner. The trash barrel was full. Grease congealed on the dirty dishes. The walls had peeling paint, dark wood showed under the torn linoleum. The ill-fitting secondhand curtains were too heavy for the rods. Everything looked worse, which, I supposed, made us look as if we really needed the help.

The noncommittal social worker was the first American to see the way we lived, her visit an invasion of what little privacy we had. It stressed just how dependent we were on the opinion of a total stranger, who didn't speak our language, whose life was clearly better than ours. Otherwise, how could she pass judgment on it? I seethed, but I had no outlet for my rage, for the feeling that so long as I lived protected by Mami, my destiny lay in the hands of others whose power was absolute. If not hers, then the welfare department's. I closed myself off in my room and cried into my pillow, while my family joked and laughed and imitated the social worker's nasal voice, the way she peeked inside the cabinet under the sink, as if a man could fit there. It was not funny anymore to laugh at ourselves or at people who held our fate in their hands. It was pathetic.

I fell asleep bathed in tears and didn't hear the screams when the world went black, didn't hear Mami shuffle from her room to the front of the apartment, bumping into furniture as she counted heads to make sure we were together in the utter darkness of Brooklyn. I didn't hear her call my name as she and Tata ordered the kids to huddle close until they could figure out what had happened. When I woke up, I was blind, and opening my eyes made no difference. I thought I'd died, but I could feel. I screamed Mami's name and heard her "We're in the front!" I groped my way out of my room, through the kitchen to the open living room windows, where my whole family was crammed against each other. People were on the street, talking in subdued, intimate voices. The warm yellow light of candles flickered in our neighbors' windows.

"What happened?" I asked.

Delsa shushed me. Through the static of her battery-operated radio, we heard the news. New York and the entire Northeast were blacked out. I went back to the window. Above the scrawny trees, over the ragged flat lines of buildings, tiny bright lights beckoned and danced, the first stars I'd seen since we'd come to Brooklyn.

"It must be a sin to be so disrespectful to the Virgin."

In the depths of winter we moved to a single-family house on Stanhope Street. I no longer had a room to myself but shared with Delsa, Norma, Alicia, and Edna while the boys — Héctor Raymond, and Franky — slept in another room. Mami put the soon-to-be-born baby's crib, her double bed, and the dressers in the middle bedroom, the only one with a door. The downstairs had a small living room and dining area and a good-size kitchen. Tata's cot went into the pantry, across from the rice, flour, dry beans, cans of tomato sauce.

Having a whole house to ourselves made us feel rich. No downstairs neighbors to bang on the ceilings because we made too much noise. No one upstairs walking heavily overhead, shaking the light fixtures. But it also meant no super if the toilet broke, and when there wasn't enough heat, it was because we hadn't paid the bill, not because the landlord was stingy.

We lived close to the relatives again, and I could visit Alma and Corazón on the way home from school. They too had moved, to a roomy but dark apartment on Flushing Avenue, half a block from the elevated train. Alma had graduated from high school and worked as a secretary for a sock wholesaler. Her office was a few blocks from Performing Arts, and every week we met for dinner in the city. We got along so well that we soon came up with a plan to share an apartment as soon as I graduated from high school and could find a job.

"It'll have to be a two-bedroom," Alma said, "I need privacy."

"Yes, and I hope you know I can't cook."

"Neither can I. We'll eat out," she suggested.

We combed the classifieds for a sense of what we'd have to pay in the Upper East Side, our first choice. Alma had read somewhere that we shouldn't spend more than the equivalent of one week's salary, and it was soon clear that a two-bedroom apartment anywhere in Manhattan was out of the question.

"We might have to look in Queens," she suggested, to which I objected. "I don't want to live in the outer boroughs."

"We'll keep looking, then." The next week we went over the listings again. We figured out how much to put aside for a security deposit, the first month's rent, furniture, towels, sheets, curtains, and rugs. If we were thrifty, if Alma got a raise, if I found a good job, we'd be able to afford an apartment six months after I graduated.

"We'll move in for Christmas," I said, "and throw a housewarming party." I imagined an apartment not unlike Mrs. Kormendi's, filled with people whose faces were a blur because I didn't know them yet.

It was so much fun to plan our lives as single girls in Manhattan that we didn't think of asking our mothers.

"The only way you're leaving my house," Mami vowed when I broached the subject, "is as a married woman."

"But I don't want to get married."

"Decent girls don't live alone in the city."

"We won't be living alone. Alma and I will be together, in the same apartment."

"Still," she spat out, and when I was about to make another point, she held up her finger in my direction, "just because you're in that school for *blanquitos*," at which point I tuned out.

Alma had the same argument with Titi Ana, and we had to accept that, according to our mothers, two young women living

together were still alone if there was no man to keep an eye on
them.

⟳

Charlie was born in February, and Don Carlos used the birth of
his son to insinuate himself back into our lives. He showed up
with a scarf for Mami one day, a birthday present for Franky, an
outfit for Charlie. He played gin rummy with us, or sat with Tata
and Don Julio until late at night, then climbed the stairs to Mami's
bedroom when he thought we were asleep. As soon as he left for
work, Tata ragged on Mami for taking Don Carlos back. When he
returned at night, she served him supper, muttering insults under
her breath. "Sinvergüenza," she said as she set down his rice and
beans, "desgraciado," as she poured his coffee.

Mami was embarrassed by Tata's candor, but Don Carlos
didn't seem to care. He ignored Tata, his eyes trapped behind his
tinted glasses, a half-smile on his lips as if what she said were
amusing but not offensive. He tried to win her over with presents:
a jug of Gallo wine, a carton of cigarettes, a velvet painting of John
F. Kennedy and Martin Luther King facing each other across the
bleeding heart of Jesus. Tata took his offerings but didn't let up,
until I wondered if Don Carlos enjoyed the abuse Tata heaped on
him, if part of the reason he wanted to live with us was to hear an
honest accounting of what kind of person he was. I figured he
must love Mami to put up with her eight children and bristly
mother. And she loved him, because pretty soon, Don Carlos's
dark suits hung in her closet like giant bats, and her fingers caressed the cuffs and collars of his white cotton shirts as she ironed
them every morning.

⟳

Luigi and La Muda couldn't live together, but neither could they
live apart. They separated, reunited, separated again, came to-

gether in teary reunions when he'd just happen to drop in during a family gathering. La Muda, Mami, and Tata had long conversations that we were not allowed to watch. I managed to need something from the kitchen whenever La Muda visited, and since I was *casi mujer*, Mami didn't shoo me off as she did my younger sisters. During one of her visits, La Muda swatted the side of her face, which seemed to mean that Luigi hit her. It was hard to believe that such a quiet, gentle man would hit anyone, least of all the woman he loved. But it was even harder to believe that La Muda would lie about something like that.

A few days later, he came to see us, his sad figure stooped inside his suit as if he'd shrunk and his clothes had grown around him. He had decided to return to Puerto Rico. We begged him not to go, but he said he couldn't stand the cold any more.

"Look at my hands," he moaned. The bumps on his knuckles were huge, the fingers curled over one another into loose fists. I looked away.

He walked back to the train station, his steps a painful shuffle down the street. He'd aged so much in five years that it was hard to imagine he'd been young, had performed card tricks, had been vibrant La Muda's lover. I sensed we'd never see him again, and less than a month later, we learned he was dead. It wasn't clear what killed him. Arthritis, someone said. He died in excruciating pain under the warm Puerto Rican sun. Someone else whispered that Luigi was so in love with La Muda that, unable to live without her, he had committed suicide. He had drunk himself to death, went a third theory, less believable because we'd never seen him drunk. We never knew. He simply disappeared from our lives, consumed by pain, grief, or liquor, a memory of pale graceful fingers scattering magic into the air.

The spring of my senior year of high school brought daily updates from my classmates on acceptances to colleges they had applied to and I hadn't. Mrs. Provet, Dr. Dycke, and the school guidance counselor encouraged me to continue my education.

"I can't afford to go to college," I said to them. "I need a job so I can help my mother."

"Maybe you can work part-time," Dr. Dycke suggested.

"Most colleges have work-study programs," Mrs. Provet added.

But I wasn't interested in college just yet. I wanted to be out in the world, to earn my own living, to help Mami, yes, but also to stop depending on her for my every need.

Mr. Murphy offered me full-time work in his lab in Brooklyn, but I'd already decided to seek work in Manhattan, in one of the gleaming new office towers that sprouted from the ground like defiant, austere fortresses. The only problem was that I had no skills to bring to a business.

Performing Arts offered a typing course, designed to teach us a practical skill should our talents not be recognized the minute we graduated. I sat in the front row of the classroom, feet flat on the floor, back straight, head up, eyes focused ahead, fingers poised over the keyboard, as Mrs. Barnes called out the letters we were to press without looking.

"Capital *T*, lowercase *r*, capital *J*, lowercase *m*, Shift Lock, *H P S V*, semicolon."

Each keystroke was a nail that hammered my future onto a rubber platen. If not an actress, a secretary. If not a dancer, a secretary. If not a secretary, what?

～～～

Senior Showcase was the last time my class performed in front of the whole school. I had expected to portray another Cleopatra in an obscure play by an unknown playwright, since I'd already interpreted all the famous Cleopatras. But I was surprised to be cast as the Virgin Mary to Laura Rama's Bernadette of Lourdes.

When I told Mami I was to play the Virgin Mary, she was

ecstatic. Unlike Cleopatra, queen of the Nile, Mami knew the Virgin to be a respectable character who didn't wear outlandish clothes or heavy makeup. She offered to make the costume, but the school provided it.

The first day of rehearsals I learned that my part didn't require acting in the traditional sense. I was to be a dancing Mary, with no dialogue. While my classmates blocked their scenes, Miss Cahan and I worked on a dance of apparition in a corner of the Basement.

Mine was not a religious family, so my idea of the Virgin Mary was based on what I'd picked up from devoutly Catholic Abuela, my father's mother, who went to church every morning and prayed the rosary every evening. "*Santa Maria, madre de Dios,*" she'd taught me, and in my dance improvisations, I tried to come up with decorous, evocative movements, befitting Holy Mary, Mother of God.

Miss Cahan, however, offered a less pious interpretation. Her vision of Mary was according to the Martha Graham school of movement: geometric, hard-edged, abstract. I made my entrance in one deep lunge, firmly planted my right leg, straightened it as the left rose parallel to the floor. Eyes focused on the ground, arms outstretched, back flat, I balanced on the right leg, while the rest of my body formed the cross-stroke of a *T*. I held this position until Bernadette of Lourdes noticed me and went into a trance. Then, still on one leg, I straightened my body, while my left leg swung up, up, up into a standing split, which I held with my right hand. Not very modest, this Virgin Mary with her privates exposed.

Laura Rama knelt at the foot of the stage, while I circled the back like a hungry tigress, my long robes hissing, Bernadette's terrible vision. Not once in the entire dance did my hands come together in the traditional prayer pose, nor did my arms gently open to encompass humanity. I was a warrior Virgin, mourning my Son. Torso contracted, I sought Him in my empty womb. Arms stretched back, I arched my heart toward Heaven, daring God to take me instead of Him, who suffered on a cross. When I made my exit, in the same powerful lunge that brought me on stage, there was a pause, followed by scattered claps and, finally, real applause. I ran down the stage steps, through the back door into the makeup room, where I collapsed into a nervous heap. Northern ran over from the wings.

"That was great!" he said with a grin. "Great costume too!"

I laughed and thanked him, under the impression that he was joking about how I had finally left behind the yellow tablecloth of my Cleopatra days. As the next group of actors ran out for their scene, I bent over from the hips to stretch my back, my legs apart in second position, and noticed that, with the lights of the makeup mirror behind me, my virginal robes were transparent. I rose in a panic. During my dance, I'd been lit from behind to enhance the dramatic effect of the Grahamesque choreography.

I dropped to my knees, covered my face with my hands. Around me, my classmates ran back and forth, preparing for their moment on the stage, while I tried to make myself disappear.

After the performances, everyone gathered for a reception in the Basement. When I came down, Mami, my sisters and brothers, and Don Carlos circled me.

"*Ay, Santo Dios,*" Mami was breathless, "it must be a sin to be so disrespectful to the Virgin." She was flushed, scanned the crowd as if God Himself were walking toward us to punish me on the spot.

"We saw right through the dress," Delsa announced, and people clustered around another student turned toward us and chuckled.

Miss Cahan came over. "It was wonderful." She kissed me. "Lovely."

"My costume . . ." I burbled on the edge of tears, "the robes . . ."

"Don't worry," she assured me. "You were great."

The Basement hummed with the chatter of proud teachers and excited students. For three years we'd been one another's critics, but this night everyone loved everybody's work. As we hugged, kissed cheeks, and applauded ourselves, my family backed away. The distance was not much, a few feet at most, but it was a continent. I felt their pull from where they bunched in a corner of the room, talking and laughing, isolated in the noisy crowd of voluble actors and jovial teachers. I couldn't walk away from them, but neither did I want to be with them and miss the camaraderie of actors after a show. I was pulled by Mami, Don Carlos, and my siblings in one direction, while my peers and teachers towed me in another. Immobile, I stood halfway between both, unable to choose, hoping the party wouldn't move one inch away from me and that my family would stay solidly where they were. In the end, I stood alone between both, and when it was clear no one missed me in the spirited gathering of actors and teachers, I ambled back to Mami, and in a few minutes we were on the train to Brooklyn.

Back home, I suffered through a depiction of my dance by my sisters for the benefit of Tata, Don Julio, and the kids who hadn't come. Seeing them recreate my Virgin Mary was so funny that I laughed until tears sprouted. Later, when we'd all gone to bed and the house was still, I cried for real. I didn't know why, didn't want to know. I just let the tears fall and hoped that in the morning my swollen eyes wouldn't give me away.

~~~~~~~

I asked Papi to come to my graduation. He wrote back that he'd see. "We'll see" usually meant no, so I didn't insist, but I was disappointed. In the five years I hadn't seen Papi, I'd grown at least five inches, had learned to use makeup, had acquired another language, had become independent enough to travel around Brooklyn and Manhattan on my own, had worked at two jobs, had become a dancer, had managed to avoid the *algos* that could happen to a girl in the city. And he hadn't been there.

I wondered if he had any idea what our lives were like in New York. My letters seldom described the conditions under which we lived. Even when things were at their worst, I didn't ask for help.

It was his responsibility to determine his children's needs, not ours to beg him to take care of us.

Sometimes I was so angry with him, I wished there were a way to tell him, but I couldn't bring myself to be disrespectful, to risk his anger. My letters responded to his newsy chatter, but I expected more from him. I longed for the small, tender acts that marked our life in Puerto Rico. The time he took to explain things. The hours we spent side by side hammering nails into walls. His patience when he taught me to mix cement, to place a cinder block over squishy concrete, to scrape the mud oozing from the bottom of the block with a triangular spade. I missed the poems he wrote, the silly jokes he told, the melodies he hummed as he worked. Now that I was almost a woman, I missed my father more than ever. But I couldn't tell him, afraid that my need resembled a demand, or looked like a criticism of Mami's ability to take care of us. Instead, I stifled the hunger for a father who had become more and more of an abstraction, as illusory as the green flash of a tropical sunset.

⌒⌒⌒

Just before final exams, men in fitted suits appeared at Performing Arts. Within minutes a rumor spread that they were Hollywood producers casting a movie. They visited a few classes but were more interested in the architecture of the school than in the students or teachers. A few days later, however, some of us were told that we'd been chosen to audition for the film version of Bel Kaufman's *Up the Down Staircase.*

"Mami, I've been discovered!" I crowed as soon as I came home.

"Discovered doing what?" she asked.

I explained what little I knew. They were making a movie of a famous book about a school. The writer had once been a teacher at Performing Arts. The producers had come to look around, because they might film there and might choose kids to play students in the movie.

"¡Ay que bueno!"

"You'd better be careful," Tata broke in. "Sometimes those movie people just want to meet young girls."

Tata had never met any movie people. As far as I knew, she'd never been to the movies, so her warning went in one ear and out the other. Still, it was a relief when I went up to Warner Brothers for my interview and there were no couches in the casting director's office.

Mr. Jeffers was a square-jawed, ageless man whose practiced smile nevertheless elicited a toothy response. He sat behind a huge desk piled with black-and-white photographs of every aspiring actor in New York City. I didn't have a head shot, but he said that wasn't necessary.

"We're looking for real people," he said, "not necessarily professional actors."

He didn't give me a script to read from but instead asked questions designed to get me to talk. I figured he wanted to make sure I didn't have an accent, so I enunciated every word in standard speech, modulating my voice as I'd been taught. Satisfied, Mr. Jeffers stood to show me out, and I was surprised by how short he was. He took a business card from a wallet in his pocket and handed it to me. When I reached to take it, he took my hand in his, curled my fingers around the card.

"This is my direct line," he said. I nodded but didn't dare look him in the eye. Was he flirting, or was he being nice? He led me through a maze of halls and offices toward the reception lobby.

"Call me tomorrow," he said and flashed his perfect smile.

That night I met Alma for dinner and we talked about the interview.

"It's weird. He didn't do anything, other than hold my hand a little too long."

"You think he was coming on to you?"

"I think so, but I'm not sure."

"We can't be suspicious of every man we meet," Alma suggested.

"Maybe I was reading too much into it. But I keep hearing,

'Men only want one thing,'" I mimicked Mami's voice, but Alma didn't notice.

"It's the same with me." She thought for a few moments. "Maybe our mothers just haven't met any nice men."

"They're nice at the beginning," I reminded Alma. "Then, when they get what they want . . ."

"Now you sound just like your mother!" Alma laughed, and I was embarrassed but had to agree.

Since Mami and Titi Ana had shot down our plan to move in together, men had replaced apartments as the main topic of conversations during our dinners out. In my household, there were Don Julio and Don Carlos, and we had frequent visits from Mami's male uncles and cousins, who came alone as often as they showed up with wives or girlfriends. But Titi Ana didn't encourage male relatives to come around, especially if Alma and Corazón were alone while she was at work. When it came to men, I had firsthand knowledge and long experience compared with Alma, whose main contact with men was her boss, the sock wholesaler. Sometimes we talked about what kind of man we'd like to marry.

"Rich," I said when she asked.

"But how about other qualities? A sense of humor, kindness?"

"No," I insisted, "just rich." She laughed because she thought I was kidding. "Let's say our mothers are right and men only want one thing," I continued, "what's the point of giving it to just anybody? It's the only thing we have to offer."

"No, I don't agree with you," Alma's dark eyes grew larger. "You can't think that way."

"Why, not? Men think that way about us."

"No, Negi, that's wrong." She shook her head back and forth as if trying to dislodge my words from her brain.

"I'm not kidding. When I'm ready to give up my virginity, it's going to the highest bidder."

"Oh, my God, that's terrible! Don't joke about it. It's not funny."

I loved seeing her flustered. With Alma I could be outrageous and say things I wouldn't dare say in front of anyone else. What made it fun was that she believed me. I tried out the craziest ideas on her and she took them seriously. I spoke without thinking, for the sheer joy of seeing her reaction, of arguing a point with her, of hearing myself express opinions I didn't know I had until they spilled out of my mouth.

"Just wait," I said. "The first man I do it with will be a millionaire."

"Just make sure you love him," she warned.

"Of course," I said. "Once I know he's rich, I'll fall in love with him." And then we laughed.

⌣⁓⌐

When I called Mr. Jeffers, he said he'd like me to try out for Carole Blanca, a featured role, the most prominent part for a Puerto Rican actress in the movie.

"Come prepared to perform a short monologue," he said. "And call me afterwards."

"But won't you be there?"

"No, that's not my department," he chuckled. "Good luck."

The audition was in a rehearsal studio on West 49th Street. Several chairs were set up against the wall of a hallway that led to a closed door. As I reached the top, a woman flew out from inside, asked my name, checked me off a list attached to a clipboard, pointed to the last unoccupied chair, and then disappeared behind the door.

Three actors were ahead of me. They dismissed me as soon as they realized I wasn't competition. They were called into the audition room one at a time, and I moved up the line. When my turn came, the woman who had first greeted me led me into a small, dark theater with a tiny stage that wasn't even raised off the audience level.

Several people huddled in the back. Miss Silver introduced me to an elegant man, Mr. Pakula, who was the producer, and to a rumpled man with a thick mustache, Mr. Mulligan, the director. We talked for a few minutes as they asked the usual questions; then Mr. Pakula pointed to the stage and said they were ready for me.

"You can use any props that you find down there," Mr. Mulligan suggested, which meant he wanted to see me handle a prop. I'd chosen the scene from *Member of the Wedding* in which Frankie tells John Henry she wants to leave their small town. I hadn't practiced the scene with props, but I found a bench against a wall and incorporated it into the monologue. When I sat down in the middle of it, the bench shuddered on its hinges, and I jumped up but stayed in character and played it as if the whole thing had been planned. It was the best audition I'd ever given. Mr. Pakula and Mr. Mulligan shook my hand, told me I'd done well, and said Mr. Jeffers would let me know in a couple of days, as soon as they met everyone being considered for the part.

I was proud of myself. I'd reacted appropriately to every situation, and I hoped to get the role. Even though it was after five, I called Mr. Jeffers, who sounded friendly and excited.

"You did great this morning," he said.

"You mean this afternoon," I corrected him.

"If they were making a decision right now, you'd be it," he assured me, and I could almost see his brilliant smile over the phone. "Come in tomorrow afternoon. I'll probably have good news for you."

That night I couldn't sleep. I had images of myself as Carole Blanca, my first major role in a movie, made by Warner Brothers, a famous Hollywood company. It wasn't legitimate theater, but my training at Performing Arts would ensure that I rose above the indicated performances of movie actors. I'd be brilliant. It would be the first time in my short acting career that I would play a Puerto Rican. Not Maria or Anita or any of the Sharks' girlfriends. I was to be a character with a name, a smart girl, someone my age.

The next day, when I went to Mr. Jeffers's office, he seemed surprised to see me.

"You said I should come today," I reminded him.

"Yes, of course," he was flustered, appeared confused, as if I were the last person he expected. "You're Esmeralda Santiago?"

"Yes."

"Right. Give me a second." He shuffled through some papers. It took him a while, and I had the impression that he was stalling. Finally he asked if I'd brought a head shot.

"You said I didn't need one."

"Right, I did." He shuffled his stacks some more.

"If this is not a good time," I offered, "I could come back."

"Yes. No. It's fine. That's fine." He took a couple of deep breaths, held them in, placed his hands in a prayer pose in front of his nose, stared at me for a few seconds until I looked away. "The truth is," he exhaled, "I had you confused with another girl."

"Oh."

"The other girl . . ." He leaned in, as if about to whisper, but his voice was the same as before. "The truth is," he repeated, "you're not right for the part."

"But you said . . ."

"The other girl, she looks more, how do I say this? Well, the truth is," he said for the third time, and I wished he'd lie because the strain in his voice told me that, whatever he was about to say, I didn't want to hear.

"The other girl looks more Puerto Rican."

"What?"

"You just don't have the look. You're a pretty girl. This is the movies. It's about the look."

"I'm too pretty to be Puerto Rican? Is that what you're saying?"

"You don't look Puerto Rican enough. But you'll be in the movie, don't worry about that. There are many other parts . . . a whole classroom of kids . . ."

I felt myself leave my body and rise to a corner of the room. There was Mr. Jeffers, looking somewhat hapless and small, and I, across from him my hands gripping the armrests of the chair as if loosening them would make me hurtle through space. He was blubbering, or so it seemed, his brilliant smile fading more and more every time he flashed it. He wrote something on notepaper, handed it over the desk, and the me sitting on the chair took it, read it, folded it, put it inside the small pocketbook on my lap. He stood up, stretched his hand out, and I was no longer above my head. I was shaking his hand as if he'd done me a favor. I walked out of the building in a daze; went straight to the library; found a picture of Rita Moreno, another of Chita Rivera, a third of José Ferrer. They were not ugly people. They were beautiful Puerto Ricans. But did they, I asked myself, "look" Puerto Rican? Had I not known that they were, would I have said, there goes a *compatriota?* Knowing who they were, I could not know what I would have done if I hadn't known. I only knew that according to Mr. Jeffers, my one connection with the entire motion picture industry, Puerto Ricans were not pretty people.

When I came home, I didn't mention the humiliation. I announced in chirpy tones that I'd been hired to act in the movie, that I'd be paid, that the ten-year rule obviously didn't apply to me. One week before graduation, and I already had a job as an actress. I convinced myself that it was more than I could have hoped. As we'd been told over and over again, rejection was part of the business. You couldn't take it personally.

⟳

The auditorium at Performing Arts was filled to capacity. When we marched in, dressed in our caps and gowns, the audience stood up to applaud. It was our final performance, the last day we'd appear in the auditorium as students. Papi wasn't there. From the corner of my eye I caught Mami's proud smiles. Next to her Don Carlos, in his suit and dark glasses, stood tall and dignified, proud too, even though I wasn't his child. I'd been allowed two guests. I'd pleaded that I was the first of nine children to graduate from high school, that my mother wanted to make an example of me and bring all the kids to watch. But the auditorium at Performing Arts was small. Only two guests per student.

During the program, many of my classmates were called up to receive special honors or prizes. My name wasn't called, but it didn't matter. I knew what I'd accomplished. Neither my mother nor my father had studied beyond elementary school. And here I was, in a foreign country, in a foreign language, graduating from a school for dreamers.

Had I stopped to think about my future, I would have been afraid. But what I felt on that bright June day was the thrill of achievement. I'd managed to get through high school without getting pregnant, without dropping out, without *algo* happening to me. I had a job as an actress in a movie, not a starring role, but at least I'd be paid, and who knew, I might be discovered.

But first I had to go home to Brooklyn with my mother and stepfather to celebrate with my sister the clerk at Woolworth's; my brother the pizza cook; my other six sisters and brothers; my grandmother and her boyfriend; my cousins the deaf mute, the wrestler, and the Americanized sisters; with my alcoholic uncle. That world in Brooklyn from which I derived both comfort and anxiety was home, as was the other world, across the ocean, where my father still wrote poems. As was the other world, the one across the river, where I intended to make my life. I'd have to learn to straddle all of them, a rider on three horses, each headed in a different direction.

"Who do you think you are?"

A week after graduating from Performing Arts, I stood in the middle of an elementary school playground in El Barrio, surrounded by other hopefuls on the first day of filming for *Up the Down Staircase*. Mr. Mulligan's assistant told us that we could expect work every day for a couple of weeks. The playground was to be our base while the crew filmed exteriors in front of the school and across the street.

Most of the other teenagers in the movie were from local schools, but a few were professionals with commercial and film credits. They'd been around sets and came prepared with books, knitting, cards, and board games to pass the time between takes.

The story line for *Up the Down Staircase* followed a young teacher, Miss Barrett, at her first job in a New York City school filled with underachievers. There was the class clown (Jewish), the ugly fat girl (white), her best friend (the part I didn't get because I didn't look Puerto Rican enough), the future young Republican (also white, also fat), the sensitive, doomed boy (Puerto Rican Negro), the Italian rebel with no cause, the slut. Sandy Dennis played the idealistic teacher. A supporting cast portrayed an assortment of other types: "Committed Teacher," "Frustrated Spinster," "Fascist Principal," "Alcoholic Poet."

Every time I learned the name of someone associated with the movie, I went to the library to look the person up. The director, Robert Mulligan, had won an Academy Award for *To Kill a Mock-*

ingbird, produced by Alan Pakula. Tad Mosel, a respected playwright, wrote the screenplay. And the character actors — Roy Poole, Eileen Heckart, Maureen Stapleton, Ruth White, and Vinnette Carroll (who was a teacher at Performing Arts) — were legitimate theater actors, as was the star, Sandy Dennis, who'd just costarred with Elizabeth Taylor and Richard Burton in *Who's Afraid of Virginia Woolf?* I was proud to be in the midst of so much talent.

Most of the exteriors were filmed in El Barrio, outside the elementary school and the streets around it. We were called to the location early in the morning and were often there until late afternoon. We did a scene several times and then waited for the lights, camera, and sound to be ready for another take from a different direction. It was tedious work, but it did give me a lot of time to read, to learn to play Monopoly and Scrabble, to chat with the other extras. Like me, they hoped to make such an impression in the movie that they'd be discovered, go to Hollywood and become stars. We did everything we could to gain the attention of the director, producer, and crew. We massaged sore shoulders, carried coffee, flirted, listened attentively to dumb jokes. It paid off. After the exteriors were shot, some of us were chosen to be featured in the classroom, which meant more work and higher pay.

The production moved to a high school near Lincoln Center, where the hall, stairway, and some of the classroom and office scenes were filmed. Then we were called to a sound stage in the West 20s, where the classroom was recreated complete with a giant transparency of the view outside the windows of the school we'd just left. The walls moved out of the way for the cameras, lights, and technicians who ran around between takes to adjust lights or microphones or to powder Sandy Dennis's face or spray her hair.

When she wasn't needed on the set, Miss Dennis went to her dressing room or sat in a director's chair, where she was approached for autographs by kids brave enough to risk being shooed away. She was friendly, seemed to enjoy it when one of us talked to her as if she were a normal person and not a movie star. Sometimes she did things that we didn't know how to interpret. Once, we came back from lunch to film a scene that required deep emotion and concentration on everyone's part. We rehearsed the scene numerous times, having been warned before the break that the scene was difficult to shoot, that we should listen, concentrate, follow directions carefully to make it easier for the featured actors. We were nervous, and when Miss Dennis came in, we focused and prepared for the moment. Mr. Mulligan called "Action!" in a soft voice. Sandy Dennis's face twitched, she opened her mouth, and out came a long, ripe, thunderous burp. Everyone froze in place, Mr. Mulligan called "Cut!"

Miss Dennis giggled. "I shouldn't have beer at lunch." We cracked up. It took us a while to settle down because the minute Mr. Mulligan called action, someone laughed, and pretty soon the entire cast and crew were giggling.

Usually, a stand-in Sandy Dennis's height and coloring took her place while lights and cameras were adjusted. But sometimes Miss Dennis did it. One day she sat at her desk while technicians worked around her. My desk was directly in front of hers, and every once in a while she looked up and smiled. Then, out of nowhere, she asked if I had any sisters or brothers.

"Yes, I'm the oldest of nine children," I said.

"Nine!"

"Five girls and four boys."

"Hasn't your mother heard about birth control?"

Someone behind me snickered. "She doesn't believe in it," I mumbled, because I didn't know what else to say. Miss Dennis nodded, no longer interested, and began a conversation with Liz, who sat next to me.

Birth control was in the news because of the recently developed pill to prevent pregnancy. Whenever we discussed it at home, it was agreed by the adults around the kitchen table that "the Pill" was nothing more than a license for young women to have sex without getting married. The fact that my mother, grandmother, and almost every other female relative of ours had sex without marriage was not mentioned. If I pointed that out to them, I was scolded for being disrespectful. In any case, I would never suggest that Mami avoid having babies. While being in a large family was hard for all of us, there was not a single sister or brother I'd rather not have.

For myself, however, I'd decided that I'd changed enough diapers for a lifetime and planned to sign up for the pill as soon as there was any possibility I'd need it.

Sometimes, when we were dismissed from the set of Up the Down Staircase early, I window-shopped on Fifth Avenue or spent hours at the Lincoln Center Library listening to Broadway musicals. From time to time, men approached me.

"Excuse me, is this seat taken?" They pointed to the empty chair next to me, and I felt like saying, "Yes, my invisible cousin is there," but never dared. Next thing I knew, I was carrying on a conversation with Dan or Fred or Matt or Kevin. Sometimes they invited me for a cup of coffee. We sat across from each other discussing theater, since most of the men I met in the middle of the day on weekdays in Manhattan were unemployed actors. As I listened to them expound on whether the Method was passé, or whether legitimate theater actors were selling out if they did commercials, I tried to determine if this qualified as a date. I didn't know what the rules were for dating, never having done it. And I felt pretty stupid asking people who did know about it, like the girl who played the slut in Up the Down Staircase, or Liz, my seat mate on the set. I read Sex and the Single Girl, Mary McCarthy's The Group, some Harold Robbins, trying to figure out what one did on dates, should I ever have one. But my encounters at the library never went further than coffee, and there were no other candidates.

Delsa had a boyfriend, Norma had a boyfriend, Héctor had a girlfriend. But none of them dated. My sisters' boyfriends came to our house on Sunday, had dinner with us, sat in front of the television with the younger kids, then left at a respectable hour. Héctor's girlfriend came with her mother, or Héctor went to her house and did what Delsa's and Norma's boyfriends did at ours. They were not permitted to go anywhere as couples without a chaperone, most frequently one of the younger kids because they had to be looked after, couldn't be ditched, and snitched if anything untoward took place.

Because I had the most freedom, I could get away with a solo clandestine date in the city. I hadn't tested it, since no one asked, but I began to plan for the day when I'd have to do it. Every day toward the end of summer, as *Up the Down Staircase* wound down, I stayed out later, giving one excuse or another for coming home long after expected. Most of the time Mami scrunched her brow, narrowed her eyes, pursed her lips, any of the familiar grimaces I understood meant she had misgivings but was not about to give into them yet. In the interest of not raising suspicions for what I wasn't doing, I didn't take advantage. I slowly raised the threshold of her permissiveness, and when she complained I was late too many days in a row, I didn't go out if there was no filming the next day. I played with my sisters and brothers or went shopping with Mami or hung around the house reading, my hair in curlers in an attempt at a new hairdo, and tried to act as if I had nothing to hide, which I didn't, certain that someday I would.

⌒⌒

Although I'd worked hard to be discovered on the set of *Up the Down Staircase*, when the movie wrapped there were no offers from Hollywood, so I had to figure out what to do next. I gave myself a month to be cast in another movie, a play, or as a dancer with a company. I bought *Backstage* and *Variety* every week, made a list of the auditions for which I might qualify, called casting agents, appeared at rehearsal studios where try-outs were announced. But there were no parts for a Puerto Rican ingenue/ Cleopatra/Indian classical dancer.

Late summer and early fall was a rough time for Mami because of the enormous expense of getting the kids ready for school and another winter. I'd made a lot of money over the summer but had spent most of it on dance classes and a wardrobe appropriate for an actress/dancer who needed to make a good impression at auditions. I gave Mami a portion of each paycheck, and Don Carlos also helped, especially now that Mami was pregnant again. But it wasn't enough, so we moved from our house to a smaller, third-floor apartment where the rent included utilities.

The owner of the house, Doña Lila, lived on the second floor with her two sons, one of whom was a couple of years older than me. Neftalí was slender, with a dark *café con leche* complexion and startling green eyes. He was the handsomest man I'd ever seen, and his deferential manner, soft voice, and tender smile made me flutter and tingle whenever he looked my way.

My sisters and brothers noticed I liked Neftalí.

"How come you don't sit around the house with your hair in curlers any more?" Héctor asked.

"Yeah, and you go up and down the stairs twenty times a day," added Alicia.

"You used to pay us to take the garbage out when it was your turn," Raymond complained.

"Come on, Negi," Norma begged. "I'm not making any money from you."

Neftalí came upstairs frequently, joined the domino and gin rummy games around the kitchen table that competed with laughter from the television set in the other room. He was a terrible player, which made him fun to play with, since we wagered on every game. He came on Sundays, like Delsa's and Norma's boyfriends. He liked to read, which I appreciated, but his favorite books were serial science fiction novels, which I didn't understand. He was a high school graduate and talked about going to college. In the meantime, he worked in the garment center, pushing carts loaded with newly made clothes from the factory where they were made to the warehouse from where they were shipped. He said it was like lifting weights and let my younger brothers dangle from his bent arm to show off his biceps.

"You're in love! I knew you didn't mean it when you said . . . you know," Alma blushed, "about your virginity going to the highest bidder."

"I'm not going to have sex with him or anything," I protested, but I blushed too, though for a different reason. For days I'd fantasized about kisses from Neftalí's *café con leche* lips. And more than once I'd let my hands skitter across my body, imagining they were his. "Anyway," I continued, "we haven't even been alone yet. Mami doesn't take her eyes off me whenever he's around."

Which was true. But it was also true that Neftalí didn't show any interest in being alone with me. There were plenty of opportunities. He could have walked with me when I went on one of the many errands I volunteered to do for Mami. He could have waited for me at the train station when I came back from work. He could have come up while Mami was at work and the kids and Tata watched television. But he did none of that. He seemed content to join my family, to gaze at me from time to time with his unnerving green eyes, to gamble lavishly against the hand dealt me in gin rummy.

"He'll act when the time is right," Alma guessed. "He knows your mother expects things to be done a certain way."

"I wish I knew if he liked me, at least."

"He wouldn't visit so much if he didn't like you."

But I wasn't so sure. If he liked me, he should show it. He should send flowers, hire mariachis to serenade me, bring me chocolates, write poems. He should do something romantic that proved he cared about me in a way he didn't care about anyone else. When he did nothing, I followed the advice in *Sex and the Single Girl* and played hard to get. If I heard his step up the stairs, I disappeared into my room. I paid my sisters and brothers to do my errands again, so that I no longer went past his door four or five times a day. I stopped announcing when I'd be home.

One day I came back to find Doña Lila at our kitchen table. "He's not violent," she murmured between tears. "He never hurt a fly." Mami and Tata huddled by her, rubbed her shoulders, made humming sounds meant to soothe. I thought one of her sons had been accused of killing somebody and silently prayed that it hadn't been Neftalí.

"A *Neftalí lo llamaron del servicio*," Mami answered my silent question, but I had no idea what she meant by "Neftalí was called by the service."

"He's been drafted," Delsa interpreted.

Mami and Tata rubbed Doña Lila's shoulders, tried to convince her that just because Neftalí was drafted didn't mean he'd go to Vietnam. But none of us believed that. More than once Mami thanked *Dios* and the *Vírgenes* that Héctor was only fourteen. She and Tata prayed out loud that the war would end before he was old enough to be drafted and sent to what we feared was certain death.

It was hard to make sense of what was going on in Vietnam. The images were so incongruous. We watched news reports of soldiers having a great time, soldiers who laughed and made rabbit ears behind one another's heads as sober newsmen talked about casualties. We saw the landscape, lush and tropical, the long beaches lined with palm trees that reminded us of Luquillo, on Puerto Rico's northern coast. Cheerful soldiers, picturesque rice paddies, reporters who leaned manfully against army trucks, spoke into the camera while behind them young men in fatigues cavorted or carried one another in stretchers. It didn't seem real.

But here it was, my first potential boyfriend, about to go to war. It was too much like the radio *novelas* I'd listened to as a child, where the handsome hero went to war, while the beautiful heroine stayed home, wrote soulful letters, and fended off suitors not nearly as worthy as her beloved. I was torn between feeling sorry for Doña Lila and the romance of a boyfriend in a faraway country fighting for democracy.

That night Neftalí came upstairs, and I didn't hide. Don Julio and Don Carlos, both of whom had fought in Korea, told him what he could expect in basic training. "They'll make a man out of you," Don Julio joked, and Neftalí smiled shyly and looked my way.

The next day I made sure to take the garbage out, and there was Neftalí at the bottom of the stairs, with his family's trash.

"Will you wait for me?" he said, so softly that I heard "Will you weigh it for me?"

I looked at him with what must have been a stupid expression because he came closer and repeated his question.

"I'll write to you," I responded.

"I'll speak to your mother," he said, "to make it official."

I'd been waiting eagerly for pledges of love from Neftalí and the tingles and flutters that accompanied thoughts of him were now tremors and shivers. "What do you mean, official?"

"*Tú sabes,*" he murmured with a shy smile, and leaned over for a kiss.

I backed away. "No, I don't know." This was not the way I'd imagined it. He was supposed to get down on one knee, to say he loved me, to offer a diamond ring, at least to use the word "marriage" in a complete sentence. It wasn't right that he expected me to propose to myself as we stood in a dim hallway holding bags heavy with trash.

"What's the matter with you?" he said, an edge to his voice so familiar, it could have been Mami's.

I slid past him out the door to the barrels. "What's the matter with *you?*" I wanted to ask but didn't. I was sure he didn't know any more than I did. I felt like crying. He came up behind me.

"I thought you liked me," he whined, and the sound grated.

"I don't." I couldn't stop myself from being mean. A few minutes earlier he'd been a dream, and now I was telling him I didn't like him. What *was* the matter with me? I ran into the building, up the stairs, into my room, buried my face in the pillow. I sobbed as if Neftalí had done something terrible, when all he did was love me. Or did he? Why didn't he say it? I was confused, unable to understand why I'd responded as I had. I was ashamed.

He'd stood on the sidewalk holding the garbage, looking at me as if I'd lost my mind. Which is what it felt like. I was crazy, nuts, *loca*. Who'd want to come anywhere near me?

"Neftalí hasn't been up to see us in a while," Mami said a few days later, her eyes searching for a reaction. I shrugged my shoulders.

I stepped past Neftalí's door on my way to work and back on tiptoe. A part of me hoped we'd cross in the hall, and we'd talk and I'd apologize, but I didn't know what to say after that. So it was a relief when, after a week, Doña Lila came to say that Neftalí had gone to visit relatives in Puerto Rico before reporting to basic training. She watched me as she made the announcement, and there was resentment in her eyes. But she never said anything, and neither did Mami, and neither did I. There was nothing to say. I played out the scene with the trash bags in my head hundreds of times, trying to find a reason for my behavior. But it was no use. I'd behaved badly and couldn't forgive myself.

My month deadline to get an acting or dancing job came and went, and it was clear that I'd have to find another line of work. I answered a classified ad, and the week before Labor Day I was met at the door of the personnel office of Fisher Scientific by Mr. Kean, who had the characteristic turned-out, shoulders-back, lifted-from-the-hips posture of a former ballet dancer. He asked me to fill out an application, then took me into a small room with a typewriter on a small table. From a shelf by the door, he picked up a kitchen timer, a spiral-bound book, and a sheaf of paper, which he set next to the typewriter.

"We have openings in typing," he said, "so let's see how fast you do it." Mr. Kean watched as I put the paper in the typewriter and lined it up so that the edges were even. He opened the spiral-bound book to a random page, placed it next to the typewriter, set the timer, and said, "Start."

I typed as fast as I could, but I'd had no practice since the course at Performing Arts and made so many mistakes that when the bell rang, I was ashamed to show Mr. Kean the page.

"I see," he marked the mistakes in red. "Don't feel bad," he assured me, "not everyone was born to type." He laughed, and that made me feel better. "Let's see what else we can find for you." He led me to his desk in a corner of a room full of desks that reminded me of the welfare office. He riffled through a box of three-by-five cards, pulled out a couple, read the notes scribbled on them, then dialed a number. "Don't worry," he said. "There's a job in the mail room."

We took a rickety elevator to a room the width and depth of the building. Rectangles of fluorescent light fixtures cast bluish light over everything and everyone. The room was a labyrinth of gray metal desks in rows. Wide aisles divided the purchasing department from international sales from the noisy corner where typists sat, clickety-clacking for eight hours a day broken by two fifteen-minute coffee breaks and a half-hour lunch. At the far corner, in front of a row of dusty windows with a view of rooftops, was the mail room. It wasn't a room at all, but a section divided by a long table flanked by file cabinets in a horseshoe, with just enough room between them to make a passageway into the work area. Under the windows there were two more tables, and at the end a wooden desk with an armchair. Mr. Kean knocked on the table as if it were a door. A stately blonde woman stood up from behind one of the cabinets where she'd been putting folders away.

"Come in, dear," she smiled. She had an aristocratic air perfectly appropriate in spite of the setting. Mr. Kean introduced us, and Ilsa Gold interviewed me standing up, even though there were chairs under the tables by the window. Mr. Kean led me back to his office, where his phone rang, on cue, the minute we reached his desk. "You're hired," he announced in such cheery tones that I was certain he was as happy for me as I was for myself.

Ilsa explained my duties. I was to open the mail in the morning, sort it, distribute it, pick up outgoing mail in the afternoon, run it through the postage meter, and get it ready for the mailman, who came by at the end of the day. In between, I was to retrieve and file documents in any of the fifteen cabinets that formed the horseshoe of our office. By the end of the first day my fingers were shredded with paper cuts. The next morning, I showed up with Band-Aids on every finger. Ilsa looked at me curiously but didn't say a thing.

There was more work than two people could handle. Ilsa said she'd hire another person to help us, but that the right candidate hadn't come along.

"I'm very particular about who works for me," she assured me. She spoke with an accent that became heavier when she was nervous or had to talk on the telephone. I asked her where she was from.

"Far away," she said with a mysterious smile. I felt bad for prying.

The best part of my job was when I collected or delivered the mail. It gave me a chance to visit the departments, to chat with the secretaries or typists, the purchasing clerks, the salesmen. One of them, Sidney, was always at his desk when I came around.

"He's a good boy," Ilsa said, which made me giggle. "What's so funny?"

"He doesn't look like he's ever been a boy, he's so serious."

"As he should be," she said, but didn't elaborate and I didn't ask because she was frequently enigmatic, and when I asked her to explain, she clammed up or found something to do that minute.

Fisher Scientific had an employee cafeteria, but because someone had to be available should a file be needed, Ilsa and I didn't take our breaks together. In any case there was a hierarchy that determined who took breaks with whom. After a few awkward attempts to join people who were friendly when I came to drop off or pick up their mail, I learned that my place was with the clerks and other low-level employees. The supervisors, managers, and executive secretaries sat in their own groups, like high school cliques on an adult level.

There was a lot of gossip during the breaks. Gus drank too much. Phil's marriage was on the rocks. Loretta was pregnant with no husband in sight. People's problems kept us in suspense from morning coffee break to lunch to afternoon coffee break, as details emerged over the course of the eight-hour workday. When nothing juicy happened, there was the question of how women dressed for work. Brenda was too conservative and wasn't it a pity, because she had a nice figure. Lucille, however, was not nearly shapely enough for the revealing outfits she insisted on wearing. Penny's frequent hair color changes made her bald, and that was why she wore wigs. Jean's legs were too thick for miniskirts. Roberta wore too much perfume.

I worried that if I wasn't there, my coworkers would talk about me, so I rushed to the cafeteria the minute my break was due and stayed until they all headed back to their desks. At home, I repeated the gossip for the amusement of my family, who followed the stories as if they'd met the people involved. For dramatic impact, I exaggerated or added details not present in the first telling. Pretty soon I believed my version was the real thing and was surprised when facts veered from what ought to have happened, given the scenario I'd invented.

One day, as I came down the stairs of the elevated train on my way home, I was surprised to find Neftalí waiting for me. In the few weeks since he left for Puerto Rico, I'd sent him off to war, where he distinguished himself. I had received his love letters, responded with cool but interested reserve, obtained vows of enduring love, married in a cathedral with my sisters and brothers in attendance, gone on a honeymoon to Tahiti, and was about to bear twins — all in the fifteen minutes it took me to walk to and from the train station. Faced with him, I realized that the Neftalí of my imagination was taller and better dressed than the Neftalí in real life. He was also more poised. The flesh-and-blood Neftalí hung his head and mumbled hello while I asked myself what I could have seen in him a mere three weeks ago.

We walked side by side down the crowded sidewalk. It was a mild September afternoon, and the stores were open. Each door was an entrance into a cave rich with treasures: tropical fruits and vegetables; newspapers and magazines; colorful candies in shiny wrappers; racks of plastic-covered dresses, blouses, and skirts. People ducked in and out, their shopping carts squeaking behind them. Crumpled brown bags bulged with musty-smelling coats from the secondhand store. Women sat on their stoops while their children skipped rope, roller-skated, pitched bottle caps against a wall.

Neftalí and I dodged in and out of the crowd, enough space between us to fit a small child. I wished he'd try to touch me, to steal a kiss, something to indicate we were more than just neighbors. But all he did was tell me about his trip to Puerto Rico, which made me jealous.

"I hadn't been since I was kid," he said. "Those *quenepas*, man. You can't get them here."

I ignored that he'd called me "man" because I tasted the round, crackly skinned, slippery, sweet, solid-centered *quenepa* of my childhood.

He touched my shoulder and I jumped back. "You were in a trance," he explained.

"I'm sorry."

"Anyway, I was wondering if you'd like to live in Puerto Rico."

"Someday."

"Then we can settle there. In Ponce, so you can eat all the *quenepas* you like. I picked out a *solar* for a house."

"Are you planning to marry me?" I asked, incredulous.

"You like me, don't you?" Then, in an accusatory tone, "You act like you do."

"Is this a proposal?"

"You want me down on my knees?" He kneeled on the sidewalk, like in church, clutched my hand. "Is this what you want?"

People steered around us on the sidewalk. "Say yes!" somebody called, and there was laughter.

"Let go!" I pulled my hand back and ran up the street.

"Who do you think you are?" he yelled after me. "You're a big movie actress now. Is that it? I'm not good enough for you, is that it? Is that it?"

His voice faded into the clatter and thrum of the street. I ran as fast as my high heels allowed, my purse banging my side as if someone followed me with a stick. Who did I think I was? I wasn't sure, but I knew for certain I wasn't about to be Neftalí's wife.

⁓⌒

There were times when I left our apartment, caught a train, rode for an hour, rose from the subway station to the crooked streets of the Village, walked six blocks to Fisher Scientific, rode in the elevator, and realized where I was only when the doors opened to the fluorescent glow and clatter of typewriters in the huge room where I worked. It was an enormous stage lit on all sides, with an audience that could see every action from any angle. A daily theater in the round.

Ilsa professed that she had hired me because of my attitude. "You're positive and enthusiastic," she asserted. "You'll go far if you keep that up."

Sometimes my face hurt from smiling, from maintaining the alert demeanor of someone excited about what she did. But the truth was that my job was boring. Hours of filing papers that I couldn't read because Ilsa made a face if the stack in front of me hadn't decreased every time she looked in my direction. I looked forward to the half hour I spent delivering and picking up the mail, which at least allowed me to chat with the other employees. But it took enormous energy to talk without saying much about myself. People were shocked when they learned I was the oldest of nine children with a tenth on the way. Their reaction embarrassed me, as if it were my fault Mami was fertile.

When my coworkers asked for details, I made light of our living situation. "Nine children, three adults in a four-room apartment," I grinned. "It sounds worse than it feels," I insisted.

If pressed, I admitted that Mami wasn't married to the man whose baby she carried, had, in fact, not married the father of any of her children. My coworkers' eyes crinkled, their lips tightened as they judged what kind of woman Mami was and, by extension, what kind of girl I was.

"But I'm not allowed to date," I joked, to let them know I understood the irony but that my family had values that ought to command respect.

More than once I was told I didn't "sound" Puerto Rican. "You don't have an accent," Mr. Merton, one of the supervisors, remarked, and I explained about Performing Arts and standard speech. When he implied that I didn't "act" Puerto Rican, I swallowed the insult. "Maybe you haven't met enough of us," I suggested, hurt that he was surprised Puerto Ricans could be competent, chaste girls who spoke good English.

I smiled, did my job, gossiped. At the end of the day, I retraced my steps to Brooklyn, sometimes in the same haze in which I left, but exhausted, the performance having gone on too long.

"How was your day?" Mami asked each evening as I walked into our apartment.

"Good," I smiled brightly, and ducked into my room to change. Delsa, used to the routine by now, climbed down from the top bunk of our bed and left me alone.

I wiped off my makeup, then stripped. Esmeralda Santiago remained in the folds of each garment I took off and put away. Naked, nameless, I lay on my bed and slept. Half an hour later, Negi emerged, dressed in the comfortable clothes I wore at home. Another performance was about to begin, this one in Spanish.

"Pearls bring tears."

~~~~~~~~~~~

After weeks of interviewing people, Ilsa hired another clerk, Regina.

"She's beautiful, isn't she?" remarked Ilsa one day, as Regina walked away from us.

"She's giving them whiplash," I laughed.

Every man in the office craned his neck when Regina strolled by. Their eyes followed her as she moved from desk to desk, her hips and buttocks undulating in a most un-American fashion. Some of our male coworkers actually broke into a sweat when Regina came near. When she spoke, in a throaty voice with a Brazilian accent, her shushes and hums sent visible ripples through men's bodies.

Regina seemed unaware of her beauty. She dressed in long skirts, sleeved blouses with prim collars, squat-heeled shoes. She favored drab colors, wrapped her shoulder-length hair into a loose bun at the nape of her neck, wore little makeup, just a dab of lipstick and mascara.

Ilsa assigned me to train her. Regina followed me around long after she learned the simple tasks involved in our work as mail/file clerks. At first, I was annoyed that whenever I turned around, there she was, beautiful and dazed. Then one day, as we walked down for our coffee break, she thanked me.

"What did I do?"

"I am, how you say, culture shock," she confided. "In Brasil was not so." She opened her arms as if to embrace the world.

"In Puerto Rico," I said, "it was not so either."

Neither of us needed to say more to understand what the other meant, but I still didn't know why she thanked me.

"I have not friends here," she said. "Only you."

I was so touched, I hugged her.

During our breaks, we didn't sit with the other clerks but took a table by ourselves and talked about our lives. She was an only child who had nursed her mother through a three-year battle with breast cancer. When her mother died, Regina's father sent her to New York.

"I cry every day in three months," she said. "Is horrible see your mother die a little bit, a little bit." She lived with her paternal aunt, who had an important job at the Fisher Scientific offices in New Jersey. "She say me three month enough tears. I must get job. And soon I have get marry."

"Who are you going to marry?"

"I don't know."

I imagined her aunt to be the evil stepmother in fairy tales, and soon Regina's predicament was added to the stories I embellished for my family's benefit. Mami and Tata were ready to adopt her.

"Poor thing," Mami said, "motherless and alone in this city."

"And that woman," Tata added "*no tiene corazón.*"

Mami nodded that Regina's aunt did sound heartless. "*Pobrecita,*" she repeated, as she shook her head for poor Regina.

Because Regina's English wasn't very good, and because Ilsa was nervous on the phone, I was in charge of answering the calls to our office. Most of the time people called to request a file, or to warn us that they had a large mailing and we should allow extra time for pickups. One day, just as Ilsa left for her break, the phone rang. It was Sidney, who was always so pleasant to me. His office was twenty feet from ours, and he usually just walked over to ask for whatever he needed.

I turned around to make sure he was at his desk, and he waved. "How can I help you?" I waved back.

"Go out with me Friday night." He smiled.

"On a date?" I turned away because I didn't want him to see my excitement.

"Yes. Dinner, a movie, whatever you like."

"Dinner sounds good," I said into the phone, softly, because Regina had noticed what was going on and looked from me to Sidney with amusement. "Thank you," I hung up, then felt stupid for thanking him. I was afraid to look toward his desk, in case he could see me blush.

"He's very nice," Regina volunteered.

"How do I ask my mother?" I wondered aloud, and Regina laughed.

Mami wanted to know who Sidney was, what he did, where we were going, how long we'd be gone. "Bring him home so we can meet him."

"I'm just going out to dinner with him Mami. I'm not going to marry him."

"It shows respect," she said. She was right, but I couldn't imagine Sidney in our apartment filled with people and furnishings. What would he think if Tata happened to be drunk when he came by? Or if Mami wore a housecoat and rollers in her hair, as she often did when we were home? Or if Don Carlos were there, in his suit and dark glasses, sitting silently at the kitchen table, a bemused smile on his lips? Or if Don Julio, his face battered like a boxer's that had taken too many hits to the head, lounged with the kids in front of *The Lawrence Welk Show*? What if my sisters and brothers giggled about the way Sidney looked? He was short, wore thick rectangular glasses that slid down his nose and left deep red grooves along his nostrils. He spoke in a soft, whiny voice that sounded as if he were complaining, even when he wasn't. His hands stuck from the sleeves of his suit small and childlike, and never rested anywhere for more than a few seconds. I found them graceful, but Mami would surely imagine them deftly undoing my bra.

Ilsa was shocked that I was going out with Sidney.

"He asked you?" she asked, incredulous.

"Of course," I answered, annoyed she thought I had asked him.

She looked toward his desk, a somber expression on her face. "Interesting," she mused.

"Is there anything I should know about him?"

"No, dear," Ilsa said, "it's just . . . I'm surprised, that's all. He's a good boy. You have a good time."

The day before the date, Regina accompanied me to Gimbel's. I liked to shop alone, but I was worried about making a good impression and needed help in choosing something appropriate. Regina was the perfect person to restrain my impulses for theatrical, colorful, or dramatic clothing. When I came home with a new navy blue suit, low-heeled shoes, a demure handbag, Mami couldn't hide her smile.

"What's wrong with it?" I asked.

"Nothing," she said. "It's okay." She turned away to stifle a giggle.

"It's an old lady outfit," was Tata's opinion.

"I got it in the junior section," I explained, but as I looked at it, the suit seemed more Regina's style. "It's elegant," I added, repeating Regina's words. "It looks better on." I couldn't persuade anyone.

As I dressed the next morning, I told myself that it was better for me to seem conservative and old-ladyish than like a hot *tamale* right out of *West Side Story*. When I walked into the office, people stared, and some commented on how cute I looked, which made me feel better.

Sidney wasn't in his office all morning, and I worried that he'd changed his mind and wouldn't show up. During lunch, Regina pulled a small pouch from her handbag.

"Wear these," she said. Inside the pouch was a string of pearls. "They were my mother's," she explained. "They will be nice for your special night."

The pearls hung heavy in my hands, languid like a tropical

afternoon. I coveted them. My desire embarrassed me. "Regina, I can't wear these." I handed them back reluctantly. "What if I lose them?"

"You will take good care, I know," she said. "Please accept to wear them."

I hugged the pearls around my neck and she fixed the clasp. When she sat back to admire them, Regina gently straightened the collar of my blouse. She smiled sweetly, her eyes misted. "You remind me of my mother," she said. I had to swallow hard to keep from crying.

Sidney walked into the office five minutes before five. "I'm sorry. There was a lot of traffic from New Jersey in the tunnel."

I assured him it was all right, relieved that he'd shown up.

"Go," Ilsa said, "put on some lipstick. We'll finish here." I ran to the rest room and fixed my face and hair, straigthened the pearls around my neck. They shimmered pale against my cinnamon skin.

"I thought we'd eat near where I'm parked," Sidney suggested, as we walked down the street in a direction I'd never taken. The air was moist, and a cold wind blew from the Hudson, cut through my cloth coat until I shivered. We walked down a cobblestone street, around huge delivery trucks backed up to loading docks.

"Are we going far?" I asked after a few blocks.

"Just around the corner," Sidney said.

The restaurant was in a basement. An awning flapped over the door with a name written in such dark characters that it couldn't be made out. Inside, two brick walls were lined with booths, each lit with a single flickering candle inside a red glass. The cloths and napkins on the tables glowed a fluorescent white, floated in the darkness, each with its red circle of light. It reminded me of my grandmother's altar in Puerto Rico, the mystery of the rosary she recited every evening.

We were the only patrons. The bartender looked up when we walked in, nodded us to a booth. In the dim room, Sidney's features softened. His eyes, enormous behind his glasses, were kind, and there was a sadness in them that made me want to be nice to him.

A waitress appeared from the back pushing bobby pins into a frothy beehive. "I'll take your drink order," she informed us.

I'd never had an alcoholic beverage anywhere but with my family, at Christmas, when Mami made several bottles of *coquito* with fresh coconut milk and Puerto Rican rum. When I asked for a Coke, both Sidney and the waitress were disappointed. He ordered a whiskey sour.

"Don't you drink alcohol?" he asked.

"Only at home," I answered, and he laughed. It took me a while to understand why. "I didn't mean it that way. I mean . . ."

"I know what you mean, don't worry about it."

We chatted for a few minutes about life at Fisher Scientific, where he worked as a microscope salesman. He liked the work, because he visited clients in several states, instead of being stuck in the office all day. He'd recently moved out of his widowed mother's house into his own apartment.

"It's not much," he confided. "I hate living alone, but I liked it less when I lived with my mother."

We ordered dinner from the specials board, discussed movies we'd seen, places we'd like to visit, books we'd read. We talked about our coworkers, and he told me something I didn't know. Ilsa, my supervisor, was Hungarian and had survived Nazi concentration camps.

"She doesn't like to talk about that part of her life," Sidney confided.

"I don't blame her." It explained a lot. Her accent, for starters. The faraway look that came over her, as if she heard voices.

"Look at her left arm sometime," Sidney suggested. "She has numbers tattooed right here." He touched me near the inside of my elbow.

He was easy to talk to, a generous listener. We sat at our table long after we'd eaten, sipping coffee, talking about dance and music. He played the violin, and I admitted I knew nothing about classical music except what I'd heard at Performing Arts assemblies.

"MOTE-zart," he corrected my attempt to name composers. I dug a piece of paper from my handbag, wrote down more names. "How do you pronounce them?" I asked. "BATE-hoven." I repeated after him. "Rack-MANNY-nov. Pooch-EE-nee."

It was drizzling when we left the restaurant.

"How about a walk? I have an umbrella in the car."

At first, he held the umbrella so that I was protected and he wasn't. When I pointed out that he was getting wet, he drew closer, took my hand, kissed my cheek. I quivered with pleasure, with the romance of a stroll down a cobblestoned street in the rain with a sweet man who played the violin.

"If my mother knew I was out with a *shiksa*, she'd kill me," Sidney blurted out.

"A what?" I stopped so suddenly that he walked a few steps before he realized I wasn't with him.

"A *shiksa*. A girl who's not Jewish."

I didn't know if he was insulting me or if I should feel flattered that he'd gone against his mother's wishes to be with me. I understood why Ilsa was surprised that Sidney had asked me out. He wasn't supposed to. "Is it against your religion?"

"Sort of," he said, but I heard "Yes."

"Then you'd better not bring me home to meet her." He gaped at me as if the thought scared him. "It's a joke," I reassured him, and he smiled, unconvinced. "It's getting late," I decided.

We ran to where he'd parked, as if to get away from whatever had come between us. The rain picked up the minute we entered the quiet, protective hull of his car. I directed him to Brooklyn. Squinting against the glare of other cars, Sidney paid close attention to the street signs, the turns he'd have to take on his way out. I tried to make conversation, but he stopped me. "Just a second, I have to concentrate. At the pizzeria," he continued talking to himself, "I go right, then left. Got it." He turned to me. "This is your street," he grinned, "which one is your building?"

Our Venetian blinds were drawn, but, through a slit, Mami peered out of our third-floor window at the street below. I waited for Sidney to get out of the car, come around, open the door, hold the umbrella so that I wouldn't get wet. We went up the stairs — slowly, because I heard running, things shoved, doors slam. At the top landing, I fumbled for a key I didn't have, since there was always someone home, then pretended I'd forgotten it and knocked. Mami opened the door. She wore a maternity top and slacks, had combed her hair into playful curls, had dabbed her lips with color. I wondered if she had been dressed like this for hours, or if the running around I'd heard was due to the family getting ready for Sidney. My sisters and brothers sat on the couch and chairs, still as starch, their faces scrubbed, hair slicked. A flowered bed sheet divided the kitchen and living area from the front room, where I could hear Tata shushing Charlie. The kitchen smelled of freshly brewed coffee.

I introduced Sidney to Mami, then to each kid. The younger ones giggled shyly and hid behind the older ones.

"Would he like some coffee and cake?" Mami asked. On the table was a supermarket coffee cake still in its box.

"No," I answered, "he has to go." Sidney looked from me to her, expecting me to translate the exchange. "I told her you have a long drive to New Jersey."

"Oh, right, yeah." He seemed startled to be reminded of his home state. I led him to the door.

"See you Monday," I promised, letting him out. Nine pairs of eyes followed our every move. It was a relief when Sidney waved goodbye from the threshold, made his way down the stairs. Tata shuffled out from the other room, Charlie in her arms. "Is he gone?" she cackled. I closed the door and turned to face my family, who expressed their opinion.

"He's so short!"

"He has a big nose."

"His coat smelled bad."

"His glasses are so thick."

"That's how come he took Negi out. He's blind and couldn't see her."

I made a feeble attempt to defend Sidney, "He's a sweet man," but it was useless. I gave up and added to their mirth by revealing that his hobby was the violin. They thought that was really funny.

Mami looked at the clock on the kitchen wall. "At least he behaved like a gentleman and brought you home early. It's not even ten o'clock," she noted.

"Maybe Negi couldn't stand to be with him anymore," Delsa snorted.

"Where did you get those pearls?" Tata asked, suddenly serious.

"Regina lent them to me. They were her mother's."

"Take them off," she shrieked. She lurched toward me, about to remove them from my neck. I covered them with my hand. "Pearls bring tears," she warned.

"Ay, Tata, stop with your superstitions." The pearls felt warm against my neck.

"They bring tears," she repeated, "especially if they're some-one else's. And a dead woman's!" She came at me again. I ducked into my room and closed the door. The pearls felt lovely. There was no way I'd believe they brought tears. All I had to do was listen to the laughter on the other side of the door.

⁓

I thought it might be awkward to see Sidney the following week, but he was away for the first three days, and by the time he returned, I was in love with Otto.

Otto was a big man, with golden skin and hair, a deep voice that rumbled out of a barrel chest. We locked eyes when I went to deliver the mail in the International Department. For the rest of the morning, we exchanged glances across the blue-gray fluores-cence of the office. He disappeared at lunch but was there when I came to pick up the outgoing mail from his desk.

"You are Esmeralda, yes?" he asked. The way he pronounced my name, the yes at the end of the sentence, was like a song that repeated in my brain for hours. "I am Otto," he said. I stretched my hand to shake, and he held on to it, squeezed it gently before releasing it. I almost melted on the spot. He handed me a stack of letters addressed to Germany. I thanked him and continued my rounds, aware that he watched me. Although I'd always resented it when men brazenly scanned my body, I welcomed it from Otto, made sure to stay within his sight the whole time I picked up the mail. That night I fantasized about what it would feel like to be in Otto's arms and continued to dream about him over the days that he didn't return to the office.

Christmas blinked red and green in the neighborhoods of New York City. At home, we folded notebook paper into triangles, then cut out fanciful shapes to create snowflakes. Héctor carried Raymond on his shoulders as he taped the snowflakes to a corner of the ceiling. Don Carlos lifted Franky up to impale a blonde angel atop the Christmas tree. Tinsel tears dripped over the plastic branches laden with fragile balls in brilliant colors.

It was an abundant Christmas. Everyone in our household old enough to work had a job. Sundays vibrated with the thump-thump-thump of relatives climbing the three flights of stairs to our apartment. Most of them carried wrapped boxes to be placed under the tree, near which the younger kids kept watch as if the bounty might disappear if left unguarded for a few minutes.

La Muda and Gury came up one day with a bag of clothes, which Delsa, Norma, and I divided among ourselves, since Mami was pregnant and couldn't fit into any of them. From the bottom I pulled out a pale pink chiffon and taffeta party dress, the cuffs of its long sleeves and modestly scooped collar dotted with pearly beads.

"Is it bad luck," I grinned toward Tata, "to wear these pearls?"

"Not the fake ones," she chuckled, and La Muda gestured snipping off the collar and sleeves of the dress to indicate that if the pearls were real, I'd have a sleeveless dress with a very low neckline.

"You can wear it to the dance at the Armory," Mami suggested, and my sisters and I cheered, because we hadn't been dancing in months.

Sometimes I met Alma, and we spent hours on Fifth Avenue, among tourists who shoved and pushed each other before the elaborate displays the stores put on to lure us inside. When it came to spending our money, however, Alma and I went to Herald Square, where our salaries stretched further. One day, as we browsed the shoe bin in Ohrbach's basement, I looked up to a familiar face. I froze, struck by the sight of Greta Garbo bent over a stack of flat gillies at 30 percent off. She wore a black turtleneck and coat, her pale, angular face luminous under the brim of a soft black hat. When she felt me stare, she turned and disappeared in the crowd. By the time I signaled to Alma, Garbo was a memory.

That week I went to a hairdresser and had my shoulder-length hair cut blunt to chin level and parted in the middle, like Garbo's. I bought a black felt cloche, which I pulled over my ears, trying to duplicate the effect of Garbo's soft hat. It was useless, I looked nothing like her, and all the hat did was squish my hair. When I took it off, it looked as if I'd been wearing a bowl over my head.

The presents I bought were stored at Alma's, so that my family wouldn't discover what Santa Claus-Negi was to bring them. In Titi Ana's apartment, Christmas was observed quietly, with a few strands of colored lights around the windows, a small tree by the television set, a modest pile of gifts wrapped in bright paper. I spent the night in the small room off the kitchen thirty yards from the elevated train tracks. After Titi Ana, Alma, and Corazón went to bed, I stood at the window and watched trains rattle past. The people inside were ghosts, gray specters framed in darkness. Their anonymity made me homesick for the warmth of our noisy apartment. I crawled into bed, lonesome and invisible behind the lace curtain of Titi Ana's window.

The dance at the Armory was on a Sunday night. We stayed until the band played its last note, then had an early morning breakfast at a diner. Back home, I had just enough time to shower, change into daytime clothes, and head back into the city and my job at Fisher Scientific. Only half awake, I stumbled through the morning until Ilsa suggested I go home and get some rest. It was already dark as I walked to the subway station, strangely quiet for midafternoon. The cold air revived me just enough to keep me upright. My feet, sore from hours of *salsa* and *merengue* in high heels, throbbed with every step.

I was about to cross Hudson Street when someone grabbed me from behind and pulled me back to the sidewalk. I struck back with my elbow, hitting my attacker in the face, and started in the opposite direction, but stopped as a truck barreled past. Then I realized the man behind me was trying to keep me from being run over. When I turned around, there was Otto, his fingers pressed to his lips.

"Oh, my God, I'm so sorry!"

"I thought I was a hero." He tried to smile but the cut on his lip hurt.

"There's a little blood on the side." I offered a tissue, but he bent his face in my direction. I was too embarrassed to look him in the eye as I wiped the blood off the rapidly swelling lip. "You need ice."

"There's a coffee shop," he said, guiding me in its direction.

As we walked, his hand at my elbow, I wished the previous night hadn't been so much fun. My eyes were swollen from lack of sleep, my hair, in its Garbo cut, stuck out in frizzy curls because I hadn't had time to wash and straighten it. I'd worn no makeup, had grabbed the first thing I reached in my closet—the suit I'd worn on my date with Sidney—which made me look, I now realized, like a nun in street clothes.

But Otto didn't care. We sat across from each other at a window booth. "Charming," he kept saying, and I had no idea how to respond except to stammer "Thank you," which he found even more endearing.

Unlike Sidney, Otto wasn't easy to talk to, because his accent was heavy, his grammar confusing, and the pack of ice at his lips caused him to mumble. He liked restaurants or restoring, cooking or küchen, Audubon or autobahn. After many attempts, I understood he wanted me to go to a Christmas party with him at his sister's house in Long Island.

"I have to ask my mother," I said, embarrassed that at eighteen I needed permission to go to a party.

"Charming," he repeated.

He walked me to the train, and on the way to Brooklyn, I remembered his strong hands on my shoulders. He'd saved me from being run over by a truck. It was the most romantic thing that had ever happened to me.

"Not alone!" Mami said, when I asked her if I could go to Long Island with Otto.

"It's to his sister's house."

"I don't care if you're going to see the pope. You can take one of your brothers with you, or one of your sisters. But you're not going that far alone with a man I've never met." No argument could persuade her that I was old enough to take care of myself.

Regina sympathized with my problem and came up with the perfect solution. "I will come," she suggested. Although Mami had never met Regina, she agreed that a young woman who had been so recently orphaned and had picked the unflattering navy blue suit as appropriate wear for a date was the perfect chaperone. Otto thought it was a wonderful idea that Regina come with us. His cousin Gilbert needed a date for the party.

"He will like your friend," Otto assured me, and the date was fixed.

He offered to pick me up in Brooklyn, which I knew would impress Mami. The evening of the party, Don Carlos and Don Julio decided to stay home, doubtless at Mami's suggestion. Dressed in his black suit, Don Carlos sat across the kitchen table from Don Julio, also dressed up in a pressed shirt and new pants. They were joined by Héctor and Raymond, the two oldest boys in the family, their faces scrubbed, hair newly washed and combed back. I dreaded the moment Otto would walk into this pitiful attempt to protect my virtue.

I was ready twenty minutes before Otto was to arrive. My intention was to introduce him to everyone and then get out of there as fast as possible.

When Otto and Gilbert appeared at our door, however, it was clear that it would take longer to leave than I had planned. They dominated the room — two large, Teutonic men who spoke little English. They wore suits, which, rather than make them look respectable, added to their bulk, their maleness. Mami frowned and exchanged a look with Tata, who smiled vaguely and left the room to attend to a screaming Charlie.

Otto handed me an orchid in a plastic box. I pinned it on myself because there was no way I was going to let him get that close in front of Mami. The concern on her face was worrisome. I wished Otto and Gilbert had picked up Regina on the way so that Mami wouldn't envision me alone in a car with two men for so long as a second. But it was too late. Don Carlos, who spoke good English, managed to get a phone number and address for where we'd be. He handed Otto his business card, made him take down our phone number — as if I didn't know it — while Mami made sure I had identification on me.

"*Por favor*, Mami," I pleaded, "you're embarrassing me."

"What do you mean embarrassing you?" she asked, her voice rising enough for Otto and Gilbert to take their eyes off Don Carlo's green lenses and look in our direction. Mami smiled at them, then turned to frown on me.

"We better go," I suggested, avoiding her gaze, "or Regina will think we're lost." I hoped that mention of Regina would remind Mami I had a chaperone and that she'd relax a bit.

"Call when you get there," Mami said, as she watched us trudge down the stairs in silence.

Otto and Gilbert spoke German to one another, laughed. I waited for a translation, but none came. Before climbing into

Gilbert's car, I looked up. My entire family was at the window, surrounded by blinking Christmas lights.

Maybe this was a mistake. These two men I barely knew could drive me somewhere, rape me, throw me off a bridge. I couldn't relax the entire drive to Lefrak City, where we were to pick up Regina. It didn't register when Otto mentioned that Gilbert and Regina had already been out on a date until we parked in front of her building and she ran out. She looked spectacular, dressed in a form-fitting dress under a fur, spike heels, her mother's pearls gleaming at her throat. Her perfume invaded the car, a flowery scent that lingered in the air.

"Wow," I commented, and she laughed.

"Is not every day I go to party," she said, and even the men were delighted with the happiness in her voice.

Otto's sister lived in a street of identical houses behind broad lawns. Santa Claus, reindeer, elves, and miniature carolers vied for attention with thousands of tiny lights on the roofs, eaves, and window shutters of almost every house. Something about the neighborhood was familiar. Then I remembered that Archie and Veronica, Betty, Reggie, and Jughead strolled along an identical street, without the decorations, in the comic books I'd devoured during my first year in Brooklyn.

It was easy to tell the house where the party was, because many cars were parked in front of it and the window shades were up. We came up a walk lit by strings of Christmas lights on the ground. Inside, the house was warm, smelled of cinnamon, cloves, and burning wood in a fireplace. A blonde, big-boned woman met us at the door, and Otto kissed her on both cheeks. She was Minna, his older sister. They looked alike, but Minna spoke much better English.

"I'm so happy you're here," she said, pressing my hand, "Otto has told me so much about you." Regina and I exchanged a look, wondering what he could have said, as we barely knew each other.

Minna treated us like honored guests, introduced us to everyone there, offered us drinks and miniature sausages from a tray.

Her husband, Jim, was American, but as blond, blue-eyed, and German-looking as everyone else in the room. He wore *lederhosen*, and I wasn't sure if it was really a national costume or a joke. His principal job was to keep everyone's glass full, which he did with gusto. From time to time he broke into song, and the company joined in what I took to be German Christmas carols.

We'd arrived as dinner was being served. The dining room table was heaped with food arranged by type. A turkey, a ham, a platter of meatballs, and cold cuts were set next to a variety of cheeses, whipped cream, butter. Beside them were colorful bowls of vegetables: chunks of yellow squash, milky mashed potatoes, green string beans dotted with tiny white onions, blood-red beets. Several trays held crusty breads, rolls, seeded buns. A sideboard was devoted to cakes, puddings, cookies, chocolate-covered nuts, and fruits. It was the most bountiful spread I'd ever seen, each food group set off from the other with ribbons and pine boughs.

Otto and Gilbert led us through the buffet, encouraged us to taste everything. They laughed at how diligently I kept the different flavors from contaminating one another, and at Regina's face when she tasted the whipped cream and it turned out to be not sweet, but spiced with horseradish.

After dinner, we went down to a finished basement with chairs along the walls, a bar, a Hi-fi with a stack of records that dropped one by one onto a lazy turntable. Nancy Sinatra insisted that her boots were made for walking, the Monkees were daydream believers, and the Young Rascals promised good lovin'. Otto and Gilbert flailed their arms and legs in a style I'd come to associate with American dancing, which now appeared to be an international technique. Used to the graceful, seductive movements of *salsa, merengue,* and *chachacha,* I was frustrated by the distance between our bodies, the sense that we weren't dancing together, but near each other. That changed when Percy Sledge wailed about when a man loves a woman. Someone turned the lights down. Otto took off his jacket, pulled me close, and I was finally in his arms, my head resting on his broad chest. Each time

Percy Sledge's voice rose, Otto drew me closer, and I didn't resist. As the song ended, Otto took me by the hand and led me up the stairs. Regina watched us, smiled, buried her head in Gilbert's shoulder.

"Where are we going?" I asked, but Otto didn't answer. We went down a hall. He opened a door into a dark room, but I refused to go inside. "Let's go back," I suggested. He pressed me against the wall and kissed me.

It was wonderful, his kiss. Soft, warm lips. The heat between our bodies. The slow insinuation of his tongue into my mouth. Irresistible. Each time we came up for air, he guided me closer to the door. A couple went past us into another room, and I caught a whiff of Regina's perfume. Otto mumbled some words into my ear, which I didn't get. "Please," he begged and I understood that I'd better get out from between him and the wall. His kisses were insistent, his hands strayed. I was overwhelmed, certain that if I waited a moment longer, I wouldn't be able to resist his curious fingers, his hot tongue, the desire to rip my clothes off and present myself naked before him. He was a big man, but I was a muscled dancer. With effort, I pushed him away and ran back to the crowded basement, where the Troggs sang about their wild thing.

I sat on one of the chairs against the wall, tried to calm my breathing. Otto had not followed. I was grateful not to have to face him just then.

Minna came over and sat next to me. "Are you having a good time?" she asked.

"Very nice," I responded, my voice tight. She didn't notice.

"My brother really likes you," she confided. "He's never brought a girl for us to meet before."

"I like him too," I admitted, hoping that if she conveyed that message, he might forgive me for what I'd just done.

Two small windows high on the wall faced out to the walkway in front of the house. Huge snowflakes twinkled among the Christmas lights. Minna followed my gaze. "How lovely!" she exclaimed. "Look, everyone," she called, "it's snowing."

Several couples stopped dancing to ooh at the sight. Otto came down the steps. I expected him to be angry, but he wore a sheepish expression, smiled sweetly, sat on my other side, squeezed my hand. He turned to the window where everyone was staring, and I turned in its direction. To my horror, there were my mother and Don Carlos marching toward the front door, fat snowflakes pelting their resolute faces.

~⌒◦

"Oh my God," I stood up so fast, I slipped and fell to my knees. Otto helped me up, and I ran up the stairs. I opened the door before they could knock. "What are you doing here?" I shrieked. Mami's lips were pressed together. She looked behind me at the festive house, the leftovers of the meal still on the holiday table, the curious faces that followed us to the door.

"You didn't call," Don Carlos responded. "We were worried about you."

A giant hot wave of humiliation, relief, and shame, rolled over me. Ten minutes earlier I'd almost given myself to Otto. What if Mami had found me naked in bed with him?

Minna appeared at my side, put her arm around my shoulder, invited them in, offered them a drink. But Mami declined with a strained smile, pointed to the taxi at the bottom of the walkway.

"And your friend?" she asked.

"She's in the bathroom," Minna said, too quickly.

"Where's my coat?" I croaked. Jim retrieved it from a closet by the front door. Mami stared at him — a grown man in green leather shorts with suspenders, red knee socks with dangly felt balls on the side. Otto helped me into my coat, tipped his head sympathetically when I pulled it closed and crushed what was left of the corsage he'd given me. "Thank you," I said to no one in particular.

I wanted to die, wished that on the way home, the taxi would crash and kill us, so that I never had to face Otto again. But the driver was careful, drove slowly, which gave me plenty of time to scream at Mami and Don Carlos.

"How could you do this? I'm old enough to take care of myself!"

"Lower your voice or I'll shut your mouth for you."

The source of Mami's anger was an enigma. I argued that I'd asked her permission, had brought Otto home for her to meet, had found a chaperone. She knew where I'd be, who I'd be with, when I'd be back. Don Carlos repeated that I'd forgotten to call when I got there, but I reminded him they had Otto's sister's number. Why hadn't they called to see if I'd arrived safely? They'd gone to great trouble and expense to come get me, to humiliate me in front of my friends, to teach me a lesson I didn't need. I was hysterical all the way back to Brooklyn. As soon as we got home, I tore the pink dress with the fake pearls off me and ripped it to shreds. The tiny pearls dislodged from the fabric, plinked onto the linoleum floor, rolled into the crevices along the baseboard where roaches lurked.

⸻

Regina didn't come to work on Monday, but Otto was there. Ilsa and I were scrambling to open and sort piles of mail by ourselves when he approached the long table that divided our department from Purchasing. He was the same person as two days before, but now I saw him through Mami's eyes. Unlike Neftalí and Sidney, Otto was a man, not a boy. That didn't make him less attractive. As he stood in front of me, I couldn't stop blushing. Shame and desire alternated, fused until they were the same.

"We can have coffee, yes?" he asked. Ilsa frowned from her desk.

"My break is at 10:30." I was happy that he'd talk to me after Saturday night's fiasco. Ilsa coughed discreetly to let me know I should go back to work. Before he left, Otto bowed in her direction, which I found gallant but she found infuriating. She muttered a few words in her language that sounded hostile.

"Why don't you go out with Sidney anymore?" she asked later.

"I'm a *shiksa.*" The defensive tone in my voice surprised me as much as it did Ilsa, whose eyes flickered wildly for a few seconds, then looked away.

Everyone in the cafeteria stared at Otto and me sitting by ourselves in a far table. He held my hand through the fifteen minutes I was allowed for coffee. In his halting English, he apologized for getting "fresh," which astounded me, since I had had as much to do with it as he had.

"Your mother and father is very good," he assured me, "they take good care."

"They treat me like a child."

"It is good," he consoled me. "You are not American girl. They are very free."

"I want to be free," I hinted, but he didn't get it.

"You are perfect," he smiled. "My girlfriend," he murmured, and, had I been standing, my knees would have buckled under me.

Later, we had lunch in the coffee shop where he had once nursed the wound I caused him. He had to go to Switzerland next, he informed me.

"We write each other," he offered.

I was late getting back, and Ilsa put on a face. She glared at the piles on the tables. My apology didn't affect her mood. Later, as we filed a stack of documents in side-by-side cabinets, I apologized again.

"It wasn't right," she relented, "for me to be so cross. It's not you I'm mad at, it's him." She tipped her head in the direction of the International Department. "And it's not him," she amended. "It's them." I had no idea what she was talking about. She fixed me with her blue eyes. "I had a very bad experience with Germans," she explained. Then I understood.

"But Ilsa," I argued, "they can't all be bad."

"To me they're all the same."

"But it's not fair."

"Fair? Was the murder of six million Jews fair?" Her voice rose, but not so loud that anyone else heard. I stammered that no, it wasn't, but that it was equally wrong to judge a whole nation by the actions of a few.

"A few!" She was appalled. "The whole country stood by as Jews were murdered. My mother, my father, my sisters and brother." The passion in her voice was hypnotic, and I remained silent, hoping she'd continue, but she bit her lips and said no more.

"I'm so sorry, Ilsa." I touched her arm, and she pressed my fingers and smiled sadly.

"I hope you never have to hate," she murmured.

<hr />

Regina came back two days later, still weak from a bad cold. She'd heard about Mami and Don Carlos coming to rescue me in Long Island.

"How horrible for you! Minna said you were so shamed. Everybody felt bad."

"It's all right. Otto was impressed," I laughed.

"Gilbert and me, we see each other more." Regina blushed.

"Don't tell Ilsa," I warned.

Unable to convince Mami to let me stay out after I was due home, I could see Otto only at work. Over the next few days, we took lunch or coffee breaks together. Ilsa scowled every time she saw me leave without Regina, but I didn't care. Whatever feelings she had about Germans were hers, not mine. Used to being judged because some Puerto Ricans did bad things, I wasn't about to do the same to Otto.

I expected Otto to want something to remember me by. I snipped a few strands of my hair, tied them in a thin red ribbon. But he didn't ask, and I was too embarrassed to admit such a silly thing had occurred to me. He left right after the New Year. Other than holding my hand and giving me an occasional peck on the cheek, he never touched me as he had the night of the Christmas party. His gentlemanly behavior proved that Mami was right: "A man who really cares about you respects you." I appreciated it but couldn't erase the sensations of his tongue in my mouth, his hands on my breast, his probing fingers. He was a man, and his kiss had made me feel like a woman.

"The music inside her ..."

Fisher Scientific was to move its offices to New Jersey after the first of the year. Regina, Ilsa, and I were offered promotions if we transferred to the new location. With the promise of a job in New Jersey, I made a case for moving closer to work, as Regina's roommate. Mami vetoed the plan. "There's plenty of work in New York," she claimed.

Before the company moved, I took advantage of a benefit they offered. They paid part of the tuition for employees who wished to continue their education. Don Carlos, who studied accounting in night school, encouraged me to look into a community college. They were less expensive than the famous New York universities, he said. They also offered evening and weekend classes, which meant I could work and study.

I applied to Manhattan Community College because it was on 51st Street, off Sixth Avenue, close to the theater district and dance studios where I still took lessons. Courses focused on business, advertising, and marketing. I signed up for those that allowed me to be out of classes by one o'clock in the afternoon. After school, I picked up temporary jobs as a receptionist in nearby offices.

Soon after classes started, I went to the college bookstore to buy supplies. On line ahead of me stood a young woman about my age whose presence overpowered the hallway leading into the bookstore. She wore knee-high brown boots, a leather miniskirt, a brown chiffon blouse through which her black bra showed. Her hair was ratted into a mass of golden curls held back with a leopard print chiffon scarf whose ends draped over her shoulder. Her makeup was elaborate, complete with false eyelashes.

Tired with the long line ahead of them, the two people in front of me left in disgust. The young woman turned around, smiled radiantly, and introduced herself as Shoshana. "We're in the same English Composition class," she informed me.

We chatted while we waited our turn, continued over lunch at the Horn & Hardart. She lived in Queens with her parents, who were as old-fashioned as Mami.

"It's stupid. I spend half my time arguing with them," she complained. Her mother was particularly critical of the way Shoshana dressed, which didn't surprise me. If I were to wear anything half as flashy as Shoshana's most conservative outfits, Mami would lock me up.

Shoshana was born in Israel, came to the United States the same year I did. Her parents were Holocaust survivors, so it took me a while to tell her about my German boyfriend.

"It's true then," she mused, "that Puerto Rican girls prefer blond, blue-eyed men."

"Where did you hear that?"

"In school. A classmate told me."

"Maybe she was speaking for herself."

"You have a blond, blue-eyed boyfriend," she pointed out.

"Yeah, but it just worked out that way. The first guy I dated was Jewish," I added. "But he couldn't bring me home to his mother."

"What, and give her a heart attack?"

When I was with Shoshana, I felt happy, even if she sometimes made assumptions, like Puerto Rican girls wanting blond boyfriends. If she offended me and I set her straight, she nodded as if she understood and moved on to other things. I did the same with her.

Shoshana could date, if she dated Jewish men.

"I'm being loyal to Otto," I gave as my reason for not going out with anyone.

"Do you think," she asked, "that he just sits at home on weekends thinking of you?"

Otto's letters weren't as frequent as I would have liked, but they brought news of evenings at the opera, the symphony, museums. He described hikes in the woods in such detail that it felt as though I were there. My news was less interesting, mostly reports on my courses, the New York weather, and the people I met as a part-time receptionist. Occasionally, I fabricated this or that highly accomplished man who took an interest in me. Otto never responded to my attempts to make him jealous. I also invented friends happily married to foreign men, stories about marriage by proxy, in which the bride and groom were in different cities (the Corín Tellado romances I still read had lots of those), and marriages in which everything was arranged by the bride while the groom lived in Europe. He never responded to those hints either.

Shoshana insisted that as far as she could tell, Otto and I were pen pals, in which case, I should go out with whomever I chose.

"My mother doesn't want me alone with men until after I get married," I admitted.

"My mom's the same," Shoshana chuckled. "It's because they're from the old country."

Shoshana said the reason our mothers said no so much was that we asked them too many questions. "Does she have to know everything you do?" Shoshana asked. She suggested we get part-time night jobs, but that we should tell our mothers we worked every night. That way, the nights we didn't work, we could go out.

We answered an ad for telephone operators, evenings only, and were interviewed by Mr. Vince, a perfumed, coiffed, man who wore a pinkie ring, tight-fitting pants, and a shirt unbuttoned to display his hairy chest. He hired us on the spot and put us to work that same night.

Our job was to return phone calls from people who'd inquired about how to win a fabulous vacation. The company advertised destinations on television. Viewers called a special number, actually an answering service, and were asked their names, phone numbers, the best time to call, and which commercial they'd seen.

Mr. Vince said that we couldn't use our real names when returning the calls. We should each pick one that was short and easy to remember. Shoshana became Miss Green and I Miss Brown. He gave us a script. "You're an actress, you shouldn't have any trouble with this," he grinned.

We read aloud before Mr. Vince let us make the first call.

"Good evening Mr. (or Mrs.) _____. This is _____, returning your call. How are you tonight?" (Give them a chance to respond. If they ask how you are, thank them.)
"You inquired about a chance to win a vacation in _____. Have you ever been to _____?" (Yes: "It's a fabulous place, isn't it?" No: "Oh, you'll love it.")

To qualify for the prize, the prospect had to agree to a sales visit. If they accepted, we transferred them to Mr. Vince, who set the date and time. We were paid by the hour, but if Mr. Vince sold a certain number of vacations to prospects we'd contacted, we received a commission and the chance to go on the fabulous vacation ourselves.

"How many do you have to sell?" Shoshana asked.

"I'll let you know when I sell them," Mr. Vince laughed.

We worked in cubicles, each with a phone, a stack of pink message slips, a few #2 pencils, and notepads. At first Mr. Vince monitored our end of the conversation by standing behind us when we talked to prospects or by listening on an extension. But once he was sure we were talking to his clients and not our friends ("You do that, you're fired," he threatened), he wasn't as strict. Sometimes he left us in the office alone, since he was not kept very busy. In spite of our best efforts, most prospects refused a sales call to make them eligible, if they purchased another trip from Mr. Vince, to win the fabulous vacation. As soon as he left the office, Shoshana called her boyfriends. I didn't have anyone to call, so I talked to her boyfriends, too.

"Are you as beautiful as Shoshana?" they asked, and I answered that no one was as beautiful as Shoshana, which she loved.

Many of the calls we returned were from people with no intention of ever going on vacation. "You can't let them waste your time," Mr. Vince scolded. "I'm not paying you to be their friend."

But I liked listening. Given interested silence, people talked. They complained about inattentive spouses, ungrateful children, undeserving nieces and nephews, greedy neighbors. The dead were recalled with regrets.

"I didn't know how much I depended on him until he was gone."

"She was an angel, and I didn't appreciate her."

"He never knew how much I loved him."

More than once I was brought to tears by the voices that floated out of the darkness into my ear. No one was happy. I let them talk, asked questions, pointed out the snares they'd stumbled into that left them sad and lonely. If I listened carefully, I might hear myself speak twenty years from now, or thirty, or even fifty. Would my life be summed up in a series of regrets and resentments? Would I wish to turn back time, to relive this or that moment, as so many of my callers did, to change the outcome? How could I tell if a decision I made today would haunt me for years to come?

"I hope you never have to go through what I went through," a woman began her tale, and I paid close attention. Each life was a message I had to decode, clues for what lay ahead. Not a blueprint, but a road map from which to choose a path.

When we weren't in classes or working, Shoshana and I went to tapings of television shows. Manhattan Community College was only a few blocks from the CBS and ABC studios and two blocks from NBC. In the daytime, we sat in the audience of game shows, hoping we'd be picked as contestants. We never were. After a while, the NBC pages recognized us and moved us to the front of the ticket line or saved places for us in the studios. They were pleasant, clean-cut young men in neat blue uniforms. We each had a favorite. Mine was Andy, a pudgy redhead with freckles on every visible part of his body, including his earlobes and knuckles. He worked the evening shift most of the time and always made sure I got in to watch tapings of *The Johnny Carson Show*. Andy reminded me of comic book Archie. He had the same goofy grin and dreamed of writing the jokes Johnny Carson read off cue cards during his monologue.

"You mean those are not his jokes?"

"There's a whole army of writers who make Johnny funny," he confided.

"But the ad libs . . ."

"Oh, those are his," Andy said. "The man is funny. But the writers make him funnier."

Because he worked nights like me, Andy and I could only go out days, if I didn't have a class. We visited museums and art galleries, ate lunch from hot dog vendors on Fifth Avenue, sat in coffee shops for hours, each engrossed in a different book.

"That's what you do on dates?" Shoshana asked. "You read next to each other?"

I explained that with Andy, what I had was a friendship, not a romance.

"Oy!" she slapped her forehead. "You're hopeless."

"He's all I've got," I laughed.

"I know some guys," she offered.

Sammy and Josh were Israeli premed students. Shoshana had dated Josh a couple of times, and he had asked her to introduce his best friend to a girl. That's how, on a damp Sunday morning in June, I sat stiff and fearful atop a horse in Van Cortland Park.

"You have to show the horse who is boss," Sammy asserted, his speech garbled by the cigarette in his mouth.

"He's the boss," I said.

"No, no, no, no." Sammy shook his head, and ashes flew in every direction. "You are the boss. You!"

It was hard for me to believe I could dominate the quivering creature between my legs. His malevolent eyes rolled back wetly to focus on me, petrified on his sagging back. He stomped his hooves into the gravel the way Trigger did when Roy Rogers asked him to count, only this horse wasn't counting. He was, I was certain, anticipating the moment Sammy handed me the reins to take off, with me helplessly bouncing atop him, or dragged alongside, still attached to the stirrups. I suggested to Sammy, Shoshana, and Josh that I'd be happy to sit on a bench and wait for them to come back from their ride. But Shoshana insisted that this was a fun date. The horses in Van Cortland Park, Josh claimed, were old, docile, one false step from the glue factory. Sammy swore he was an expert horseman and would ride alongside, in case I needed him.

The horse knew where he was going. No matter what I did with the reins, he trudged forward, followed Josh and Shoshana's horses as if he were attached to them. I loosened my grip and looked around. Beside me, Sammy chatted in a low murmur about his experiences on kibbutz, where he worked as an electrician. He was very thin, with abundant black hair and eyes that probed from beneath luxurious eyebrows. He sucked unfiltered cigarettes one after the other. His fingertips and teeth were stained an opaque mustard color, and from time to time he doubled over with rumbling coughs that turned his face red.

The path was wooded near the stables, but as we came around a curve, it opened into a long stretch alongside a busy avenue. Cars and trucks rumbled past, but the horses were used to the congestion and paid no attention to it. They ambled along placidly, the clop of their hooves an incongruous contrast to the whir and horns of traffic. Josh and Sammy spoke to each other in Hebrew, and Shoshana and Sammy changed places, so that she rode next to me.

"The guys want to canter," she explained.

"What's that?"

"When the horses go fast."

I gripped the reins again. I expected a "Hi-yo, Silver," or some other exclamation to make the horses go, but Josh and Sammy simply dug their heels into the animals' sides, and they took off. Shoshana's horse and mine pursued them, even though I, at least, did nothing to encourage mine. I pulled the reins with all the power in my arms, but the horse ignored me. Shoshana's horse was even faster and soon whizzed past me. Then, way ahead, I saw Shoshana fly through the air and land on her side, inches from the avenue. In a move to make Annie Oakley proud, I slid off my horse while he was still moving and rushed to her side. She was unconscious. Within seconds, traffic stopped on the avenue, Josh and Sammy appeared, and the horses could be seen cantering (if that's what they did when they ran fast) toward the stables, their reins flapping uselessly along the ground.

"I'm a doctor, I'm a doctor," Sammy and Josh yelled, to keep people away from Shoshana.

"You're not supposed to move someone . . ." I started when Sammy turned her over, but he gave me a look to wither poison ivy, and I backed away.

She moaned, opened her eyes, and it was a relief to see she was alive. Josh and Sammy hovered over her until an ambulance wailed its way to us, then I rode with her while the guys followed in Sammy's car. She was pale but conscious. I held her hand all the way to the hospital, and when they took her away to be examined, I called Mami.

"Has someone told her mother?" Mami asked. I hadn't, and probably Sammy and Josh hadn't either. Mami said it was Shoshana's mother I should be calling and not mine.

Josh and Sammy ran in, and while Josh went into the room where they'd taken Shoshana ("I'm a doctor, I'm a doctor!"), Sammy called her mother. Josh was escorted to the waiting room, and we sat in silence until a doctor came out and led us back to

Shoshana. She lay on a high bed, her golden curls framing her face like a halo. The white sheets added to the angelic effect. She looked both vulnerable and sexy, and the three men were jelly. The guys spoke to her in Hebrew, and then she asked if she could be alone with me. Once they left, she smiled mischievously.

"He's cute, isn't he?"

"Which one?"

"The doctor."

"Which one?"

"The real one, silly. We're going out next week."

Shoshana was in the hospital a few days. She was released in time for her date with Dr. Diamond, who testified when she sued the people who rented the horses. They settled for enough money to allow Shoshana to spend the rest of the summer in Israel. "But you should go out with Sammy while I'm gone," she suggested.

Dashing as Sammy was, I preferred my quiet afternoons with Andy. Shoshana rolled her eyes. "You'll die an old maid!" We laughed. We were both nineteen, and although we were desperate for love, we knew there was still time. After all, this was America, not the old country.

⌣

I hadn't seen Neftalí since the day he had tried to propose on the street. His mother, Doña Lila, still came up to visit, but I rarely saw her. Then, shortly after Cibi was born, Mami decided the apartment above Doña Lila's was too small. We moved to a single-family house with a huge yard and large, bright rooms with high ceilings. At the rear of the house was a small room off the kitchen, which I claimed. It was big enough for a single bed, a desk, my mirrored vanity table and matching chair. I spent the "summer of love" in that room, loveless, writing term papers about the history of public relations and the use of humor in outdoor advertising.

One day I came home and Mami and Tata were at the dining room table, their faces so somber I knew someone had died.

"Who?" I asked.

"Neftalí." Mami said.

I dropped onto a chair, overwhelmed with images of Neftalí riddled with bullets in a foxhole in faraway Vietnam. But that's not how it happened. Neftalí, Mami informed me, had been rejected by the army because he was a heroin addict.

"He was arrested," she said, "and he jumped out the window of the police station."

"There were spikes on the fence . . ." Tata added.

I raised my hands and motioned for them to stop. It was too much, too fast. My brain was still working on Neftalí being rejected by the service. Mami and Tata waited for me to signal I was ready for more, and then they repeated the information, as if it hadn't been clear enough, and filled in the details.

Doña Lila had such an attack of *los nervios* when she was called by the police that she was hospitalized. Neftalí hadn't told anyone the army didn't want him. When he was arrested, he jumped, according to Doña Lila, because he was ashamed everyone would find out he was on heroin.

"That's why he always wore long-sleeved shirts," Tata mused, and I stared at her.

"I never noticed that," I cried, and went into my room, followed by Mami and Tata's concerned gaze.

I threw myself on the bed and closed my eyes. Images of Neftalí popped into my head in confused sequences. Neftalí hoisting my brothers on his arms to show off his muscles. Did he wince because it hurt the needle tracks? Neftalí's flat nails against Tata's Spanish playing cards. Did he always lose because he couldn't concentrate? Neftalí's green eyes that made me shudder. Was the look I interpreted as mysterious actually blank? It was hard to reconcile the romantic hero I had wanted him to be with who he had been: an addict who'd rather jump out a window than confront his problem.

One Sunday afternoon, my half sister, Margie, came to visit. In the two years since she had first come to our apartment on Pitkin Avenue accompanied by her mother, we had moved four times, and Margie at least once. She had recently married Nestor, a warm, sociable man several years older. He stood behind her, his left hand lightly touching her waist, as Margie introduced him and tried to remember our names. When we had last seen her, there were only eight of us, and she was surprised that the family had grown so fast in two years.

Mami and Tata immediately began preparing *arroz con pollo* and stewed pinto beans. Nestor and Margie sat at the kitchen table talking about their new apartment in Yonkers.

"Why so far?" Mami asked.

"It's just over the border with the Bronx," Nestor said. But anything outside the confines of Brooklyn or north of the garment district in Manhattan was foreign territory to Mami. To her they might as well be living in another country.

Margie and Nestor were interested in every bit of news we could give them. They asked what schools we attended, what jobs we held, how tall we were. She apologized several times. "I don't mean to be nosy," she said. "But it's been so long since we were together." I was touched by her need to connect with us, to feel a part of our family. Nestor played with the boys as if he'd known them forever, and Margie talked to the sisters, helped Mami and Tata in the kitchen, jiggled Charlie and Cibi on her knees. She was comfortable, as if this were her house, her mother and grandmother, her siblings. I was enchanted by how open she was, how sweet and unpretentious. Before they left, Margie asked Mami if we could visit her now that she had her own place.

"Of course!" Mami said, and hugged her.

A few weeks later, Margie met me at the Yonkers train station. We walked the few blocks to the yellow brick building on a hill where she and Nestor lived in a sunny, cheerful apartment decorated with the optimism of newlyweds.

"This is where you'll sleep." She opened a door to a small

room near the kitchen. A single bed was covered by a fluffy comforter and matching pillows. A lamp topped a wicker side table with drawers. At the foot of the bed lay a set of towels, a basket with tiny soaps, a shower cap. She reached under the bed and pulled out a small basket. "If you get your period, here are the tampons." A box of Tampax was propped into a well of pink tissue paper like an offering to the goddess of menstruation.

I'd never touched a tampon, since Mami warned I could lose my virginity if I used them. Just having Margie think that I wore them made me feel grown up, privy to the secrets of a married woman. She no longer needed to worry about her virginity, and I wondered if offering me the tampon was a test to see if I worried about mine.

Nestor was due from work, so Margie asked me to set the table. At home, setting the table meant putting platters of food in the center so that everyone could come and get their share. Margie used place mats, knives, forks, a dinner plate, a salad plate, a water glass, a coffee cup and saucer. She had to remind me to put each on the table. A pitcher had to be filled with ice water. Paper napkins had to be folded into a triangle, placed to the left of the plate. Matching salt and pepper shakers had to be retrieved from the cabinet and lined up with the bottle of ketchup, the sugar bowl. It took me as long to set the table for three people as it took her to cook the entire meal, because I kept getting things wrong. I closed my eyes and tried to remember restaurant settings, but that was no help. Most of my dining-out experience was in coffee shops and the Automat, where one was lucky to get utensils.

"No, the water glass goes to the right of the plate," Margie corrected me. "The salad plate on the left, like this." She was kind, but I took her criticism personally, which made me sullen and uncomfortable during the meal. I offered to clean up, to make up for my ineptitude in other areas. She stayed in the kitchen with me, which under other circumstances I would have welcomed. But I was so self-conscious that I was bound to break something. She cleaned up the glass from the floor and sent me to watch Red

Skelton with Nestor. I was glad they went to bed early and curled up under the plush bedcovers, neither comforted nor consoled.

The next morning I woke to the smell of fried eggs and coffee. Margie bustled in the kitchen while Nestor read the paper and sipped his *café con leche*. I ducked into the bathroom to wash up. On the counter top a Water Pik gleamed white and clinical on the shelf next to the sink. I was afraid to touch it, because I didn't know what part of Margie or Nestor's body the tiny hose went into. It looked marital, as intimate as the cottony tampons wrapped in white paper. When I came out, Nestor was finishing his breakfast.

"I better get ready for work," he said, moving toward the bathroom. Margie set a plate in front of me neatly arranged with two fried eggs, a slice of ham, toast cut into triangles. Then she sat at the table and nibbled on a piece of bread, chatting about what we would do later. It was hard to concentrate on what she said because of the sounds coming from behind the bathroom door. The hum of electrical appliances, gargles, running water were a counterpoint to Margie's plans to walk to the park, have lunch at a local diner, shop. When Nestor came out, a fresh, clean scent of peppermint and orange saturated the room. Margie accompanied him to the door, where they kissed and muttered endearments. Once he was gone, Margie went into the bathroom, and the buzzing and gurgling resumed.

"Don't you wash up after every meal?" she asked when she came out, and I mumbled yes, which wasn't true, but I knew I should. "You can use the Water Pik if you like," she said. Still afraid to touch the hose, I pushed a button; water squirted out of it in a stream like a baby pissing. "Do you know how to use it?" she called from the kitchen, and I was thrilled that my older sister was about to impart adult knowledge. She came into the room, unhooked the hose, squirted water inside her mouth, the way the dentist did when he fixed my cavities. I was disappointed beyond words, which must have shown because, halfway through her demonstration of the proper technique, she crossed her eyes, curled her lips into a weird grimace, and let water dribble down her chin. Our eyes met in the mirror, and we set each other off in a fit of giggles that lasted the better part of the morning because, every time I looked at her, she put a finger in her mouth, hummed and gurgled, crossed her eyes, and pretended to brush her teeth.

We talked a lot about our father, whom she hadn't seen in years, but with whom she corresponded. I had lived with him many more years than she had, and she was surprised to learn that he sang well, and that he wrote poems and *décimas*.

"His handwriting is so tiny," she laughed, and showed me a sheet in his slanted script, each letter neatly drawn, the accents over the *is* nearly horizontal. It was Papi who gave her our address. "He loves your letters," she told me, which made me feel good and guilty at the same time, because I never wrote as much as I should have.

Over the next few weeks, my sisters and I took turns spending time with Margie and Nestor. They came to visit, and we went home with them. Or she met one of us at the train station, and in a couple of days they'd both return with us to Brooklyn and have some of Mami's good cooking. She once wrapped her arms around Mami and muttered that she wished she were her mother. Mami repeated the comment every time one of us was especially annoying or disrespectful, to let us know other people appreciated her when it seemed that we didn't.

One Sunday afternoon, Nestor informed us that they were moving to Miami. "Of course, you're welcome to come see us there," Margie offered. That was unlikely. If we had any money for travel, our goal was always Puerto Rico, where none of us had been in seven years. When we hugged goodbye, I knew it would be a long time before I'd see Margie again.

⌒

In mid-August, I received an invitation to the premiere of *Up the Down Staircase* at Radio City Music Hall, to be followed by a party at the Warwick Hotel. Almost all the actors who had played students in the classroom were there, dressed up. We were asked to come early so that we could be photographed on the grand staircase. Like me, many of the other students had never been inside Radio City, and we tried our best not to appear too amazed. But once in the upholstered seats of the theater, I couldn't help myself. I gawked at the high ceiling, the gilded decorations, the hundreds of seats sloped toward the enormous stage. For the first time I saw the Rockettes' precise kick line, the long legs that moved as one, the tappety-tap that seemed to come from every corner of the room.

Once the movie was shown, it was difficult to concentrate on it, because my fellow actors and I cheered or giggled every time we saw ourselves or one another. At the party, we exchanged stories about what we'd been up to since the movie wrapped. Sandy Dennis had won an Oscar for *Who's Afraid of Virginia Woolf?*, and the rest of us did our best to make our paltry accomplishments sound equally splendid.

My performance would not earn any awards, would more than likely not be noticed. But seeing myself on the screen renewed the desire to stand before an audience. After more than a year of office jobs and uninspiring college courses, I longed for the nervous excitement before the curtain rose, the hums and rustle of an expectant audience, the applause.

Once more I scoured audition notices in *Backstage* and *Show Business*, and on the bulletin boards of the International School of Dance, where I took classes. I had visions of dancing with an established group like Matteo's, but I was soon discouraged. While I'd come a long way as a dancer in four years, my competition began as children. They could take classes every day, could devote their lives to dance. Many of the traditional beginner dances, like Allarippu, had become second nature to them, and they'd moved on to more complex choreography that required a wider range of expression and technical expertise.

I went to dance class whenever I could afford the time or

expense, practiced at home even when my family complained that
the jangling ankle bells and atonal Indian music drove them crazy.
Every time I considered dropping out of college and using my
money from temporary jobs to support my art, I rebuked myself
for being self-indulgent and unrealistic. An artist should sacrifice
for her art, I knew that. A part of me loved the romance of being
a starving artist. But the voice that spoke loudest asked what
chance an undertrained Puerto Rican Indian classical dancer had
of supporting herself.

Our house on Glenmore had a finished basement as well as a
second floor, where Mami set up the kids' beds. We had room to
spare, Mami said. Maybe that's why one day her cousin Lólin
appeared at our door on the arm of the man she had eloped with.

Lólin was thin, with dark soulful eyes and a quiet manner.
She was delicate and graceful, wore her long hair down, a wide
black ribbon between narrow shoulders. She spoke in a hushed,
kittenish voice, made frequent use of the Spanish diminutive, as if
she could make herself smaller through speech. It didn't surprise
me that she introduced her "husband" as Toñito rather than An-
tonio.

He was as slight and quiet as she was, with nutmeg skin, dark
hair, Taíno features. They came with few belongings and no
money, but they were obviously in love. Every time he looked at
her, she blushed and dropped her lids. When she did look at him,
her gaze was like a caress, soft and slow and full of meaning.

Mami wasn't thrilled to have them at our house. She liked
Lólin, but she wasn't comfortable with a handsome, lusty young
man — not our brother — in his undershirt near me and my sisters.
I was nineteen, Delsa seventeen, Norma sixteen, Alicia fourteen,
Edna thirteen. We knew what Lólin and Toñito did at night in the
room in the basement that Mami assigned to them. And although
they did their best to be discreet, it was difficult to ignore the soft

moans and whispers coming from their room, the way her hand stroked his thigh when they sat together, the way his arm kept her close when they watched television.

Mami's aunts and uncles, cousins—Gury, La Muda, and Margot—and other relatives who rarely showed up at our house all came to see Lólin and Toñito as if they were the main attraction at a circus. In Puerto Rico, Tío Pedro was not happy with his eldest daughter's choice of husband. The many telephone conversations I overheard were pleas for him to be flexible, to accept Toñito, to respect Lólin enough to allow her the consequences of her decision. But Tío Pedro was stubborn. The aunts and uncles, the cousins, Mami and Tata sat at our kitchen table for hours, discussing what to do. From time to time, the romantic chords of a guitar were heard from the basement, where Toñito strummed love songs while Lólin reclined on her side.

The relatives complained that Toñito was irresponsible, because he showed up with nothing to his name but that blasted guitar. They predicted the relationship couldn't last. Lólin was used to comfort, they noted, since Tío Pedro was a merchant who provided well for his family. She was temporarily blind to Toñito's charm, they suggested, and as soon as she realized what a laggard he was, she'd crawl back to Puerto Rico to ask her father's forgiveness. Of course, it was assumed Tío Pedro would never forgive her or accept Toñito, so the gossip was tinged with compassion for poor, misguided Lólin.

My sisters and I watched the drama. For years Lólin and her sister Tati had been held up as examples of "good" girls, and here was Lólin, having eloped with a good-looking guy who, by all accounts, had no skills with which to support her. And in Puerto Rico, Tati, who was younger, had already married, borne a son, and been abandoned. Tati, who was so pretty, lively, and always carefree, was now a tragic figure. Lólin's disobedience didn't conform to her mild, serene nature. The female aunts and cousins still used Tati and Lólin as examples—only this time they were negative models.

About Tati they said, "See what happens when a girl is too eager to get out from under her parents' care and protection?" Lólin's defiance they blamed on her docile ways. "All this time she was the perfect daughter," they mused. *"Pero llevava la música por dentro."* When they said that Lólin carried "the music inside her," they looked at us hard, to let us know that if we were too well behaved, they suspected we were up to no good.

When Tío Pedro relented and Lólin and Toñito returned to Puerto Rico, the relatives shook their heads and suggested it was Tío Pedro and Titi Sara's overprotectiveness that had caused so much trouble for their daughters. Had they been more permissive, Tati might have waited to get married, thereby avoiding abandonment at a young age. Lólin would have met many men and not fallen for the first *manganzón* to make eyes at her.

My sisters and I were advised to learn from their mistakes, to place ourselves between Tati's impatience and Lólin's audacity. It was a path with no precedent in our family. Each aunt and uncle, each adult cousin was a model of impulsiveness and contradiction. Not to mention Mami and Tata, who both spouted rules they didn't live by and were prime examples of the aphorism, "Do as I say and not as I do." Tata warned us not to smoke or drink as she sat at the kitchen table with a cigarette in one hand and a beer in the other. Mami talked about church weddings for us, then used herself as an example of how tenuous nonsanctified unions were.

"But Don Carlos was married to that woman, and he divorced her to be with you," I started, and she shushed me.

"That marriage was over long before he met me," she said, which was true, but that wasn't my point.

"Get an education so that you can get jobs in offices, not factories," Mami frequently advised us. The next day she showed us a beautifully stitched bra. Her face flushed with pride, she went over every seam, pointed out how tricky it was to get the double needles to turn just so, how delicate the fabric was to work with, how unusual the new closures. She made useful and lovely things with her own hands. When she was laid off, she lamented that her skills were not enough to support her children.

"Don't be like me," she insisted, "learn a profession, don't depend on factories for your livelihood."

The more time I spent at home, the more confused I became. We never went to church, but I should marry in a cathedral. A good girl, I should not be too good or my goodness was suspect. If I was too anxious to leave home, my life could turn to tragedy. If I lingered under Mami's protection, I was sure to be deceived by those more knowledgeable in the ways of the world.

There were times I left the house for school or work with the intention of never coming back, but I didn't have the courage to run away. Sometimes I stared at the shiny subway tracks, at how easy it would be to throw myself upon them, but the thought of being mangled by tons of moving metal made me step back when the train rumbled near.

The home that had been a refuge from the city's danger was now a prison I longed to escape. I was exhausted by the intensity of my family life, by the drama that never ceased, the crises that rose out of nowhere, subsided, made way for others that in their turn were mere preludes. I was tired of the constant tug between the life I wanted and the life I had. I dreaded the loneliness that attached itself to me in the middle of my raucous family. I didn't blame them for my unhappiness, but neither did I want to contaminate them with it. I wanted to be, like Garbo, alone. I wanted to become La Sorda, deaf to my family's voices, their contradictory messages, their expectations. I longed to cup my hand to my mouth, the way singers did, and listen to myself. To hear one voice, my own, even if it was filled with fear and uncertainty. Even if it were to lead me where I ought not to go.

"What size bra do you wear?"

The second semester at Manhattan Community College, Shoshana and I signed up for Fundamentals of Mathematics. The
course was not required of business majors, but in the fall of 1967,
it was taught by gorgeous Mr. Grunwald. Shoshana was thrilled,
because he was not only the handsomest man she'd ever seen but
also Jewish. She reasoned that since the class met three times a
week and Mr. Grunwald had office hours for extra help, there
would be many opportunities for him to fall in love with one
of us.

"But what if he falls in love with you and I get jealous?"

Shoshana considered this a moment. "Let's not do that. Let's
say that what's good for you is good for me and vice versa. That
way there's no jealousy."

Shoshana had no sisters, and I did. Her proposal was noble
but unrealistic, and I told her so.

"All right then. If he chooses me over you, then you have to
promise to back off. I'll do the same."

"That sounds better," I agreed.

The first day of classes, Shoshana and I took seats side by side
in the front row of the room, which was filled with females
dressed, like us, in our best outfits. When Mr. Grunwald walked
in, we sighed as one. Not too tall, not too short, perfectly proportioned from head to toe, Mr. Grunwald was as gorgeous as
Shoshana had promised. His dark blue, nearly violet eyes were

intelligent and gentle. His sandy hair curled around his ears and below the collar of his shirt. He was clean shaven, with a wide, chiseled jaw, sensuous lips, a perfect nose. He wore a light brown corduroy jacket with suede elbow patches, tight jeans, a button-down indigo shirt with a subtly patterned tie. When he wrote his inscrutable formulas on the chalkboard, his handwriting was crisp, the numbers perfectly formed, the *x* forceful and mysterious. He claimed he wasn't teaching us math, that he taught logic; but it looked like math to me.

"He's good-looking and everything," I said to Shoshana, "but the course looks too hard. I'm dropping it."

Shoshana would have none of that. "All you need is a C − to pass," she said. "I'll help you."

After class, Shoshana consulted her careful notes and re-peated almost everything Mr. Grunwald had just said. Twice a week, I went to his office, and he corrected my dismal quizzes and tests in front of me. He wore cologne, a fruity scent that filled my nostrils as he leaned in to show me how the sine and cosine related to the tangent. He spoke with a drawl, the vowels long, soothing as a siesta. I wanted to live in his diphthongs, engulfed by his *o*s and *u*s, caressed by his *i*s. But Mr. Grunwald's passion was in convex regions and the vertex of a parabola. Just as it didn't occur to Shoshana that Mr. Grunwald wouldn't fall in love with any of us, it didn't seem to occur to Mr. Grunwald that I, and every other girl in his class, was in love with him.

One day, as he tried to help me understand what would never make sense, Mr. Grunwald leaned back in his chair. "Let's not work on this anymore," he suggested.

Humiliated that he should give up on me, I apologized. "Math has never been my subject."

He rubbed his face with both hands. "What is it that you hope to do with your college education?" he asked from inside his fingers.

"Get a good job," I answered.

He dropped his hands, glared at me. "Doing what, exactly?"

"Advertising, I guess." Sweat collected on my forehead, my upper lip. "Or marketing . . ."

"You have no idea, do you?" The tone of his voice, its low register, the soft look that accompanied his words, made tears come to my eyes. I shook my head. "What would you like to do?" he asked, and I wanted to say kiss you all over, which was what I was thinking, but I shrugged my shoulders instead. "Shoshana mentioned you're a dancer," he added. "Are you any good?"

No one had asked me that, and it took a few seconds to decide to answer honestly, without false modesty. "I'm very good," I said. "Considering how late I started."

He smiled. "Modern dance? Ballet?"

I smiled back. "I'm probably the only Puerto Rican Indian classical dancer you've ever met."

The rest of the extra help period was spent describing to Mr. Grunwald the subtleties of Bharata Natyam. He was attentive, made comments that let me know he was listening.

"Indian music progresses mathematically," he interjected once, and I stopped talking to consider it. He watched me think, as if it were a new experience.

"I . . . I guess so," I finally said. Mr. Grunwald chuckled, which made me feel stupid for coming up with such a dumb response.

When I told Shoshana that I had spent my extra help session talking to Mr. Grunwald about dance, she was ecstatic. "He likes you! Now he'll probably ask you to a musical."

"That's not the kind of dancing I do," I protested.

Shoshana was over her infatuation with Mr. Grunwald now that she was dazzled by the Principles of Advertising teacher. Mr. Delmar was older than most of the professors at Manhattan Community College. He had salt-and-pepper hair, gray eyes, features embellished with wrinkles deliberately placed to enhance his handsome face. He wore expensive, fitted suits that accentuated an elegant physique, slim and long legged. Mr. Delmar strolled the halls of the college as if he owned the place and drew admiring glances from males and females alike, young or old. I disliked him instantly, found his finished air too self-conscious and calculated. But Shoshana said that was because I'd never been anywhere. "He's so sophisticated, so European," she sighed.

With each of us mooning over a different teacher, there was no jealousy. Our conversations focused on how far we'd go if one of them asked us out. We were both willing to give up our virginity if Mr. Grunwald or Mr. Delmar gave us the slightest hint that they wanted it. After repeated attempts to gain his attention, Shoshana decided Mr. Delmar wouldn't date her while she was still his student. She gave up on him for the fall semester and set her hopes on the spring. As for me, the only way to impress Mr. Grunwald was to become immersed in reflection symmetric figures. I wasn't about to do that, even with the promise of a night of passion as its outcome. I continued my long, rambling letters to Otto, whose responses were shorter and less frequent.

"You should break up with him before he breaks up with you," Shoshana suggested. I stopped writing, and I could almost hear the relief all the way from Switzerland.

Just down the hall from our lockers at Manhattan Community College was a student lounge. Shoshana and I never went in there to study, because loud music came from behind its heavy, closed doors. We liked music, but we also liked to hear ourselves talk. Between classes, we preferred to walk to a nearby coffee shop or to the Automat, or we'd meet our page boys at the NBC commissary. But one day I needed coffee in a hurry and made my way to the lounge. The room was big, with a few battered chairs, a sagging couch, a row of vending machines that offered candy, soda, pastries wrapped in plastic. Under the lone window was a small table with a coffee maker, packets of sugar, a stack of paper cups, a jar of Cremora.

As I entered, it felt as if I had strayed into another country. To my left, the room vibrated with Motown music from a portable record player. Black students sat or stood in small groups arguing politics as the Supremes sang about "The Happening." To my left, at an equally loud volume, Eddie Palmieri's rhythms punctuated the sounds of Spanglish. The center of the room was nearly empty, except for a few white students adrift between the two lively continents. Most of the people in the room were familiar to me because we saw one another in classes or in the halls. One of them, Gloria, waved me over to the mambo side of the room.

"Are you Puerto Rican?" she asked. When I said yes, she turned to the group. "You see!" She turned to me again. "These guys here didn't believe me." One of the boys, Felix, was in a class with me.

"You knew I was Puerto Rican," I chided him.

"I told them," he chuckled, then turned his hand palm up toward another guy, who slapped it.

"You were in that movie about the school, right?" another girl asked.

I flushed with pleasure at being recognized. "*Up the Down Staircase*, yes I was."

"Told you!" another round of palm slapping. The bell to signal the start of a period rang, and all of them scrambled to gather their belongings.

"See you later," I said. No one responded. I left, surprised that there was talk about me but that the minute they met me, no one cared. I wondered if I had left a poor impression and replayed the scene several times. Was I friendly and open enough? Did I appear too proud of having been in a movie? Was there anything I could have done to make them like me? They had stood close together in a semicircle as we talked, as if I were being interviewed. But then they dispersed, dismissed me.

Perhaps I was oversensitive, Shoshana suggested later, because most of the students at Manhattan Community College were black or Puerto Rican and my best friend was Jewish.

"Maybe deep down inside you feel you should be friends with them and not me," she pouted.

"Remind me to skip Psychology next semester," I responded.

Since she had started that course, everything anyone said or did was open to interpretation. But it did bother me that Shoshana felt that way and that a part of me — a tiny, hidden part — agreed.

⌒⌒⌒⌒

A few weeks after school started, I lost my night job because Mr. Vince went out of business. In spite of months of advertising and thousands of calls to prospective clients, he hadn't sold enough vacations to keep me and the other telephone solicitors employed. Shoshana had quit the job months earlier, before she went to Israel for the summer. Several men and women came and left, but I worked with Mr. Vince until the end, and he was close to tears the day he let me go.

"Soon as I get on my feet again," he promised, "I'll give you a call." He paid me an extra week's wages as a bonus.

I went to the student employment office at the college, which had a program through which I could get credit for work related to my major. The counselor sent me to the Advertising Checking Bureau. My supervisor, Mrs. Davis, promised me a flexible schedule. "Your education is more important than a job," she assured me.

Mrs. Davis was a petite, gray-haired lady who dressed in A-line skirts and frilly blouses with tightly secured cuffs and collars. Her desk was close to the entrance door, turned toward the room lined with glass-paneled offices for managers and higher-ranked supervisors. The three employees in her department faced Mrs. Davis along the only row of windows. Each desk and shelf over the radiators under the windows was covered with mounds of newspapers, magazines, folded posters, radio and television copy.

My job was to check that the ads for accounts assigned to me ran according to the arrangement between the manufacturer of the product and the retailer. The manufacturer paid for part of the advertisement. My job was to ensure that if Amana paid 30 percent of the cost, the Amana product took up at least 30 percent of the

column inches for the newspapers or magazines, or 30 percent of
the radio and television copy. Each "checker" kept track of several
accounts in a geographic area. I handled large and small appliances in the Upper Midwest. Every day I came into the office,
there was a stack of clippings on my desk and a list of which
accounts had which arrangements with which retailers. Often,
instead of a clipping, there was an entire newspaper, which I
skimmed until I found the advertisement for my client. I came to
know the vagaries of weather in Ypsilanti, Michigan, the price of
wheat in Kankakee, Illinois, the results of local elections in Ona-
laska, Wisconsin. For the third year in a row, Tracey Dobbins of
Rock Rapids, Iowa, won top prize for her calf at the 4-H exposition.
Mrs. Sada Ulton's pickled rhubarb was the best-selling food item
at the county fair. Danny Finley scored the winning touchdown at
the Emmetsburg High School Homecoming game. It was a world
so far from Brooklyn that I was lost in it, awash in church suppers,
agricultural fairs, births, deaths, local theatricals. From time to
time, Mrs. Davis stopped by our desks to ask how things were
going, or to wonder if the RCA logo was prominent in the ad for
Sam's Appliance Mart. But like her three employees, she was a
reader, and she often chuckled at the antics of Blondie and Dag-
wood, or snipped recipes from the pages of the *Philadelphia In-
quirer.*

Without the excuse of a night job, I came home every evening. I had supper, then closed myself in my room to do my
homework, most of which involved preimage objects to which Mr.
Grunwald had us apply identity transformations.

The more time I spent away from home, the more it felt as if
I were a visitor in my family. Our house, with its noise and bustle,
was like a pause between parts of my real life in Manhattan, in
dance studios, in adventures with Shoshana, in college, in the
social calendar of Mishawaka, Indiana. Weekends when I didn't
have school or work, I caught up with my siblings' lives. Delsa had
a boyfriend named George. Héctor excelled at gymnastics in high
school. Alicia sang in the school choir.

Mami, thirty-six years old and pregnant with her eleventh child, looked worn. Her step was slow, her skin had lost its luster, her hair, cut short to frame her face, was brittle and broken at the ends. After being unable to afford dental care for years, she went to the dentist during the summer, and he pulled out her teeth. Her face collapsed into her mouth, her youthful look vanished. The dentures didn't fit well, and she was in pain for months before the dentist agreed to fix them.

Tata moved out for a few weeks to live with Don Julio, came back, moved out on her own again. I went to see her at the boarding house where she lived in one room crammed with a bed, an easy chair with torn upholstery, a hot plate, some chipped dishes and glasses. By the window she had set up her altar of family relics and saints, who were supposed to bring her luck when she played *bolita*. She won enough times to keep her faith in them. The bathroom was in the downstairs hallway, and she kept a chamber pot under her bed so that she wouldn't have to make the trip up and down the stairs more often than necessary. After a few weeks there, she returned to the basement once occupied by Lólin and Toñito. She grumbled and complained about the activity in the house. Now that we were older, she didn't find us as charming as when we were little. The only one she still doted on was Franky, who at four years old was still cute and didn't talk back when she scolded him.

I floated in and out of family activities, took note of major changes. Don Carlos lived with us. Norma dyed her hair red. Don Carlos moved out. Cousin Paco gave up wrestling. Don Carlos came back. Delsa achieved straight As in math. Héctor helped Raymond get a job at a pizza shop. Crises rose, subsided, rose again, kept Sunday afternoons lively as aunts, uncles, cousins, and their families appeared unannounced to share in the good food and gossip that kept everyone entertained from week to week. I made excuses, disappeared into my room, or left the house as soon as I could get away, sometimes with one of my sisters or brothers but more often alone. I took in a double feature, lost in Hollywood's version of life, with its elegant women, manly men, nonexistent children, predicaments resolved by guns or marriage, and sometimes both. Sometimes I went to visit Alma and Corazón, sat in their quiet apartment talking about books and listening to American rock and roll.

Corazón loved the Doors and the Bee Gees. "Listen to this," she said, as she put on an LP. She sat back on the couch, I plopped next to her, and we closed our eyes and listened. She understood the lyrics of the songs, I didn't. "What does the chorus say?" she asked.

"Come and maybe like my buyer?" I guessed, and she roared with laughter.

Alma wrote poetry. One of her poems was published in an anthology. She placed a sliver of paper as a bookmark on the page where her name in italics looked authoritative and precise. The poem was titled "They," a sonnet about impotence and powerlessness. The last line, "They will not let me," was such a surprise that I looked up at her to ask whom she meant, but her face was so proud and pleased with herself that I didn't dare.

On the bulletin board of the International School of Dance, someone posted a "Models Wanted" flyer, no experience necessary. I called the number and was told that the models were for a photography school. In exchange for posing, models received an eight-by-ten glossy from each student who took a picture. There was no nudity involved. Models brought a couple of changes of clothes and their own makeup. I told Shoshana, who immediately agreed we should do it.

The school was in a loft in the West Forties. There was a small dressing room with a lighted mirror and a closet for the models to hang their clothes. We were asked to put on "natural" makeup and wait to be called. There were two other girls, Sharon and Beverly, who planned to use their pictures in modeling portfolios. They were taller, with better cheekbones, so they ignored me. Shoshana they eyed with envy. She was as tall as they were but more shapely, and her features, well proportioned and very pretty, were designed to be photographed.

We sat in a row of chairs outside the dressing room. Within a few minutes the instructor appeared, trailed by a group of young men.

"Ladies," he began. "The way this works is, for the first hour or so everyone gets to pose, and everyone gets to take a picture. But if one of the students and one of the models develop a special affinity, then you may work together individually over there in the seamless." He pointed to a huge roll of white paper dangling from the ceiling onto the floor, "Or on the set." His hands fluttered in the direction of a dark gray backdrop with cloudlike blotches painted on it. "Is everyone ready?" We nodded, and he led us to another lit seamless area, where we posed in assorted groupings while the students clicked furiously, moved around for different angles, and tried to stay out of one another's way.

I felt silly striking "Mod" girl poses, but Sharon and Beverly were expert at it. When the instructor asked me and Shoshana to step out so that they could be photographed first together, then individually, I saw what a difference aptitude for modeling made. Sharon butterflied her elbows, placed her hands on her hips, and somehow made herself look two-dimensional. Beverly's specialty was motion. She jumped, and she managed to float in the air long enough for the photographers to take many more pictures than they could take of me standing still. It was impressive to see how effortlessly Sharon and Beverly went from pose to pose, each one different, each one striking. Shoshana and I looked at each other in dismay. No way could we do that.

We were surprised when, at the end of the first session, Sharon and Beverly were told to go, but three young men asked to photograph me and Shoshana together. We were posed in profile, first facing each other, then both looking in the same direction. The three young men worked as a team, set up lights for one another, took turns at a portrait camera set up on a tripod, while the instructor stood in the background and offered suggestions for how to pose or light us. We were also photographed individually, in different clothes and with changes in our makeup and hair, which Shoshana and I did for each other. The session took the entire morning. At the end, we were exhausted, but the instructor asked us to come back on a different day for another group of students, and we agreed on the spot.

"Can you believe it?" Shoshana exulted. "They sent the professionals away and liked us better!" A career we'd never considered was now possible. "If we get good pictures," Shoshana suggested, "we can put together a portfolio and go to the agencies." We imagined that Eileen Ford herself would sign us and put us on the cover of *Vogue*.

"Competition for Twiggy!" I crowed.

"Although I think you're more *Seventeen*," Shoshana mused.

"I've never seen a model with my complexion on that cover," I sulked.

We did several more sessions at the photography school. The eight by tens the students gave us were high-contrast, black-and-white glossies, different from what we had imagined as we posed.

"Do you think we can really use these for a modeling portfolio?" I asked Shoshana one day as we went over our photographs. Deep shadows distorted our features, dramatic juxtapositions made us turn the pictures on their side to see if we could recognize ourselves.

"They're arty." She was as unconvinced as I was. Nevertheless, we each bought a black portfolio and arranged our pictures with the "arty" ones in the back. It was Shoshana's idea that once we got our portfolios together, we should consult our advertising teachers. "After all, they have agencies and see thousands of models," she reasoned.

Her professor was the dashing Mr. Delmar. Mine was Dr. Henning, long as a basketball player, with huge feet and hands, a massive head topped by curls of gray hair. He wore suits that hung in folds and drapes around his body like tweed togas.

When I asked him if he could look at my portfolio, he suggested I come to his office, which was over a Tad's Steaks on Seventh Avenue. It was a small dark room at the end of an equally dim hallway that smelled of grilled meat. Mr. Henning sat behind a massive oak desk in front of a window. Smoky gray light fell on him from behind, highlighted the dust that floated in the air. He pointed to a leather chair across his desk, and I sank into its musty rasps and squeaks.

"These are very nice," he said, poring over the pictures. He turned the portfolio over, as Shoshana and I did, to figure out the more artistic photographs. He looked up. "How tall are you?"

"Five feet, four inches."

"Fashion models are taller," he said. "At least five-eight. But you might be able to do catalogue work. What size bra do you wear?"

"I beg your pardon?"

"I'm not being fresh," he reassured me. "There's a market for models who do women's intimate apparel, bras and girdles, that sort of thing." I was aghast, and it must have shown, because Dr. Henning raised his palms toward me, as if to protect himself from something I might throw. "This is for respectable catalogues like Sears and J. C. Penney's." He unfurled himself from his chair to reach for a thick book behind him. "Let me show you."

I waited until I could speak without breaking into tears. "Thank you, but . . ."

He leafed through until he reached the back pages. "They don't usually photograph the face, so no one will recognize you." He tipped the catalogue toward me. Black and white images of female torsos wearing cotton bras were printed along the left and right margins. Blocks of print gave particulars for styles, price, sizes available. "There's quite a bit of money in it," he promised.

"It's not the kind of modeling I had in mind," I said, trying to stay composed. I shook with anger and humiliation, but I didn't want to say or do anything stupid. After all, he was my teacher and would grade me at the end of the semester. "Thank you, anyway."

"Don't decide right now. I know it's not the sort of thing a girl jumps into." He returned the catalogue to its place.

"I'm sure it's not my thing." I took my portfolio. He walked me to the door. "I appreciate the time you took."

The long hall felt longer with him staring after me from the threshold. I tried to walk so that my hips didn't swing from side to side, my breasts didn't jiggle. No part of my body should appear suggestive in any way to someone who had just recommended a career for me as a bra model. Had the thought just occurred to him as he looked at my pictures? Or had he checked me out from every angle while I sat in class jotting down famous advertising slogans? How could I face him again? Never in tight clothes, that was for sure.

Shoshana didn't think I should have been offended. "Someone has to model bras," she reasoned. "Why not you?"

"I'm not even allowed to wear a bikini. How can I tell my mother I model bras?"

"You tell her too much," she said.

"That's not the point, Shoshana!"

She ignored my irritation. "Doesn't she make bras?"

"Yes she does. But that doesn't mean she wants me to wear them without a shirt."

Shoshana's appointment with Mr. Delmar went much better. He thought she could be a model, but she needed more pictures. "Get some that are straightforward, less of this artsy-fartsy stuff," was his assessment.

Since I was about four inches too short to be a model, I didn't want to be photographed any more.

"You can use them when you go on auditions," Shoshana suggested. "Didn't you say they always ask for a head shot?"

I'd long felt at a disadvantage during auditions because I didn't have a composite or a head shot, which cost more than I was willing to invest in my career as an actress. But these photographs were nothing like the head shots other people brought to auditions. We made another appointment to be photographed, and this time, we brought simple clothes, wore little makeup. Again we were snapped together, but at the end of the session, different students asked us to pose for them individually.

The young man who asked me was Indian. He was bony, slightly taller than I, stoop-shouldered. He spoke in a soft, deferential voice, a musical English that at first sounded too fast for me to understand. Once I became used to it, I liked his forceful explosives and snappy vowels, the way every syllable was differentiated from the other.

"My name is Shanti," he said, as he set up lights for a portrait.

We worked well together. He was gentle and considerate, gave me breaks between setups, made little gestures with his lips, or his head, or his bony fingers to get me to move, or to hold a pose. It was as if we'd known each other a long time, and at the end of the session, he asked if it might be possible to do some exteriors.

"Is that okay with the school?" I asked.

"Yes, sure," he said. "We're supposed to learn that too."

We met that Sunday afternoon in Central Park. We walked around, and when he saw a nice background, he had me pose before it. After a couple of hours, he had enough pictures, and we went home, but not before he had asked me to meet him again the following weekend, this time in the Village.

The next Sunday we wandered around, and he snapped me next to a group of hippies in outlandish clothes and unkempt hair. I was uncomfortable around them, which showed in the photographs. The hippies made faces at the camera while I stood primly in front of them, my purse clasped to my bosom. He then photographed me in the midst of a group of old men observing a chess game. I had no idea how chess was played and watched the game intently to see if I could get a sense of it. But there was such little action, it was impossible to figure out, and when I looked up to see if Shanti was done photographing me, I gazed into the eyes of my math teacher, Mr. Grunwald. Behind him, Shanti snapped a picture of me looking shocked.

"Hi!" Mr. Grunwald seemed happy to see me, strangely, since in class he ignored me so that he could focus on people who understood scalar multiplication. He grinned. "Do you always travel with a photographer?" he asked. I introduced him to Shanti, and the three of us walked down the rows of chess tables crowded with spectators, as if the game held real excitement. Mr. Grunwald said he lived nearby and often walked to the park to see the players. He laughed when I suggested there was nothing to watch. Beside us, Shanti neither spoke nor took pictures, and I felt his sullenness grow like a balloon being pumped with air. Mr. Grunwald felt it too, because after a couple of blocks, he excused himself and went in the opposite direction.

"Is he your boyfriend?" Shanti asked, the minute Mr. Grunwald was out of hearing.

"No. He's my math teacher," I blushed.

"I see." He sounded annoyed, which made me mad. What business was it of his whether Mr. Grunwald was my boyfriend or my math teacher? "Maybe we're done for the day," he said.

"All right." I looked in the direction Mr. Grunwald had taken, wondering if I might catch up with him.

"Fine, then," Shanti said, and stalked off. He quickly disappeared in the crowd, while I stood in place, surprised at his reaction. In the two weeks we'd worked together, it hadn't occurred to me that Shanti's interest might be more than professional. It was hard to imagine that when he looked at me through the lens, he saw more than a model. I walked around the Village for a while asking myself whether I wanted to be the object of Shanti's affection as well as his art. When I realized that my wanderings were meant to run into Mr. Grunwald again, I knew the answer.

The following week Mr. Grunwald asked me to stay after class. As everyone filed out, he handed me a copy of *Backstage* with an audition notice circled in red.

"I saw this," he said, "and it sounded perfect for you."

"Are you an actor?" I should have known that such a handsome man was in the theater.

"No," he said, "but my roommate is."

Shoshana waited outside, and I shared the news that Mr. Grunwald had a roommate. Her face fell. When I asked her why she looked so disappointed, she gave me her opinion.

"He's homosexual."

"Oh, please!"

"Think about it. He's single, lives in the Village, has a roommate."

It was the most ridiculous reasoning I'd ever heard. If anyone should know about homosexuals, it was me, I argued, since I was surrounded by them in dance classes. But Shoshana could not be dissuaded. She said some homosexuals didn't look it. "I bet his roommate," she curled her tongue around the word, "is swishy."

There was only one way to tell. We must see the roommate. If we followed Mr. Grunwald from school, we'd see where he lived. We might be able to catch a glimpse of the roommate through the window. Or, if we waited outside Mr. Grunwald's door, we might see them come out together.

In the excitement of planning how to follow Mr. Grunwald without being seen, I almost forgot why he asked me to stay after class. The audition notice in *Backstage* called for an ingenue for a children's theater company casting a Broadway-bound production of an Indian fable. It was a dream come true—a part I was qualified to play that took advantage of my looks and training. I called to set up a time and was told I didn't need to prepare anything because I'd read from the script.

If Shanti would talk to me again, I could learn an Indian accent and throw in a few Hindi words if necessary. We met for lunch, and as he showed me the pictures he had taken the previous week, I listened to his inflections, tried to capture the rhythm of his speech. He laughed at my attempts to mimic his accent.

"You can't learn it in one day," he chuckled. "It takes a lifetime."

The audition was at Michaels Rehearsal Studio on Eighth Avenue. Several other actresses waited ahead of me, but a couple were too old to be ingenues, and none looked as Indian as I did. I'd made myself up to appear as Indian as possible without wearing a sari, my hair parted in the middle and braided, eyes done up with kohl, a dot of red nail polish in the middle of my forehead.

When I was called in, Bill, the director, and Vera, the producer, exchanged a look. They asked some questions about my prior experience, then said they were ready to hear me read from the script. In the scene, a character named Soni explained to a character named Babu that she was a prisoner in a tower because her uncle planned to marry her to a rajah. Soni was allowed to leave the tower to pray at a temple, but she had a chain around her waist, which her uncle pulled when it was time for her to return.

As soon as he heard my poorly executed Indian accent, Bill interrupted and asked if I could read it straight. Vera then asked me to improvise a scene in which a monkey entered through a window and offered to help Soni escape from the tower. I did my best to appear surprised, scared, curious, grateful. At the end, Vera took my phone number and said she'd get back to me.

Bill and Vera were professional and noncommittal, didn't give me a clear sense of whether or not they liked my audition. I wanted to play Soni more than anything in the world, and as I left the studio, I reviewed everything I'd done and said, tried to figure out if there was more I could have done to assure me the part. It was a Saturday, almost time for matinee performances. I walked on Broadway, past the marquees with the names of famous plays and actors, the tourists who gawked at tawdry posters in front of the pornography shops vying with legitimate theaters. I turned the corner and stood in front of Performing Arts's chocolate facade with its heavy red doors. I pressed my forehead against the glass. The familiar wooden boxes were stacked near the lockers in the Basement, the desks arranged in a semicircle, as if a scene were about to be performed for students and teachers. I shook with anxiety and had to lean against the front pillars of the shuttered school until I no longer felt lightheaded and the trembling had stopped.

⌒⌒ᴐ

I hung up the phone and slumped against the wall of our kitchen. Mami panicked. "What's the matter?"

"I got the part," I spoke to myself, unbelieving. "I'm going to be in a play." I looked up at her. "On Broadway."

"Is that good?" she wondered. She knew it was when I pulled Cibi from the playpen in the middle of the kitchen and danced her around the house. "I'm going to be on Broadway. I'm going to be a star," I sang. Cibi chortled, drooled on me. I put her back.

Tata dragged herself from her room in the basement, Delsa and Norma left the television on in the living room and ran into the kitchen. Raymond and Franky appeared from the yard. The rest of my sisters and brothers came down from the bedrooms. The house was full of people I loved eager to hear good news. Without knowing what the fuss was about, my sisters and brothers, my mother and grandmother, could tell it was a wonderful thing because I was so happy. I repeated what Vera told me. The play was for young audiences. It was one of a repertory of other plays performed in schools and theaters around the Northeast. The company, Children's Theater International, had won several honors and awards.

My family was impressed. They didn't ask if I'd wear any of the bizarre costumes they'd seen on me, the bells strapped to my ankles, the nail polish dots in the middle of my forehead that had to be removed with acetone. They didn't joke about the strange sounds that came from my room when I practiced my Indian dances, which would increase now that I was to perform regularly. They were as glad as I was, which made my joy greater because it was wonderful to do something that not only made me feel good but made everyone else smile.

I called Shoshana, Shanti, Alma and Corazón, everyone I knew. I would have told total strangers if I had had the courage.

Rehearsals began that week, in a loft on Christopher Street in the Village. Some of the cast had performed in other Children's Theater International productions, *Petey and the Pogo Stick* and *Hans Brinker*. The play I'd be in, *Babu*, had been in repertory the year before.

"You might know the girl who played Soni," Vera said. "She went to your school. Priscilla López."

"Yes, she graduated a year before me." I was thrilled to be playing a part originated by Priscilla, one of the most talented actors at Performing Arts when I was a student there. Vera also told me that, while they liked the fact that I was an Indian classical dancer, my role didn't require dancing.

"There is one scene where a dancer performs," she said, "but we already have someone to do that." I was disappointed, but got over it after I had read the entire script, which made it clear that my character, Soni, had a bigger role to play in the story than the dancer who attended the rajah.

The title role of Babu was played by Allan, an actor and singer whose openness and warmth won me over instantly. In the play, he rescued Soni from her prison tower, and it didn't take much acting for me to fall in love with him at each performance, and to remain besotted between shows.

Allan and Bill had known each other for years, had worked together, and were good friends. Both had marvelous, trained voices, and I often asked one or the other a question just to hear them speak.

The other member of the cast I came to know well was Tom. In the first scene of the play, when Soni and Babu met, Tom, in his role as the monkey god, sat in the lotus position in a niche on the set. After Soni was dragged offstage by her evil uncle, Babu prayed for a way to help her escape. The audience screeched when Tom opened his eyes and spoke, because they didn't expect a statue to come to life.

After rehearsals I often joined Bill, Allan, or Tom for a cup of coffee or a late dinner. They'd been in the theater much longer than I and told funny, poignant stories about mishaps and humiliations onstage and off.

Vera lived in Westchester County and commuted to rehearsals. She was like an anxious mother one moment, all business the next. If one of us coughed, she handed out lozenges retrieved from her ample bag, but if we were late, she made sure to let us know that next time we should try harder. She frequently reminded us about our responsibilities as actors. "Just because this is children's theater," she often said, "doesn't mean we patronize or talk down to our audience."

We rehearsed evenings and weekends, and each time I left the studio I felt lucky to be among such gifted, committed people. It was fun to improvise with Allan and Tom, then to work from the script with Bill, who worked us hard but made us feel as if we were the most brilliant people he'd ever directed. Over the weeks of rehearsal, the character of Soni evolved as I better understood what Bill expected from my performance.

"Not so stylized," he scolded, when I tried to introduce Indian dance movements into Soni's actions.

With college in the morning, the Advertising Checking Bureau in the afternoons, and Children's Theater International evenings and weekends, I again spent most of my time away from home. I met Shoshana in classes, and we often had lunch together before I went to work.

We didn't forget Mr. Grunwald. One day we followed him in the subway to his stop at Waverly Place. He was easy to stalk. He was oblivious to his environment, seemed lost in deep mathematical thoughts, and kept his eyes focused on the obstacles in front of him but no further. Once he entered the subway, he immersed himself in a thick book with a parabola and formulas on the cover. From the next car, Shoshana and I watched until he got up from his seat and stood by the doors. As soon as they opened, he got off. We waited, then followed at a distance, trying not to draw attention to ourselves in spite of the nervous giggles that attacked us every time we realized what we were doing. Mr. Grunwald climbed the station steps, and we lost him in the throng on the street. But soon Shoshana spotted him buying a paper at a newsstand. He dropped some coins in the vendor's hand, turned a corner, and vanished.

"Now that's weird," said Shoshana, as we peeked around a building to a street of brownstones with neat stoops and flowerpots in the windows. "He must have gone into one of the houses."

"It must have been the first one," I pointed out, "he didn't have time to walk too far." No sooner had I spoken than Mr. Grunwald emerged from the first door on the street, led by a fluffy white dog in a hurry to get to a hydrant.

"What did I tell you?" Shoshana said, triumphant. Whether Mr. Grunwald was homosexual or not, his choice of dog certainly balanced the equation, as he would have said, in the direction of Shoshana's suspicions. "A swishy dog," she proclaimed, as if I hadn't noticed. "Oh, I'm so sorry," she pouted, when she noticed my expression.

"He doesn't look like the kind of man to have that type of dog," was all I could say.

Shoshana walked me to a nearby restaurant, where she ordered a cup of soup and a sandwich to make up for my disappointment. When I was fortified, we talked about how hard it was to find the right man.

"Maybe we're too choosy," she mused. "We'll end up old maids."

"He could at least have had a German shepherd," I said, fixed on the image of the magnificent Mr. Grunwald attached to the fussy dog.

The restaurant window faced a busy intersection near the subway entrance. A mishmash of hippies, businesspeople, ancient men and women, beggars, and street musicians paraded up and down for our entertainment. In the middle of Shoshana's description of her ideal man, she yelped as if pricked and pointed behind me. On the sidewalk, walking in our direction from the train station, was Mr. Grunwald, still led by the fluffy dog, his arm tight around the waist of a leggy, redheaded woman. Every few steps they stopped and kissed, to the annoyance of people behind, who were forced to circle around them, their faces crimped in displeasure. They passed no more than three feet from us, oblivious to the rest of humanity.

"The dog is hers," I guessed.

When I told Bill and Allan the story, they laughed.

"Do you like German shepherds?" Allan asked.

"At least they're real dogs, not walking mops." Bill and Allan looked at each other, then laughed some more. It was weeks before I realized what was so funny. One day Allan had to rush back to his apartment on the Upper West Side. He lived on the second floor at the rear of a brownstone, and as we came up, the deep-throated barking of what could only be a huge dog filled the hallway. "Wait here," Allan said, as he clicked open the three locks on his door. He slid into the apartment while I waited in the hall. In a few seconds, he opened the door, his left hand on the collar of the biggest German shepherd I had ever seen. "This is Tristan," he said. The dog's nose dove into my crotch, and Allan had to restrain it to keep it from pushing me further against the wall. "He likes girls," Allan grinned. He clipped on the dog's leash, and we walked half a block to Central Park, where Allan played with Tristan while I leaned against a tree. It was touching to see the warmth between them, the way the dog followed Allan's every move, stopped if Allan stopped, moved when Allan did. Watching them, I knew that this was the first man outside my family I had felt affection for. I'd fallen in love with several — Neftalí, Otto, Mr. Grunwald — but what I felt for Allan was unlike the romantic fantasies I had created around other men. I didn't daydream about marrying Allan, or even kissing him. I wanted to be with him, to talk and be silly and hear his stories. I loved his laugh, the way his eyes sparkled when he was pleased or proud. Between us, there were no sexual games. Had there been, I would have been disillusioned.

Shoshana didn't understand my relationship with Allan. She and I often discussed whether it was possible for a man and a woman to be friends without being sexual. She didn't think so; I did. Or rather, I hoped it was possible. I couldn't imagine that for the rest of my life, every encounter with a man was to be appraised against a possible sexual tryst. As an example of my ability to have male friends who were not boyfriends, I pointed to my frequent meetings with Shanti.

"He's in love with you," Shoshana insisted. "You just refuse to admit it."

Shanti's devotion was flattering. We worked well together and continued our collaboration, in spite of the fact that we were often testy around each other. He constantly criticized my diet, which consisted primarily of street-vendor hot dogs smothered with sauerkraut, washed down with a Yoo-Hoo, or pizza and grape ade, or creamy eclairs and coffee.

"You're a dancer," Shanti reminded me, "you should eat better."

"At least," I retorted with a disdainful look at his cigarette, "I don't smoke."

On a warm and sunny winter day, we sat on the steps of the Main Library on Fifth Avenue after he took a series of pictures of me atop the lions that guarded the entrance. "You're not the most beautiful girl I've photographed," he admitted. "But when I look at you through the lens, I see myself."

"Don't scare me that way," I snapped.

Whenever Shanti went metaphysical on me, I turned nasty. He once said our souls were connected, and I stared at him as if he were crazy. "I have no soul," I finally spit out.

He was silent for a long time, then spoke in a near whisper. "I see your soul even if you don't."

It was my turn to be speechless. His faith in something within me that he could see and I couldn't made me feel inadequate and immature. I had to defend myself. "You see what you want to see, not what's there."

Another time he insisted on reading my hand. "Over here is the life line," he stroked a curve from between my thumb and index finger to the crease on the inside of my wrist. "It will be a long life," he assured me. "But these," he pointed to a series of ragged lines, "indicate illness."

I pulled my hand away. "That's nonsense," I said. "I don't believe any of it." The truth was that it scared me to think he could know anything about me from my hands. If so, were there other signs, in the shape of my lips or eyebrows, the way my hair curled? If there were, I didn't want to know what they meant. What difference did it make if I had ten, twenty, fifty years to live? Or if the next day I'd be run over by a car? Why would I want to know what lay ahead?

"I can't predict what will happen," he protested, "I can only interpret what has happened already."

"I can do that," I retorted.

No matter how mean I was to him, or how much he criticized me, we always found time to be together. We knew that the pictures he took were not commercial, would never end up in a magazine, or be printed by the hundreds as head shots for auditions. Weekends, we still met in Central Park, or Lincoln Center, or the Empire State Building, where he took pictures of me looking as remote and inaccessible as I was to him. Every week, he handed me a few eight-by-ten glossies, which I studied as if they were a puzzle, each feature, shadow, line a piece of a larger, undefined whole. I felt protected by their formality, their solemn stillness. But it unnerved me when he captured another me, whose eyes beseeched the onlooker for something I couldn't define.

⸻

As the day neared for my Broadway debut, I settled into my role as Soni. We performed at local schools, which gave me a chance to become familiar with the set and comfortable in my two costumes. Bill and Vera planned several more shows after the New

York run, and a tour out of town. I prepared Mami for the possibility that I'd go away for two weeks or more with the cast of *Babu*. Other than occasional overnight stays with my cousins Alma and Corazón and the visits to Margie in Yonkers, I'd never slept away from home. I expected Mami to make a fuss, but she just asked a few questions about where we'd be going and seemed at ease with the possibility.

Even though Mr. Grunwald gave me a C as my final grade in his class, I invited him to the opening. After all, he was responsible for the audition that had won me the part. We both knew a C was generous, considering my negative progress in mathematics or, as he called it, analytical thinking. For the final paper, we were supposed to state a theory and, using logical progression, prove it. I set out to prove that civilization began in Puerto Rico.

"But you said the theory didn't have to be true," I argued when we discussed my paper. "You just wanted us to make a logical case for it."

"You didn't do that," he maintained.

The play was to open for a limited run at the Longacre Theater during the Christmas holidays. Just a few months before, Sandy Dennis had starred in *Daphne in Cottage D* on the same stage. At the first dress rehearsal, I was assigned her dressing room, which featured a star on the door. Every time I pushed the door open, the star right before my eyes filled me with pride, which I had to contain so as not to appear conceited. I wanted to share my happiness with someone without seeming vain or boastful, so I wrote to Papi in Puerto Rico. I sent him a copy of the program, which featured Allan and me in our "crown jewels," the elaborately sequined and embroidered costumes Robert De Mora had designed for the finale. I described the hours of work it took to put a show together, the people involved, the fanciful plot. I told him about the dressing room, the wall-size mirror surrounded by lights, the private bathroom, the rug, the rundown but comfortable couch in which I took naps between performances. Because he wasn't there to see it with his own eyes, Papi saw it through mine, and for the first time I was glad he didn't live with us, because now there was someone whose vision of my world depended on my version of it.

The stage of the Longacre was huge. A few hours before the opening, I stood in the center, peered at the rows of empty seats, and saw not a deserted theater, but a challenge. My task was to transform a roomful of adults worn out from Christmas shopping and children fidgety with expectation into an audience. If I believed that I, a Puerto Rican girl from Brooklyn, was an Indian princess captive in a tower, rescued by a monkey, married to a prince, my audience would believe. If I could do that, I could do anything.

Mami and my sisters and brothers came to the first show. I was so nervous that I raced through it and was dazed and exhausted for the curtain calls. When I returned to the dressing room to change, I was greeted by a huge bouquet of flowers from Bill and Vera, another from Mr. Grunwald, a third from Shanti. Within minutes, the room filled with people. When she came backstage, Mami carried more flowers, somewhat wilted from having to share her arms with Franky. Mr. Grunwald stopped by, waved at the confusion from the door, disappeared.

Bill and Vera made a point of being nice to Mami, and she later told me she could see they were respectable, sober people.

"You take good care my daughter," Mami told Vera, when she mentioned the tour.

"I'm a mother, too," Vera responded. "Don't worry." Mami hugged her.

Don Carlos brought his kids. La Muda showed up. Shoshana came with Josh and Sammy. Shanti took pictures of me putting on makeup, as well as in the captive-in-a-tower costume.

"This looks nothing like what Indian girls wear," he complained. "It's for a harem."

"The designer took creative liberties," I said, "but the costume works on stage, which is what matters." He shrugged his shoulders.

Every day before a show, I got off the subway from Brooklyn, walked slowly along Broadway, listened to the commotion as if it were a marvelous song. Taxi horns blared. Tourists chattered in a plethora of dialects, all of them incomprehensible but familiar. The Hare Krishnas clinked their finger cymbals, pounded their drums, chanted their joyful tune. Peddlers offered legal and illegal bargains. I turned the corner and smiled at the bold *Babu* on the marquee of the Longacre. In front, there were huge posters of Allan and me, of Tom as the monkey god, of the rajah and his dancer. I entered the theater through the stage door, floated as if in a dream into my leading-lady dressing room, and caught an image of myself in the enormous mirror. I was not the most beautiful girl Shanti had ever photographed, nor the most talented actress graduated from Performing Arts. Alone with my reflection, I wondered what had brought me here. I was grateful, but I didn't know whom to thank.

"It wouldn't look right."

Because Vera lived in Westchester County and ran a children's theater series there, she organized several performances of *Babu* at schools in her area. The cast met at the rehearsal studio, and Bill drove a brown-and-beige Volkswagen van along the Hudson River north toward Scarsdale or Bronxville, Tarrytown or Elmsford, Mamaroneck or White Plains. We didn't spend much time in the communities where we performed, because the cast couldn't wait to get back to the city. Some claimed pollen allergies, exacerbated by the mere sight of trees. Others remembered childhoods in similar communities and were morose and pensive the whole way there and back.

The polite, mostly white audiences of Westchester County were a contrast to the outspoken children of New York City schools. When the curtain parted to reveal me praying before a stone god on the stage of an auditorium in a suburban school, there was appreciative applause and intense attention. At the Brooklyn Academy of Music, Town Hall, or schools in New York City, the applause of third, fourth, and fifth graders was accompanied by whistles and commentary. It took great concentration to wait while teachers tried to control students who called out "Hot mamma!", "Baby!", or "Hey, sweet thing!" Once the audience was relatively quiet, Allan made his entrance, discovered the captive Soni, a chain tied around her waist. As we discussed my predicament, a yank startled me and the audience, who couldn't see Bill or the stage manager dragging me off while I pleaded with Babu to help me. In the suburbs, this was a moment of high drama. In the city, the kids screeched. "Follow her, man!" they yelled— obvious, though not dramatically efficient, advice.

The schedule of performances intensified as spring neared and the promised tour developed. I took time off from college and from the Advertising Checking Bureau to go to Maine, New Hampshire, Massachusetts. The plan was to drive north to Bangor, then perform our way down the coast toward New York. Bill, Vera, and the cast traveled in the VW bus, while the stage manager followed in a truck that carried the set and costumes.

Early on a Sunday morning, we met on the corner of 55th Street and Sixth Avenue. The familiar VW bus was parked on the curb, a rental truck behind it.

"Nanook of the North!" Allan joked when he saw me, bundled up as if our destination were the North Pole and not New England. It was mid-March, and although New York was beginning to bloom, I had consulted regional newspapers at the Advertising Checking Bureau and knew to prepare for foul weather, from snow to sleet to implacable rain.

The cast negotiated where to sit, a process Vera likened to her four children bickering about who'd be in front and who needed frequent bathroom stops and who must sit by a window or they'd throw up. The city peeled away as we drove north on Interstate 95. Every time a familiar exit appeared, someone told a story about a summer stock playhouse, or about being stranded in New Haven in a blizzard, or about out-of-town tryouts that never made it into town. Lee, who played Soni's nurse, began a round of camp songs, none of which I knew. While everyone sang, I clapped my hands or whistled.

We stopped for meals at diners sometimes five or ten miles from the highway. Millie's Coffee Haus, Aunt Polly's Place, the Towne Line Diner, the Harbor View (with no water in sight)—all offered delicious, inexpensive food on enormous platters. We were a coffee-drinking group and usually entered diners in the throes of caffeine withdrawal, which made us irritable and impatient until the fragrant black liquid hit our systems. Veteran waitresses recognized our dazed looks the minute we walked in, desperately sniffing the air. They didn't ask if we wanted coffee. They poured full cups as we sat down, then handed us chatty menus with a long list of offerings. Along the back of the counter, refrigerated cases held golden-crust apple pies, lemon meringues, crunchy cobblers, puddings, creamy tapioca. Except for Lee, who was a strict vegetarian, we were indiscriminate eaters, eager to taste local specialties, like Rhode Island's coffee milk, Massachusetts's clam chowder, New Hampshire quahogs, Maine steamers.

We spent our first night in Lewiston, Maine. Bill and Vera were nervous about the accommodations in local bed and breakfasts. They relaxed when we pulled up to a pretty Victorian house on a hill.

"It looks like a storybook house," I exclaimed, charmed by the lace curtains in the windows, the gingerbread eaves, the etched glass door. The owner of the house, a rosy woman named Mrs. Hoch, had a fire going and muffins in the oven. Lee, Allan, and I stayed with Mrs. Hoch; the rest of the cast and crew went to other houses nearby.

We went to dinner at a local restaurant. The minute we walked in, I sensed how much we — ten New York types in urban wear — stood out from the rest of the patrons. I was the darkest person in the room, and the stares I drew felt like darts. The waitresses joined a couple of tables as we huddled at the door. I was embarrassed by the commotion we caused, conscious that we were out-of-towners in a small community. Every action was noticed by the locals, who blinked us away whenever one of us looked in their direction. I made a point of sitting between Allan and Bill.

"I feel so dark," I muttered. Bill smiled and put his arm around me.

The color of my skin was something I noticed every day when I stripped naked for a shower or bath. When I tried on new clothes, the color of my skin determined whether I could wear certain greens or yellows. Black, I noticed, made me look paler, white had the opposite effect. Hot pink gave me a healthy glow, whereas certain blues created ashen shadows around my eyes and lips. It was important for me to know these things when choosing costumes, because at Performing Arts we were taught that a character's choice of color said a great deal about her. The principles I learned there seeped into my choice of everyday clothes. I favored bright, tropical hues but avoided distracting patterns. Other than the color of my clothes, there was nothing about the style to make me stand out. My skirts were never too short, nor my pants too tight, nor my blouses too low-cut. So it was the shade of my skin, I thought, that caused people to stare in Lewiston, Bangor, and Portland, in New Hampshire, Massachusetts, Rhode Island, and Connecticut. Wherever we stopped to perform our Indian fable, I was the darkest person in the room, the diner, the school, the store, the entire town.

"I must be the only Puerto Rican ever to have visited Woonsocket," I joked once, after a particularly tense visit to a diner. The others chuckled, but no one said more. The color of my skin, my Puerto Rican background, were not topics in the garrulous discussions in the VW bus or at meals. Just as the others took their whiteness for granted, I was to do the same for my darkness. Only they didn't draw stares as I did.

At first I was intimidated by the attention. As the tour progressed, I grew defiant, interpreted the stares as a challenge, made sure that at restaurants I sat where everyone could see me, a dark face among light ones. When that didn't change the way I felt, I decided to educate people about Puerto Rico. A blustery morning in Salem, Massachusetts, recalled the warm, soft dawns of the Puerto Rican countryside. As I walked the shore in Newport, Rhode Island, with my fellow actors, I felt compelled to describe San Juan harbor. A side of pilaf next to my meat loaf elicited memories of my mother's tender rice. I took every opportunity to mention Puerto Rico and Puerto Ricans, even when the subject of conversation had nothing to do with ethnicity or culture. Waiters, school custodians, the doorman at one of the hotels where we stayed, the clerk at a pharmacy where I went to buy sanitary pads, a cashier at L. L. Bean—all learned that I was Puerto Rican, that Puerto Rico was in the Caribbean, that Puerto Ricans were American citizens at birth, that we spoke Spanish as our first language, that English was a required subject in our schools. Yes, there were a lot of Puerto Ricans in New York, but there were also many in other cities, such as Chicago and Miami. If I relieved their ignorance about me, maybe they would look at the next Puerto Rican who came through with respect rather than suspicion.

When the tour was over and we returned to New York, I felt worldly. I'd traveled into the vast horizon of the United States that I couldn't see from the ground, but the trip made me wary of venturing farther into the continent. What would it be like if, as Vera and Bill planned, we toured the South? Could I be forbidden from restaurants? I knew the laws didn't allow that, thanks in part to Martin Luther King, Jr., whose portrait hung in our living room. But I also knew laws meant nothing to people who hated. I wasn't black, I wasn't white. The racial middle in which I existed meant that people evaluated me on the spot. Their eyes flickered, their brains calibrated the level of pigmentation they'd find acceptable. Is she light enough to be white? Is she so dark as to be black? In New York I was Puerto Rican, an identity that carried with it a whole set of negative stereotypes I continually struggled to overcome. But in other places, where Puerto Ricans were in lower numbers, where I was from didn't matter. I was simply too dark to be white, too white to be black.

❦

The weeks following the tour were a flurry of catching up. I had been absent from college for fifteen days and returned to assignments missed and hundreds of pages to be read in order to get to where my classmates were. At the Advertising Checking

Bureau, a daunting stack of clippings on my desk had to be examined and approved. Mrs. Davis smiled as I scanned the pages without catching up on the latest news from Grand Rapids, Michigan, or Baraboo, Wisconsin.

Shanti called to arrange more sessions, but I couldn't do it. He'd quit the school of photography to take a job in a lab, enlarging other people's pictures. "I can develop color now," he said proudly.

We performed *Babu* a few more times, and then everyone bade a teary goodbye for the summer and dispersed to other repertory or stock companies away from New York. Bill and Vera promised us work in the fall, a tour in the Washington, D.C., area. A new production was to be added to the program, a Japanese fable this time, with a part for an ingenue.

I planned a summer devoted to work and college, so that I could take the fall semester off to perform in *Babu* and, hopefully, in the new production. One of the courses I signed up for, Survey of Art History, required weekly visits to museums. Sometimes I dragged one of my sisters with me, usually Edna, and we spent Saturday or Sunday afternoons staring at paintings neither of us understood. At home, I wrote a paper about the art work assigned that week. My weekends became stressful, because although I appreciated the art, I couldn't explain it. From time to time, Tata or Mami knocked on the door of my room because they heard moans. I was frustrated by the challenge of paintings to which I had an emotional reaction but about which I could find nothing to say.

"If the artist wanted to say other than what's in the picture," I argued with my teacher, "he should have been a writer, not a painter." She insisted that painting was filled with vital clues and subtleties that rendered meaning but that each detail had to be studied individually.

"If you stand in front of a painting long enough," Miss Prince assured me, "its meaning will become clear."

One Sunday afternoon, as I stared at Seurat's dots, a woman

approached me. "I'm sorry to disturb you," she smiled sweetly, "but do you have any idea how to get to the restaurant from here?" She had blonde hair teased into a bouffant made famous by Jacqueline Kennedy eight years earlier.

I dug out the brochure with a map of the museum galleries out of my purse and traced the route she should take to the first floor. As we were bent over the map, a man approached. "Hi," he grinned. He was obviously related to her, with the same alert eyes, sandy hair, cheery smile, and mellifluous southern accent. She introduced him as her brother Avery Lee, herself as Patsy. "You've been so kahhnd," she said, stretching the word until it seemed endless. "Would you join us for coffee?"

We walked downstairs, and she told me she lived in El Paso. "But I just love coming to New York," she said, "the museums, the wonderful restaurants . . . Do you live here?"

By the time we arrived on the first floor, Patsy had extracted from me that I lived in Brooklyn, was single, a college student, a dancer and actress. "Oh, my goodness," she gushed, "you sure do have an interesting life." As we joined the cafeteria line, she remembered she had to call her husband. I directed her to the telephones and was alone with Avery Lee, who'd followed us in attentive silence the whole time Patsy elicited my history.

"Shouldn't we get something for her?" I offered, but Avery Lee said he didn't know what she liked. The next few minutes were awkward as I waited for Patsy to return.

"I have to be honest with you," Avery Lee confided. "She's not coming back."

"Why not?"

"Because we planned it this way."

Had we not been in as public a place as the Met's cafeteria, I would have panicked. "What do you mean?"

"You were by that painting a long time," he said. "I stood next to you, but you just stared and stared."

"I was doing my homework," I admitted.

"I didn't want to scare you, so I asked Patsy to see what she could do."

"*Are* you related to each other?" I asked.

"Of course. She's my sister." Despite his ploy, there was about Avery Lee an openness that I liked, and his accent, so slow and easy, was reminiscent of the adorable Mr. Grunwald. Avery Lee looked nothing like the math teacher, however. Physically, he was more like Otto — big and muscular, with thin, determined lips and a square jaw.

"You probably know the shows to see in New York," he guessed, "because you're an actress." He was also under the impression that I could recommend the best restaurants. I had to admit that the cultural life of the city was something I read about but didn't participate in because of its cost.

"Then you can be our guide," he suggested, "You know where to go, and we're here to have a good time." When I hesitated, he insisted. "Come on. Patsy has her husband, and I'm here by myself. You can be my date," he grinned.

I told Mami that I had a job as a guide to Texan tourists. The next morning, I appeared at the apartment building where Avery Lee and Patsy were staying with friends. The doorman called up my name, and in a while Avery Lee came down alone. When I asked after Patsy, he said she had a migraine.

We hopped in and out of taxis, visited the Empire State Building, the Museum of Modern Art, Lincoln Center. We had lunch at the Waldorf Astoria. He wanted to have dinner at the Plaza, but I wasn't dressed up enough. So we went to Bloomingdale's.

"Avery Lee, I'm not comfortable with you buying me clothes," I protested. "I'll go home and change." But he wouldn't hear of it.

I chose a simple dress on sale, but then we had to get shoes and a purse to match. I was torn between the pleasure of buying what I could never afford with my own money and worry about its real cost.

"I know what you're thinking," he read my mind, "but believe me, I love doing this for you. I love to see you smile."

So I smiled my way through the junior department, where

Avery Lee bought me an outfit for the next day too, when we'd see *Man of La Mancha*, and a bikini and coverup I was to wear to the beach the day after.

It felt strange to check two shopping bags at a fancy restaurant, but that's what we did. The candlelight, the wine he ordered for dinner, the slow drawl of his speech were all intoxicating. I had to excuse myself several times and go to the ladies' room, where I leaned my face against the cool wall until my head didn't spin any more and I could speak without slurring my words. After dinner, we walked hand in hand around the fountain in front of the hotel. The last man I'd kissed had been Otto, a year and a half earlier. Avery Lee was an equally passionate kisser whose hands strayed, the way Otto's had.

"I'll get us a room," Avery Lee offered, and headed toward the Plaza.

I sobered up right quick. "No. I better go home."

He squinted, as if the colored lights of the fountain weren't bright enough to see me. He turned his back, stuck his hands in his pockets, took a few steps away from me, and I fully expected him to kick the ground, hang his head, and say "Aw, shucks."

"Home?" he asked instead, as if the word were newly minted.

I sputtered that the subways were dangerous if I waited much longer. My shopping bags were still at the hotel, but I was reluctant to go back there with him, afraid to weaken and agree to follow him upstairs. I waited outside while he retrieved them. In the back of my mind I heard Shoshana's voice, "You idiot! He's a Texas millionaire!" Losing my virginity at the Plaza would have been the perfect end to the perfect day, but I couldn't bring myself to do it. As Avery Lee walked me to the train station, gloomy and silent, I felt the need to explain.

"You should know that I haven't come this close to giving in with anyone before," I confessed.

He grinned, kissed my forehead, handed me my shopping bags. "See you tomorrow," he said.

For the next three days we met, ate, saw plays, walked in Central Park, kissed at every opportunity. It rained the day we were supposed to go to Jones Beach, so we went to the movies instead. "This is what they call petting, right?" I whispered, after a particularly breathtaking session of kisses and caresses.

"Yeah," he huffed.

"What's the difference between necking and petting?" I asked, and he demonstrated. Each evening he tried to get me to come to a hotel with him, and each time I resisted. One night he accompanied me all the way to Brooklyn. We kissed, we talked, kissed some more.

"Come with me to Texas," he offered, as the subway rumbled near my station. "I'll get you an apartment, a car, whatever you need."

"Are you asking me to be your mistress?" I asked coyly, because I thought he was kidding.

"Yeah!" He grinned, but this time I wasn't charmed.

"If you're going to all that trouble, why not marry me?"

"Because it wouldn't look right," he confessed, "for me to have a Spanish wife."

I was so stunned I almost missed my stop. The doors rattled open, were about to clang shut when I jumped out, too fast for Avery Lee to lumber after me. The train pulled away and left him still sitting on the plastic bench, astonished at my agility.

I must have misunderstood. He couldn't have meant what he said. Not once in the past few days had I sensed Avery Lee's impression of me to be tainted by the stereotype of the hot-tomato Latina. I was the virginal Maria of *West Side Story*, but he envisioned me as the promiscuous Anita.

I walked home through the dark Brooklyn streets to our house, let myself in the door, changed into my pajamas, and lay face up, staring into the dark. It was wrong to have accepted the clothes he bought me, the dinners, the theater, the romantic ride in the horse-drawn carriage through Central Park. Necking and petting, I learned from Shoshana, were okay so long as I wasn't just teasing him. But I was ashamed of how close I had come to tangling with him on a bed.

Early the next morning, he called, begged me to meet him.

"I have to explain," he said, and I agreed to meet him at a coffee shop near my job.

"It didn't sound right," he stammered as soon as we sat down, "the way I said what I did."

"Can you make it sound better?" I was determined to make him squirm, as I had all night long, remembering his kisses, feeling dirty and used.

"Hell!" he exclaimed, blushing when patrons at the coffee shop turned to look at us. He leaned toward me. "My daddy has had a Mexican for twenty years," he confided. "He loves her more than life," he added.

"A Mexican what?" I bit out.

"I'm being honest with you," Avery Lee sulked.

My eyes itched, and I was having trouble breathing. Under the table, my hands shook with the desire to strangle him. But he was impervious to my emotions. He gently turned my face toward his. In a murmur, he told me that he had political ambitions, that he had to marry a "good ole Texas gal" from a prominent family. Someone who could help him get elected. "Hell," he sat back and exclaimed again, "LBJ himself did it that way. The marriage means nothing."

I stood up, gathered my things. "I don't want to be your mistress," I hissed. "Right now, I don't even want to be in the same room with you."

"Sit down," Avery Lee ordered. "Everyone's starin'."

I sat down, defeated. It was too late to make a dramatic exit, to act self-righteous. Avery Lee wrote a phone number on his business card. "This is mah private lahhn." Oh, those long vowels! "Call me when you change your mahhnd." I stared at the paper, at his hopeful, foolish face. I wanted to spit into it. He stood up, helped me out of my chair, walked me to the Advertising Checking Bureau half a block away. At the elevator, he tried to kiss me, but I backed away. When the doors opened, I gulped some air, pushed my shoulders back, swallowed the hurt that tightened my throat, tickled my eyes. As the elevator rose, I absorbed Avery Lee's insult as thoroughly as newsprint absorbs ink. Maybe I *was* too proud and ambitious. Maybe the years at Performing Arts, the exotic dance training, the movie work, the Broadway show had caused me to develop a higher opinion of myself than I deserved. Maybe Avery Lee saw the real me, a "Spanish" girl, good enough to sleep with but not good enough to marry.

That night I pulled out Shanti's photographs and studied them. In one, I sat on the grass, my body toward the camera, my face in haughty profile, gaze on a distant horizon. A scarf was tied around my forehead — Cleopatra's diadem. When Shanti took the picture, he made me hold the pose a long time. "Be still," he murmured over and over, until I had to stop breathing to satisfy him.

In another photograph, I leaned against the granite wall at the top of the Empire State Building. Behind me, Brooklyn floated in a soupy gray cloud like the suggestion of a city, nothing but pale rectangles and bruised smudges. Between me and Brooklyn, the East River was a flat, icy sheet. That photograph was taken on a cold, blustery morning just as the sun cut through the clouds, so that half of me was overexposed, the other half obscure. My expression was desolate, as if I'd just heard bad news.

As I leafed through the portfolio of my stillborn modeling career, I didn't see myself. I saw Avery Lee's Spanish girl, earnest but sad, eyes wary, and in each picture, alone, the edges of the photographs a box encasing loneliness.

⌒‿つ

Days later, as I leaned toward an approaching bus on Fifth Avenue, a man tapped my shoulder and asked for directions to Rockefeller Center. I turned and met the sea-green eyes of Jurgen, who was clearly not lost, but captivated by my own dark brown pupils.

"I know where it is," he admitted. "There's a restaurant there. Will you join me for tea?"

I followed Jurgen to the restaurant on the lower level of

Rockefeller Center, which in winter looked out to a skating rink but in summer offered tables shaded by bright umbrellas.

Jurgen spoke excellent English with a charming accent. Whenever he made a mistake in grammar or pronunciation, he struck his lips with his index and middle fingers, as if the fault were in the mouth and not the brain. He was born in Hamburg but didn't live there. "Where, then?" I asked.

"All over," he chuckled.

His skin was translucent, its planes smooth and even. His lips frequently curled into a roguish smile that showed small teeth, flat, as if filed along the bottom.

Like many people in New York, Jurgen was just passing through. He'd buy me tea at Rockefeller Center, then return to Germany, or wherever his next stop was.

"Los Angeles," he said. "Then Egypt."

"How wonderful," I sighed, and he laughed.

As we talked, I slipped into the familiar, vague responses to the typical questions. But Jurgen was a careful listener, who asked for details no one else bothered to gather. Before the waiter refilled my glass of iced tea, I'd told Jurgen everything there was to know about me, including that I was a virgin, was not allowed to date until after I got married, and had recently been offered a position as the mistress of a Texan too ambitious to marry a "Spanish girl." He listened, chuckled, softened his eyes with concern. When tears dribbled from my eyes, he fished out a handkerchief from his pocket and pressed it to my cheeks. As he wiped away my tears, I was ashamed to have said so much and excused myself, intending to slip out another door and into the subways. But first I had to go to the bathroom, wash my face, comb my hair, apply lip gloss. When I came out, Jurgen was in the hall leading to the rest rooms. "I thought you were lost," he said.

He led me to the street, and we walked up Fifth Avenue toward Central Park. On 54th Street, he took my hand, and by the time we arrived in front of the Plaza at 59th and Fifth, his arm was around my shoulders and mine was around his waist. As we strolled through Central Park, I told him that the last German to hold my hand had saved me from being run over by a truck. He joked that Germans had great timing.

I asked where he'd been born and he told me about his childhood in Hamburg. His mother and father still lived there, he said, but he hadn't seen them in a couple of years. He asked if I missed my father, and I nearly broke down again.

"You must think I'm a crybaby," I apologized.

"No," he stroked my hair, "it's sweet."

It was easy to be with Jurgen, to talk to him about things I had never shared with anyone but Shoshana. Every once in a while I remembered we'd just met and wondered what it was about him that made me feel as if we'd known each other for ages.

We walked to a restaurant across the street from Lincoln Center. Jurgen introduced me to the bartender, Donny, at whose apartment he was staying.

"Where are you from?" I asked, upon hearing his accent.

"Ireland," Donny chuckled. He had black hair and blue eyes, was shorter than Jurgen, stocky, somewhat older, although he claimed to be the same age, twenty-nine. He and Jurgen exchanged a few words in German. I could tell Donny said something about me because of the warm, proud look Jurgen gave me.

"Where did you learn to speak German?" I asked Donny, and the men exchanged a look.

"He speaks terrible German," Jurgen laughed. "Like schoolboy." Donny blushed. We chatted for a while, and then Donny invited us to come with him and his girlfriend to Jones Beach the next day. When I hesitated, Jurgen offered to call my mother and ask permission.

"No, that's okay," I told him, certain he was laughing at me.

Jurgen said he had a meeting and asked me to come with him to Donny's apartment so that he could change.

"I can't," I said, "I should go home."

"It won't take long," Jurgen insisted. "It's very close."

Donny encouraged me from his post behind the bar. "Don't

worry, he's an honorable man. He won't bother you. You have my word."

"I'll walk with you to the corner," I offered. When we arrived there, Jurgen took my hand and led me down the street. "It's really time for me to go," I protested. "My mother will worry."

"It will only take a minute," Jurgen said, "for me to put on my suit."

The apartment was two blocks away, in a yellow brick building with no doorman but with two secure doors. Inside, the wide hall was dim and cool, the walls and floors covered with a mustard-colored tile that echoed the shash and click of our footsteps as we walked toward the elevator. We stood side by side as we rose to the fifth floor. My heart raced as I mentally reviewed every kick and strike my wrestling cousin Paco had taught me and my sisters in case we needed to defend ourselves.

The apartment was at the end of a long hall with a window that looked toward the Hudson. Inside there were two tidy, sparsely furnished rooms and a galley kitchen with no dishes, pots, or food anywhere in sight.

The minute we entered, Jurgen tried to kiss me. I resisted but then figured that if I gave in to the kiss, he'd relax, and I could make my getaway. He was gentle, didn't press himself against me, or place his hands where he shouldn't. He stepped back, took my hand, kissed it reverentially. "We are meant for each other," he said.

"Huh?"

He looked into my eyes. "Marry me."

"I beg your pardon?"

"Marry *me*," He struck his hand against his chest, as if he were saying, "Me Tarzan, you Jane."

"You must be kidding!"

"I am very serious."

I couldn't control the giggles. He stood before me, my hand in his, the roguish smile on his lips. It occurred to me then that he was a psycho and laughing at him wasn't smart.

"Yes?" he prompted.

"We met three hours ago," I reminded him.

"Yes?"

I wanted to get out of there alive. "All right, let's get married."

"Wonderful!" He hugged me, kissed my eyes, my forehead. "My wife." Now, I thought, as he tries to get me to the bedroom, I'll kick him and run. Jurgen released me, stepped back. "I go dress now," he said. "Wait one moment, please." He dragged a straight chair from its place against the wall, held it for me as I sat. Not too smart, I thought. He's going to tie me to it. "Pardon me," Jurgen said, and went into the bedroom. I sat on the edge of the chair, not ten feet from the half-open door, calculating the best moment to escape. He moved in and out of my vision as he changed his shirt, put on a tie, a jacket. Each time I was about to jump up and run, he turned toward me with a smile. He combed his hair, stepped to the hall door. "Let's go tell Donny," he said.

I jumped from the chair into the hallway, confused but glad we'd soon be outside so that I could run. On the way down, Jurgen talked about how long he'd waited for the right girl and how lucky he was to have found me. He claimed to have fallen in love with me as I stood on the curb on Fifth near 18th. "I am not impulsive man," he claimed, "but I follow my, how you say, instinct?"

We'd be married in the United States, Jurgen suggested, fly to Germany to meet his family, then settle in Egypt. It was the most surreal conversation I had ever had with anyone who didn't live inside my head. Every fantasy of princely men I'd ever dreamed up was coming true. As if there were such a thing as love at first sight, romance, intelligent, charming men with money willing to spend it on me — to marry me, even. "Can you dance?" I asked, certain there was a flaw in this too perfect plot. To prove he could, Jurgen tangoed me in the door of the restaurant where Donny still stood behind the bar serving tired businessmen.

"Married!" Donny's eyebrows rose so high they disappeared into his black hair. When he recovered, he congratulated Jurgen. "I told you he was an honorable man," he winked. "Now I'll have to propose to Laryssa," he grimaced, and we laughed.

Jurgen had to go to his meeting, but he asked me to wait with

Donny until his return, when we'd celebrate our engagement with dinner and champagne.

"Jurgen," I began, about to tell him that the game had gone on long enough, that I didn't want to marry him — or anyone — I'd only known for, let's see, four hours? What came out was, "I have to call my mother."

"Should I speak with her?" Jurgen offered, his eyes earnest. It was then I knew his proposal was no game.

Jurgen stood in front of me, waiting for an answer. He had Neftalí's green eyes and hushed voice, Otto's height, coloring, and accent, Mr. Grunwald's perfect physique. There was even a little of Avery Lee in him — the same roguish smile and confident air. In the second it took to transform Jurgen into the personification of all the men I'd ever loved, I surrendered.

We stood by the phone at the back of the restaurant getting our story together. We'd known each other a year, were introduced on the set of *Up the Down Staircase* by Sandy Dennis herself, had dinner a few times, recently met again, and decided we couldn't live without each other. "She'll want to meet you," I warned, and he offered to pick me up on Sunday when we went to the beach with Donny and Laryssa.

When I called Mami and told her I was engaged, she was suspicious, asked all the expected questions, and listened carefully to my answers. Jurgen got on the phone and told her, "I *mucho* love your daughter. Very *mucho*." When he returned the phone to me, she allowed that he sounded nice.

"Are you bringing him home now?"

"No, Mami, tomorrow. We're going to the beach. He'll come get me, and then you can meet him."

The minute I hung up, I was sorry I'd called. Before I had called Mami, I could have changed my mind, could have said goodbye to Jurgen, could have given him the wrong phone number and avoided midtown for a few days until he'd flown away. Jurgen noticed my mood.

"Come with me," he said. It seemed strange that he'd bring

me to a business meeting, but by now it was all so unreal that nothing surprised me.

We took a taxi to a luxury car dealership on Tenth Avenue. Sport cars and sedans glimmered behind the huge plate-glass windows, some with their doors open to show the interior. As we walked in, a florid man approached us. He towered over Jurgen, and I had trouble envisioning him behind the wheel of the Porsche toward which he led us. From their exchange it was clear that Jurgen was interested in a Porsche just like the blue one in the window. He was there for a test drive, and after introducing me as his "fiancé," Jurgen took a Porsche out for a spin in the crowded streets of Manhattan, where it could go no faster than a Ford. The florid man waited at the door of the dealership when we returned, fawned over Jurgen, who talked about horsepower and torque while I wondered how it was that nine hours earlier I had left Brooklyn still mourning Avery Lee's rejection and was now sitting in a Porsche dealership with my future husband.

We had an early dinner, and then Jurgen took me to see the all-black production of *Hello Dolly*, with Pearl Bailey. After the theater, he wanted to take me home, but I convinced him that wasn't necessary. He walked me to the train station, gave me Donny's phone number, and insisted I call as soon as I got home so that he'd know I'd arrived safely.

On the train home I marveled at what a strange day it had been. According to the papers, half my generation was supposedly high on LSD or other hallucinogenics. I had had nothing stronger than coffee and a couple of glasses of wine at dinner, but it felt as if I were "tripping." Any moment, I'd wake up in my bed in the back room of our house on Glenmore Street in the East New York section of Brooklyn, and the whole day would have been a dream. Or maybe I'd died, and this was Paradise. Or maybe it was hell, and my punishment for not being religious was to spend eternity having a good time in the afternoon as the fiancé of a rich, good-looking man who could afford to buy Porsches and then having to go home to Brooklyn.

As soon as I walked in the door, I called Jurgen, to make sure that he existed and that the entire afternoon had not been an extended fantasy. He sounded relieved that I had called, told me he loved me, asked for directions to my house the next day. I fabricated a history about me and Jurgen for Mami, Tata, Don Carlos, Don Julio, and those siblings who had waited up. When I finally crawled into bed, I believed every word of every lie I'd told them. Jurgen and I were in love, would marry, travel to Germany and then Egypt, where we'd live happily ever after in the shadow of the pyramids.

At the exact time when Jurgen promised to pick me up, the roar of a sports car drew my brothers to the cement yard that divided our house from the sidewalk. The family had been up for hours, cleaning and straightening up for the imminent arrival of my fiancé. He pulled up in a black Porsche, not the same one that had been on the sales floor, nor the one he had test-driven. I fretted that I might not recognize him when next I saw him, but there was no mistaking the clear complexion and rakish grin. Donny was in the passenger seat. They both kissed me on each cheek, and I introduced them to the family. I hadn't brought any men home since Otto, and I watched Mami's face for her reaction. She was taken by Jurgen's gallantry, his easy charm, the bunch of flowers he handed me, the box of chocolate-covered cherries he gave her, which endeared him to my sisters and brothers. The only one with a scowl on her face was Tata, who had been forced to change from her comfortable cotton housedress into the black lace dress she had worn to pick us up at the airport seven years earlier.

When we entered the house, every surface gleamed and smelled of Pine Sol, Pledge, or Windex. Jurgen and Donny sat on the edge of the recently purchased plastic-covered sofa in front of the new console television set. With help from those of us old enough to work, Mami had managed to decorate the house to her taste, with new furniture, pretty curtains, a lace tablecloth for the largest dining room table she could find, the seats of its high-backed chairs sealed in plastic.

Jurgen and Mami talked through me or my sisters and brothers. She asked him the same questions she'd asked me the day before over the phone, and a few more based on the information I'd made up the previous night. Jurgen was cool and relaxed, pretending that his English was worse than it actually was when he didn't know what I'd told Mami. She was both puzzled and charmed by him, but when he formally asked for my hand, she conceded it with a smile.

Jurgen informed us that because of his travel schedule, the wedding must be in less than a month. I nearly slid off the armchair, but Mami wasn't fazed by the challenge. "We'll have to order your dress tomorrow," she said.

Even though Mami and Tata had prepared a meal, I wanted to get away before Mami discovered the truth. I reminded Jurgen and Donny that we still had to pick up Laryssa. The Porsche had drawn curious neighbors to the windows and sidewalk. We came out of our house, trailed by my mother and siblings, and I couldn't hide the pride I felt. If I had been one of the neighbors, I'd have been jealous of me as I climbed into the bucket seat next to my good-looking fiancé. Donny squeezed his pudgy frame in the tiny back seat, and within seconds, Jurgen revved the many horses in his chariot and we peeled off, scattering dust and litter into the sidewalks of East New York.

It was impossible to hold a conversation in the Porsche. It was a noisy car, especially with the top down. Jurgen turned up the radio. Diana Ross wailed that a love child was never meant to be as Jurgen raced from Brooklyn to Long Island. The wind pelted my hair against my cheeks, into my eyes. I sank further into the seat, but that didn't help. Every time I moved, I received a mouthful of my own hair.

Laryssa's house sat in the middle of a pine grove in a community of homes that were copies of one another except for the landscaping and color. As we walked into the house, a cat slithered under a LA-Z-BOY in front of a console television set much larger than ours. Laryssa greeted us dressed in a yellow top and turquoise shorts, her blonde hair tied into a long ponytail. She offered us iced tea and a tuna sandwich in the sunny kitchen with a glass door that overlooked a yard with a swimming pool. Two people lounged by the pool, didn't come to greet us, and Laryssa didn't take us out there to meet them. She left us in the kitchen and went to change. A young woman came out of one of the bedrooms, her hair in curlers, her slender, well-tanned body clothed in a sheer baby doll with frilly panties. Donny and Jurgen exchanged a look.

"Hi," she purred, "I'm Jen. Laryssa's sister." The men stood up to shake her hand and, as an afterthought, introduced me. Jen poured herself a glass of tea, excused herself, went back down the hall into the door through which Laryssa disappeared. Within seconds, there was yelling, to the effect that Laryssa should have told Jen that she had guests. Laryssa countered that Jen shouldn't walk around half naked. "In the middle of the day, too!" Laryssa screeched. The men and I quietly munched our sandwiches and sipped our iced teas, our eyes on the shut door. The two sisters continued their argument, which ended when Laryssa stormed out of the room, a packed beach bag over her shoulder. "Let's go," she said. Before she led us out, she called through the door. "See you later Mom, Dad!" The two figures by the pool waved without turning around.

Laryssa and Donny went in her VW Beetle. Jurgen and I followed, and, over the roar of the Porsche's motor and the wind, Jurgen said, "That's what I don't like about American girls." He didn't elaborate, which left me to wonder if he meant Jen's near nakedness, the argument between the two sisters, or the parents who didn't care who their daughters went out with as long as they weren't disturbed.

At the beach, we drove around the parking lot a couple of times, bypassed several likely spots until Jurgen pulled up next to a copper-colored Jaguar convertible, inside which a young man was slumped fast asleep in the driver's seat. Jurgen hurdled out of the Porsche, banged the nose of the Jaguar with his fists, and the young man awoke with a start, his black eyes round with panic.

When he saw Jurgen, he jumped out, hugged Jurgen warmly, and the two chattered in German until Jurgen remembered I was there.

His friend's name was Felipe, but everyone called him Flip. "Are you Spanish?" I asked.

"Mexican," he said. He had straight black hair and slanted eyes; skin browner than mine; a muscled, slightly bowlegged body. He wore rubber flip-flops, walked with a side-to-side roll, on the outside edge of his feet. From what I could gather, Jurgen, Donny, and Flip had arranged to meet at Jones Beach. Flip had driven the Jaguar from California, which explained why he passed out on a beach blanket under Laryssa's umbrella and slept the rest of the day. Jurgen went over the car with the same attention he had invested in the Porsche the previous day. He lifted the hood, looked at the motor, opened and closed the doors, examined the body, popped the trunk and inspected it.

"It's a good car," he finally said, and shook Flip's hand.

I had on the bikini Avery Lee had bought me, yellow with white squares, not nearly as small as Laryssa's. The men also wore tiny bikinis, which made me feel overdressed, even though it was the first time I'd revealed my abdomen in public. Because I couldn't swim, I sat in the sand while Donny, Laryssa, and Jurgen cut long, elegant strokes into the waves and then floated back. In or out of the water, Laryssa and Donny were all over each other. Jurgen kissed me a few times, but I was so uneasy making out half naked in public that he gave up.

At the end of the day, Laryssa went home in her car. We pulled up in front of our house, Jurgen and I in the Porsche, Donny and Flip in the Jaguar. Mami came to the front steps, and Flip called out to Jurgen, "Watch out man. They say the daughters end up looking like their mothers." The three men laughed. Mami, who understood, scrunched her face into her most unattractive expression. I sent a killer look toward Flip, who shrugged and gave me a sheepish smile.

"He always make jokes," Jurgen said. He walked me to the

stoop. We planned to meet the next day in the city, which I confirmed in front of Mami. He backed toward the car, waved from the driver's seat, then left, followed by Flip and Donny, who laughed uproariously at something one of them said in German so that I didn't understand.

"Why didn't you ask him in?" Mami asked, looking after them.

"I'm sandy and itchy and tired," I complained. "I need a bath."

It bothered me that Flip had said something so hurtful in front of Jurgen, who indulged it. Who was Flip, anyway? He claimed to be Mexican, spoke fluent German, but other than his name, didn't say a word of Spanish to me. He drove across the country in a Jaguar, arrived that same morning at Jones Beach, of all places, and when Jurgen opened the trunk, there was nothing in it. Where was his luggage? He didn't even have a change of clothes in there.

And where did Jurgen get a Porsche? He didn't have it the day before. Why was he buying one if he already owned one? Why did he have a car in New York when he didn't live in the city? The Porsche could have been Donny's. Did bartenders make enough money to own late-model sports cars? I was confused and wary, certain that something strange was going on, not sure what it could be.

The next day, Jurgen and I walked through Central Park on our way to the Lake. He planned to rent a rowboat and take me for a ride. I reminded him that I couldn't swim, was afraid of water, dreaded the thought of being further than a few inches from firm ground. But he was adamant. We had to do this, he said, because rowing was one of his favorite sports. He was on a team, he claimed. Since we were to be husband and wife, I should learn to love the things he loved.

"Can I wear a life vest?" I asked.

"You don't need one," he laughed. "I'm an excellent swimmer."

"But I'm not!"

He said it worried him that I didn't trust him with my life. "I will save you, I promise."

The boat looked bigger once we were inside it. Jurgen placed his jacket across my lap, rolled up his sleeves, pushed off the dock. "Relax," he chuckled. "Let go of the sides."

He rowed to the center of the lake, secured the oars, leaned back with a contented sigh. He looked perfectly at home surrounded by water; his hair gleamed gold in the sunlight; his eyes deepened to a blue gray color, a bottomless ocean. I gripped the sides of the boat. "Can we go back now?"

"Not yet," he said. The graveness in his voice, the way his body tensed made me shudder. "You have been open with me," he murmured. "You have introduced me to your family. They are honest people. Your mother is a good woman. But you have not asked about me."

"Don't say any more," I covered my face with my hands. The fairy tale was about to end. Now, I thought, he'll confess he's really a waiter at that restaurant where Donny works and has a wife and five kids in Hamburg. "I don't need to know." We floated in silence for a while, I with my hands still pressed to my face. I felt his eyes on me, and when I looked up, there was a troubled expression in them. So many questions crowded my thoughts that I didn't know where to begin. "Are you married?" I finally asked. He laughed so hard the boat shook. Then he noticed I was serious.

"No, *liebchen*, I'm not married," he said softly.

I mimed picking up a notebook, a pen, adjusting invisible glasses. I tightened my lips, put on a reedy voice. "Very well, sir, do you have any children?"

He played along. "No, madame."

"Are you really from Hamburg?"

"Yes, I am, madame."

"What is your date of birth, sir?"

We were silly for a while, and then Jurgen took up the oars and brought me back to dry land. As we walked along a shaded path, I asked another question. "What is it that you do? For work, I mean."

He stopped, turned, searched my eyes. "You really want to know?"

The way he asked made me wish I didn't. I nodded.

"I fly planes," he said, then started walking again.

I guessed he was an airline pilot, but he shook his head. Did he fly for a cargo company? No. For the air force? Not that either. I gave up.

"I steal planes," he declared.

I guffawed. He smiled absently. "What do you do with the stolen airplanes?" I giggled. "Hide them in your garage?"

"I sell them."

According to Jurgen, it was easy to steal a plane. "Small ones, not jumbo jets," he stipulated. He put on a pilot's uniform, walked into a hangar, chose a plane, flew it to Mexico, sold it.

"So you steal planes and sell them in Mexico," I snickered.

"Or other places. Depends who orders one."

"You have seen too many 007 movies," I concluded.

Jurgen smiled. I was sure he was pulling my leg. "Are Flip and Donny in on this?" I joined his game.

"No. They prefer cars." Jurgen went on to tell me that he'd dreamed of flying since he was a child and had learned to do it as a young man. When he took planes, he flew very low, to avoid radar, he said. Sometimes, over the ocean, he saw enormous schools of fish, whales, dolphins. He'd flown all over the world and described dangerous air currents around mountains, sudden pockets of air, thunder-and-lightning storms he'd flown into that he feared would ground him forever. It sounded as if he were narrating a dream, but as he spoke, my skepticism ebbed until it hit me that I was about to marry a man who stole planes for a living.

"I can't believe this," I moaned. I walked over to a nearby bench and sat down because my knees couldn't hold me up. Jurgen put his arm around my shoulder.

"Don't worry," he whispered into my hair.

"Don't worry? Jurgen, now that I know this, I'm a criminal too. I'm supposed to go to the police or something. . . ."

He stroked my cheek, swore that he must be truthful with me, that it wouldn't be fair if he weren't. In any case, once we were married, I couldn't be made to testify against him should it come to that. I wanted to ask why he didn't wait to tell me until after the wedding but reminded myself that wasn't the issue.

"I'm leaving for Los Angeles," Jurgen said. "When I come back, I will marry you, if you still want me." He was sincere. I could hear it in his voice. In some twisted way, his confession was responsible. Still, a part of me wondered if he had fabricated the story to scare me away because the whole marriage thing had gone too far and he didn't want to hurt my feelings.

He escorted me to the subway station. He'd been teaching me a few words of German, and he drilled me as we walked. We pretended that our plans to get married had not changed with his disclosure. On the train back to Brooklyn, I decided that Jurgen wanted to test me. It didn't seem right that if he really did steal planes, he'd tell someone he barely knew. But then, this was the same man who had proposed after three hours. "I am not impulsive man," he'd told me a couple of days earlier. I made a mental note to look up the word, to see if there was a meaning I'd missed the first time.

Should I call the police? The story was unbelievable. I had no proof. I imagined the scene: a Puerto Rican girl walks into a police station, claims a German she met on the street and agreed to marry after three hours confessed that he steals planes and that his friends steal luxury cars. I could hear the laughter.

Jurgen left for Los Angeles. He didn't give me a phone number where I could reach him but promised to call daily. I didn't believe him, so it was a surprise when a bouquet of roses arrived, and that evening, when the phone rang, it was Jurgen. "Hello, *liebchen,*" he whispered. "Do you still want to marry me?"

"Your face is no longer innocent."

I spent the next week shopping for my wedding dress with Mami. Jurgen's daily phone calls wore away my reluctance, convinced me that we belonged together. He swore that he would no longer steal planes. He'd been considering a job offer in Egypt, piloting the private jet of an Arab prince, which he'd decided to accept. His life had been transformed, Jurgen claimed, by me. Mine was about to be transformed by him. It was a fair exchange. I'd save him from life in prison; he'd save me from life in Brooklyn.

Mami and I picked out a champagne-colored silk moiré dress and coat ensemble for me to wear when I met Jurgen's parents. As she had planned for so long, my sisters would be my bridesmaids, my brothers groomsmen. Franky, who was five, was to be the ring bearer; Donny, Jurgen's friend, the best man. I picked La Muda as the maid of honor. Papi would come from Puerto Rico to give me away. Mami found a priest to marry us even though I'd never been to his church. Jurgen kept abreast of the plans through daily phone calls. I worried about the cost of the wedding, especially when we advanced money that wouldn't be refunded. But according to the etiquette books I consulted, the bride's family bore the expense.

When not shopping for my trousseau, I echoed the phrases in the Berlitz "Teach Yourself German" long-playing records I found at the library. On my wall was a map of Egypt with a big red circle around Alexandria, where Jurgen said we would live—

not Cairo, as I had imagined. I didn't believe in karma, astrology, palm reading, handwriting analysis, reincarnation, extrasensory perception, astral projection, transcendental meditation, Nostradamus, "Chariots of the Gods," or any of the other mumbo jumbo every young person in the United States was supposed to be obsessed with in 1968. But what was I to make of the fact that I, who had spent three years perfecting the role of Cleopatra, was about to move to the city of her birth and untimely death?

Even though it seemed preordained that I should marry Jurgen, doubt niggled at me. He didn't appear to be a violent man, but by his own admission he was a criminal. What if he'd done worse things and hadn't told me about them because I didn't ask the right questions? It frightened me to think that he'd take me to Egypt and then I'd be stuck there with no one to help me if he turned out to be a drunkard or a wife beater.

There was another thing that bothered me: I couldn't convince myself that I loved Jurgen. Was I crazy to expect to love a man I'd met only a few times? It troubled me that although I looked forward to his calls, I had forgotten what he looked like. What shape were his eyes? What shade his hair? If I loved him, his features should be embedded in my memory. How tall was he? Did he write with his left hand or his right? I didn't know whether he had birthmarks, or whether he parted his hair. As the day approached for Jurgen's return, I grew nervous and wished to stretch the time so that it wouldn't happen in two weeks, ten days, five days, three.

"I can't do it," I cried on the phone two days before his arrival.

"What do you mean?" He knew exactly what I meant.

"It's happening too fast. I'm not ready. . . ."

"Don't you love me?"

I dreaded that question from him. In the two weeks we'd been engaged, no one had asked it, not even Jurgen. It was the silence that confirmed it, the fact that I didn't interrupt him and say, "No, that's not it, that's not it at all."

"I see," he said after a while.

"Maybe if we had more time to get to know each other," I hedged halfheartedly.

Jurgen heard the uncertainty in my voice, didn't attempt to change my mind. Had he tried, I might have wavered, at least for a while. "All the plans we had," he said sadly, which were Mami's exact words when I told her the wedding was off, though she was angry rather than melancholy.

We lost several hundred dollars in deposits for a wedding dress, the hall, bridesmaids' dresses. I told Mrs. Davis at the Advertising Checking Bureau not to give my job away because I wasn't moving to Egypt. At first, it was embarrassing to explain to people that I'd changed my mind, but after a while, I was proud of it. I saved myself, I thought. I've done something most women don't do until it's too late.

Shoshana had been in Israel all summer. "Are you still a virgin?" she asked the minute we saw each other again, and I had to admit I was, and so did she. "Not that I didn't have plenty of chances," she amended, which led to my telling her of my adventures with Avery Lee and Jurgen.

"What is it with you and Germans?" she wanted to know.

"I don't pick them," I defended myself, "they pick me."

She signed up for courses at Manhattan Community College, but I didn't, because I wanted my days free for Children's Theater International. To supplement my part-time salary at the Advertising Checking Bureau, I found a job distributing flyers in front of a bank on Park Avenue. One day a woman with a neatly trimmed Afro and an African print dress stopped to talk to me. She had an agency for "exotic" models and wondered if I had any interest. We made an appointment for the next day, and I showed up at her office on Sixth Avenue and 40th Street with my portfolio of photographs by Shanti. The door was locked. Every once in a while a phone rang inside, but no one answered. I waited in the hall for half an hour and then gave up, annoyed to have missed an afternoon of work for nothing.

I walked to Woolworth's on Fifth Avenue, where the public

phones were in mahogany cubicles with doors that shut tight for privacy. As I settled into the first booth, a man peered inside, and when I looked up, he moved on. He'll just have to wait, I thought. I called the temporary jobs agency to let them know I was available for the next few days. Then I called Mami to tell her I'd be home early to pack my room, since we were moving again, to a house on Fulton Street in the Brownsville section of Brooklyn. Mami was excited, because Titi Ana had agreed to rent an apartment in the house, which meant Mami could afford to buy the building. Our cousins Alma and Corazón would live with us. I came out of the phone booth in a much better mood than I entered it.

"Excuse me," a voice startled me, and when I turned around, there was the man who'd peeked into the phone booth. I was sure he was about to complain that I had talked for too long, but he smiled and pointed to the portfolio. "Are you model?"

"Trying," I grinned.

"I am film director," he said. "I am looking for leading actress for my movie." He had a heavy accent, hesitated between words as if to make sure of the pronunciation.

"Where are the auditions?" I asked, excited but trying to be businesslike.

"I write down for you." He tore an edge of paper from a note in his pocket, wrote a name and phone number, handed it to me.

"Ulvi Doğan," I read.

"Dawn," he corrected me. "Like the morning."

"Where are you from?" I asked.

"Turkey. And you?"

"Puerto Rico." I introduced myself and promised to call the next day.

"Very good," he nodded. "In the afternoon, I will be there."

That evening, I called Shoshana to tell her that a Turkish film director wanted to audition me. "Come with me," I asked.

"What if there's no part in the movie for me?"

"Just come and keep me company."

The appointment was on East 58th Street, nowhere near the

theater district or the rehearsal studios used for auditions. "This feels a little weird," I said to Shoshana as we stood in front of the white brick residential building. She suggested that maybe the film company had rented an apartment for the interviews.

The doorman called up my name, directed us upstairs. We rang the bell directly across the hall from the elevator, as he instructed. It was opened by the man from Woolworth's, whose broad smile dimmed when he saw Shoshana. He asked us in.

"I hope you don't mind," I apologized, "but my friend is an actress too. In case you need extras . . ." He nodded.

The room we walked into was in black and white. Two black leather armchairs, a matching couch, what looked like a black leather-topped table were arranged around a shag rug with black-and-white squares. On the stark white walls were four enormous posters, grainy black-and-white closeups of the same woman in the throes of sexual ecstasy. Shoshana and I looked at each other.

"Mr. Doğan," I began to excuse us and get out of there.

"Call me Ulvi, please. Have a seat, please." He ushered us to the armchairs. "May I offer you Coca-Cola?"

Shoshana said yes, and I glared at her. As Ulvi opened the refrigerator, spilled ice cubes from a tray, opened and poured the Coke, Shoshana and I whispered to each other. She thought the apartment was tasteful, the pictures as arty as the ones in our portfolios. "She's fondling herself," I hissed.

Ulvi returned with our Cokes. He sat on the couch, leaned back, crossed his legs. He wore brown leather loafers with no socks. Shoshana noticed too. While we sipped our drinks, he told us that his film was to be shot on Long Island. I asked to see the script, and he placed his hand on a neat pile of papers on the coffee table. "It is not ready yet," he said. He asked us about our acting experience. Shoshana had been in a couple of high school plays. I listed my credits, which impressed him. Shoshana wondered what he had directed, and Ulvi said his film had won top prize at the Berlin Film Festival. The posters on the wall began to look more artistic.

Ulvi leaned toward me, touched my hand. "I am sure I can use you in my movie," he said. "But we must do screen test. Yes?"

"Yes, of course," I said.

He leaned back, his hands fingertip to fingertip, and said he had a part for Shoshana too, but smaller. She beamed with gratitude. I asked when the screen test would be, and he said he had to arrange it but needed my phone number to let me know. He didn't ask for Shoshana's. He led us to the door, stood in the hall until the elevator came.

"You're going to be a star!" Shoshana shrieked, as we walked down the street.

"The screen test might be awful. . . ."

"Did you see how he looked at you? Every movement you made . . . he watched so carefully!"

"I didn't notice."

"I can say I knew you when . . ." she giggled.

I dared not hope. Ulvi talked like a director, and Shoshana pointed out it was easy to check if he really won in Berlin. We walked to the library, and sure enough, there it was on page 42 of the July 8, 1964, *New York Times*. The audiences were surprised, the paper said, that the award went to *Dry Summer*, a Turkish film. They described Ulvi as its "youthful producer," and Shoshana and I agreed that he did seem youthful, if not young.

We parted at the subway station, Shoshana still certain that Ulvi represented my big break.

He called to say that the screen test would be that Sunday, so I put on my best outfit and appeared at his door. There were no cameras in the apartment, no lights, no film crew. I wondered if I was too early, but Ulvi said no, the cameraman was late. I asked, "Should I come back?" But he suggested we talk until the crew arrived.

Was the script ready yet? I wanted to know. "My writer is very slow," he said with an indulgent smile and a shrug of the shoulders.

After five minutes of chitchat about who I was, what I did,

where I lived, the phone rang. He spoke in Turkish, a language I'd never heard. Its sound was soothing, at least, the way he spoke it, in a hushed, intimate voice, a raspy whisper. From time to time, as he listened to the caller, he lifted his hand in a "just one moment" gesture.

He had huge, very dark brown pupils; straight, fine, black hair; a high forehead. Deep lines ran from his nostrils to his lips, which seemed drawn on his face, their shape precise, flat. His nose made a straight line with his forehead, flared to a wide base. In profile, he looked like a museum fresco of an Etruscan horseman or a Mesopotamian king. The majestic air was enhanced by his movements, which were slow, studied, as if he had to be careful or he'd knock something over.

Once he hung up, he asked me about Puerto Rico. He'd never been there but had attended film festivals in Cartagena, Colombia, and in Venezuela, Costa Rica, and Mexico. Along the way, he had picked up a few words of Spanish. "*Señorita,*" he said, "*¿Cómo está?*" I congratulated him on his excellent accent. "It's English I have trouble with," he grinned.

I assured him he spoke well, that I understood everything he said. He thanked me with another self-effacing shrug. The phone rang again, and this time he spoke German. Although I couldn't understand the words, there was no hesitation in his voice, as there was in English.

When he finished his call, we discussed the film that had won the Golden Bear in Berlin. He said it was a love story, which he had produced and directed. He had also played the romantic lead. The lead actress was now a big star in Turkey. "But I discovered her," he stressed.

He said he had spotted her sitting on the steps in front of his office building. She was waiting for her mother, the cleaning woman. She'd never acted in films, but as soon as he saw her, Ulvi could tell she had star potential. When he saw me at Woolworth's, he recognized the same qualities he saw in her.

I was flattered, but aware that we were alone in his apartment decorated with posters of women masturbating. Arty or not, it was impossible to look anywhere in the apartment without my eyes landing on a nipple, an inverted navel, pubic hair. After a half hour with no film crew in sight, I stood up. "I should go."

Ulvi suggested we take a walk. "They will be here by the time we get back," he promised.

As we strolled down 58th Street toward Fifth Avenue, I asked him where he had learned German.

His eyes widened. "Do you speak too?"

"No," I laughed. "Some of my friends . . ." I waved them away.

He nodded. He had lived in Germany for years and spoke the language fluently. "Better than Turkish, sometimes," he chuckled. We lamented how hard it was to retain one's first language when there were few opportunities to practice. We agreed that the longing to go back to the home country, even after years of being away, never disappeared.

"But when you return," he said, "they don't appreciate." He became a celebrity in Turkey after his film won the awards. But the press attacked him. He held his hands palms up, seesawed them up and down, "They criticize me for this, for that, for nothing." I appreciated his thoughtful answers, enjoyed our conversation, which meandered from one subject to the next. His soft voice and relaxed manner were comforting. As Shoshana had noticed, he watched me intently. At first, I was uncomfortable with his earnest attention. But then I realized he had to do that because he read lips. Not because he was hard of hearing, but because it was another clue to interpreting what I said. I did the same. Even after seven years of intensive English, I focused on the speaker for clues other than language to help me understand. When I spoke, I still translated simultaneously from Spanish, and I was certain Ulvi had to do the same from Turkish via German. No wonder he talked so slowly.

There was a parade on Fifth Avenue. Marching bands led acrobatic cheerleaders with colorful pompons. Slow-moving floats trimmed with crepe paper streamers carried young women dressed in evening gowns. Their white-gloved hands wiped the air in perfect arcs, as they waved to the right, the left, the right again.

Later, I wondered at which point during the parade he took my hand. Or why, as a float went by filled with polka dancers, he put his arm around me. Or how it happened that, when the Middletown Police Athletic League Band marched by playing their version of "Winchester Cathedral," my face was against his chest, and I smelled his skin, clean, a nonscent really, captivating.

We returned to his apartment. While I'd been kissed, touched, had known the contours of a man through his clothes, it was different when we were naked. His skin was the color of toasted walnuts. No tan lines marred the even tones from hairline to soles. His chest was furred with a heart of straight black hair which ended in a point under his ribs. His abdomen was flat but soft, undefined by muscles, a long, smooth, flesh table on which I laid my head to listen to his life. When I moved higher, his heart thuthumped against my ear, soothed me to sleep upon his chest. Or, if I snuggled down to his navel, the sounds of a noisy brook gurgled intermittently. I traced my fingers from the top of his head, down his broad forehead across the frown line etched from temple to temple, to his nose, a wide-based pyramid above soft, cool lips. At rest, he appeared sad and solemn, but I made him smile. His chin was dimpled in the center, a shallow depression where I stuck my tongue to feel fine, prickly stubble. His neck was long, with two deep furrows webbed from ear to ear, like scars. I caressed his chest, the fuzzy valentine of straight, black hair, a heart over his heart. And the flat expanse of his unblemished belly.

After we made love he made phone calls. Naked, I wrapped myself around him, his left arm under my head, mine across his chest. I pressed close until our brown skins were one. I could not think of what I'd just done, refused to answer the voice that asked, "Why him?" Why not Otto or Avery Lee or Jurgen? Why had I not resisted, had in fact joyfully thrown off my clothes on the black leather chair?

He spoke his foreign language and I listened to the muffled words, chuckles, whispers. Once he held the phone to my lips and said, "Say hello," and I said "hi" into the speaker, not knowing who I greeted. After a while I grew jealous. I writhed this way and that, generated warmth, straddled him, rolled back onto my side until he engulfed me, until I felt his weight, until I sank under his long, dark body, until I couldn't breathe. It was when I pushed him off, gently, with a whimper, that he moved aside, stroked my face, and called me "Chiquita."

"Who?" I pushed up on one elbow, searched his face.

"You are Chiquita," he smiled, "my little one. That is what it means, the Spanish word *chiquita?*"

"Yes," I said, appeased. "Little one. Little girl," I amended and lay back.

Sated, I returned to Brooklyn, tingling with secrets. Late at night, the A train was filled with workers returning from the evening shifts. Most of them dozed or read the papers with wary intensity, seeking confirmation for their worst fears. A man in overalls slept on the seat against the conductor's booth. A woman in a nurse's uniform pulled her purse close when I sat across the aisle. Another woman, thin and nervous, tugged at the tired curls around her shoulders, the window behind me a grimy mirror into which she peered desperately. From time to time both women stared at me, then averted their eyes. Can they tell what I've been doing? I wondered. Are there telltale signs?

No, he was careful not to mark me. My skin left hotter than it arrived, but there were no marks, no signs that we'd been naked for hours. I sought his smell on me, but that too was gone. He had insisted we shower after sex. We went in together, my hair wrapped inside a thirsty towel, and on his knees, he soaped and rinsed. His hands sometimes a caress, sometimes a probe, he erased all traces of our lovemaking, all evidence that he'd been with me, inside me. Hot water pounding my back, I closed my eyes and let his fingers, slippery with soap, explore, between my toes, behind my knees, across my buttocks. I dripped with desire, but he whispered,

"Not now, no more. Enough for today." He wrapped me in his huge black towels, rubbed the corners against my skin until every drop was soaked away. I returned to Mami's house hungry, thirsty, impatient for the next day, when I'd return to his black-and-white apartment and strip down to nothing and let him touch me again where no one ever had.

⌒⌒⊃

"You did what?" Shoshana's long lashes fluttered. "When? How?"

It was hard to explain *how* it had happened. Not the mechanics of sex, but how I went from fledgling movie actress to the director's . . . what? I couldn't name what I'd become.

"Why him?" Shoshana wanted to know.

There was no way to answer that question either. No, he wasn't as handsome as Neftalí, Otto, Avery Lee, or Jurgen. In the week we'd been together he hadn't taken me to any restaurants, the theater, not even the movies. He'd spent no money on me. He hadn't asked me to be his girlfriend, his mistress, his wife. He'd made no promises whatsoever. He seemed to have no expectations except that I show up at his apartment at the agreed time. When I suggested I should get birth control, he told me not to worry. "I take care," he said, and he did.

"So," Shoshana smiled wickedly, "did you get the part?"

Ulvi admitted that he had never had any intention of putting me in a movie. "I want you for me," he said, "nobody else."

"Wow!" Shoshana was impressed.

In order to spend more time with Ulvi, I changed my schedule at work. I checked ads mornings, then spent the afternoon with Ulvi. I was usually home for dinner, then hid out in the room I shared with Delsa in our new house on Fulton Street. I didn't want to give Mami a chance to study me, afraid that she suspected, that my secret life with Ulvi showed in the way I moved or behaved.

One day I ran into Shanti on Fifth Avenue. He'd been meaning to call me, he said, because he wanted to take color photographs of me. His fingertips on my chin, he moved my face from side to side to capture the light. "Your face is no longer innocent," he concluded.

"Neither am I," I snapped back. He winced. "I have to go." I left him on the corner of Fifth and 44th, my throat tight. I ran into the Algonquin Hotel, through the bar, downstairs to the cramped ladies' room. I stared into the mirror for a long time but couldn't see what he saw. Was it only visible to others?

Vera called to discuss the Children's Theater International season. They wanted me back as Soni in *Babu* and as a Japanese princess in a play inspired by kabuki theater. After the read-through at the rehearsal studio on Christopher Street, Bill gave a couple of us a ride uptown. I was on my way to Ulvi.

"How was your summer?" Bill asked, and the others shared stories of summer stock and dinner theaters. I was the last to leave the VW van. "You've been quiet," Bill remarked as he pulled up to the corner of 58th Street and Third Avenue. I was about to tell him where I was going but was unable to speak his name.

"I can't even begin," I stammered.

He squeezed my hand, "It's amazing how one summer can change your life." I leaned over and kissed him on the cheek. I loved him, I loved Allan, I loved so many people. Did I love Ulvi? I must have, to give myself so willingly to him. Yet what I felt for him was nothing like what I felt for Bill and Allan, for my family, for Shoshana. I could easily say I loved them. About him the best that I could say was, "I make love with him."

What did that make me? After years of fantasizing about romantic love, I had landed on the black-and-white sheets of a man who was not romantic in the traditional sense. No flowers, no candlelit dinners, no talk of the future beyond the next day, when we'd be together again. Being with Ulvi was like being suspended in time. After the first long conversation we had, there were no more discussions about our lives.

"I don't care about your family, your friends," he said when I tried to tell him. "I only want you." It was freeing not to have a past with him. But it bothered me that if he weren't interested in my life away from him, how could I justify asking about his life away from me?

One Monday afternoon, I met Shoshana at the Automat. We put our coins into the slot and the square glass doors unlocked so we could pull out bowls of macaroni and cheese.

"I have to tell you something," Shoshana said, excited. Soon as I sat across from her, she spilled her news. "I did it!"

It wasn't hard to guess what "it" was. "When? Who?"

She went to a party that weekend, met a Turkish man. "Younger than your guy," she added. "Now we've both lost our virginity to Turks," she giggled.

When I told Ulvi the story, imagining he'd enjoy the coincidence, his eyebrows crept together, his lips tightened. "She is a very dumb girl," he said.

"What do you mean? Should she worry about Ali? Do you know him?"

"There are a thousand Alis," Ulvi yelled. I'd never heard him raise his voice above a murmur, and the change scared me. "How can you have such a friend?" he continued. I didn't understand what he meant. When I pointed out that she wasn't doing anything worse than what we did, Ulvi looked at me sternly. "It is not the same. She is cheap girl."

I was stunned. His assessment of Shoshana was so unfair, I argued. He'd only met her once. She was a wonderful person, warm, funny, intelligent. How could he say such a thing?

"I know million girls like that," Ulvi muttered, and the contempt in his voice made me shiver. He took me in his arms, stroked my hair, kissed me. "You are such naive girl," he said. "There are so many things I must teach you, Chiquita." He was tender, gentle. The circle within his arms was a world in which I felt protected, a place where I could admit my ignorance. Yes, I was naive, but in his arms my innocence was treasured. In his arms, I didn't have to think, didn't have to plan, didn't have to do anything but respond to his caresses. When he held me, I didn't question or challenge him, because I knew nothing. Not even the true nature of my best friend.

———

Late at night, Fulton Street was quiet, the shadows solid as walls. I walked on the side of the street closest to the playground, where the hurricane fence stretched tall and forbidding between me and the swings, slides, monkey bars. To my left, cars were snugly parked and locked for the night, but in some, people-shapes moved in wary anticipation. As I passed them, my heart beat faster than my feet could walk. I pressed close to the fence, eyes straight ahead but alert to unexpected movements. A low voice mumbled, "Hi, sweetheart," another "Hey, baby," and danger propelled me, almost lifted me off the sidewalk, but I wouldn't run, not unless chased. If I ran without provocation, they'd know how scared I was, so I walked — fast, but confident that I'd reach the door to our house, that I would have time to insert the key in the lock, turn it, push open the heavy door, and be inside before anyone could reach me.

Once safe, I leaned against the door and breathed until my backbone didn't tingle and my heart beat its normal rhythm, until my insides felt as composed as my face, wiped of its frightened expression, until my hands no longer trembled and my knees were stable. I unlocked the inside door and opened it to the dim hallway, where I listened for Mami's footsteps, for her disapproval at the end of the hall, for her dark, sad eyes heavy with disappointment and reproaches. But it was too late. She was asleep on the edge of her bed, feet still slippered, knees curled up, nylon nightgown bunched around her thighs. Her right arm was bent over her face to block out nightmares, while her left gripped the bar of Ciro's crib, where the baby slept in a tight lump.

I tiptoed past her door into the room with the bunk beds against one wall and the bed that Delsa and I shared against the other. In the airless darkness I again felt the thrill of danger, only this time it wasn't fear of an unseen attacker. The memory of Ulvi's hands was like traces on my body, charged my skin with an energy I was certain anyone could see, could feel. When I crawled into bed next to my sister, she stirred, and it was natural that I should roll over and spoon into her the way I did with him. But she was my sister, and had I wakened her for a hug, she would have flailed and cursed and pushed me off the bed. I lay face up, arms alongside my body, took up as little space on the narrow bed as possible. The deep, even breath of my sisters and brothers was as soothing a sound as I ever heard, but it didn't lull me to sleep as it once had. I was too conscious of that other breath, miles away in the sparsely furnished apartment of my lover. My lover! Again I wanted to turn over and embrace the body next to me, but it was Delsa's. I hugged myself instead, closed my eyes, imagined my arms were his, that I was in the enormous pull-out bed with the black sheets, where reaching out for warmth was greeted with a moan of pleasure, not annoyance.

In the morning, Mami pointedly kept her eyes on me as I went to and from the bathroom, but she didn't ask where I'd been. When I set up the ironing board, she moved aside without a word. Her serenity was unnerving amid the chaos of making breakfast for my sisters and brothers and helping them get ready for school. "Watch the babies," she pointed at Charlie and Cibi, who were trapped in the playpen. She walked Raymond and Franky to the door, waited there until they turned the corner, then returned to rescue Ciro from his crib, where he'd been whimpering for some time. I pressed my clothes and watched her out of the corner of my eyes, aware that her silence could explode into an argument at the slightest provocation. Her walk was a heavy shuffle across the linoleum. Three babies in two years had left her soft and fleshy, eyes permanently swollen from lack of sleep, features slack, as if her muscles didn't have the energy to animate her face. I averted my eyes from her exhausted figure, ashamed that I was adding to her burden.

I played with the babies, kept as far from Mami as the crowded kitchen permitted, then disappeared into the bedroom to change. When I came out, she was at the table with her morning cup of black coffee in front of her and Ciro on her lap.

"I'm going to work and then I have a rehearsal," I said.

She looked up, pursed her lips, nodded. I was grateful for her silent censure, for another day in which she didn't confront me with her suspicions, and left the apartment with a sense of triumph, hollow, because she refused to fight.

"Where were you last night?"

Ulvi's opinion of Shoshana didn't keep me from seeing her whenever possible. There was no one, including him, with whom I felt more comfortable or had more fun. We met for lunch, visited museums, took long walks along Fifth Avenue, chatting about our love lives. Shoshana's relationship with Ali didn't last, but it wasn't mourned. No longer his student, she began an affair with Mr. Arthur Delmar, the Principles of Advertising professor.

"Why didn't you tell me," Shoshana asked, "that sex with an older man is so much better?"

"I have no basis for comparison," I reminded her.

"I wonder how old he is," Shoshana mused. "Not as old as my father, I hope."

Papi was older than Mami, who was thirty-seven. I hadn't seen Papi in seven years and had a hard time conjuring an image of him. Was he old and wrinkled? Did he have a pot belly? Did he wear glasses? Ulvi looked younger than Mami, but he wouldn't tell me his age. Arthur had gray hair, and we figured he was Ulvi's senior, but Shoshana wasn't about to ask him directly. "I don't want to know," she said, with a flick of the wrist.

We had no illusions about a life with either Ulvi or Arthur. Even if Arthur proposed, Shoshana would never marry him, because he wasn't Jewish. "I have to think of the future of Israel," she said seriously.

I didn't have a whole nation depending on my choice of

husband, but neither did I expect Ulvi to marry me. He was blunt when he said he didn't want to involve me in his life. "Why not?"

"It is complicated," he responded, then kissed away my anxious frown. "Don't worry," he said, "it is nothing for you to concern." If I asked more questions, he silenced me with caresses. "I will never hurt you," he assured me, and so far, he hadn't.

Ulvi insisted that our lives away from his bed be private, which led me to suspect secrets much worse than Jurgen's. One afternoon when he had to go to a meeting, he asked me to wait for him in his apartment. It was the first time I'd been in his place alone, and I decided to take advantage of it. If I found anything illegal or incriminating, I swore to leave and never come back. He was so fastidious that it took a long time to search the apartment, because I had to leave everything exactly as I found it. His belongings were put away in a precise order imposed on every shelf, drawer, cabinet. The black towels were folded in thirds lengthwise, then in thirds again, stacked so that no edges overlapped. There was nothing in between, behind, or under them. He wore no undershorts, but in spite of my first impression, did wear socks, which were paired and doubled into rows at the bottom of the dresser drawer. There wasn't a gun there, nor bags of marijuana, nor love letters. His shirts, pants, and jackets hung by color, each in their own section of the closet. There was no false wall or safe behind them. His shoes lined up on the floor, each with a cedar shoe tree inside. Nothing fell out when I tipped one after the other. He wore no jewelry, used an electric razor, didn't slap on aftershave. There were no drugs in the medicine chest, not so much as an aspirin. The kitchen cabinets held a set of china for four, white dishes with a black border. There were sixteen glasses, four each in descending sizes, adorned with playing cards showing the jack, queen, king, and ace. In the refrigerator were a few vegetables, a container of orange juice, butter, a few eggs. Other than the woman masturbating on the walls, there were no pictures anywhere, no prizes for his film, no clippings, no press releases. I found no credit card receipts, no savings passbooks, no checkbook.

Everything in the apartment was brand new, carefully selected so that it all matched. Expensive too. The towels were thick and fluffy. His clothes had designer labels, were made from fine materials like wool, silk, cashmere. His shoes were thin-soled, leather-lined, soft. On the top shelf of his closet was a set of suitcases, thick black leather with brass fittings closed with a combination lock embedded in the center. There was something in the largest suitcase, but I didn't open it, because it was too heavy for me to lift down.

Used to the chaos of my home in Brooklyn, Ulvi's apartment seemed sterile, its order sinister. It was so clean, so tidy; even the corners bore no traces of dust, crumbs, or stray pieces of thread. After I examined everything and found nothing to make me suspicious, I opened the leather couch into a bed and lay in it, thinking about what it meant. He was a man with no history, ageless, rich enough to live in a luxury apartment building two blocks from Bloomingdale's but not so wealthy as to spend lavishly. There were so many questions I wanted to ask, but whenever I tried, he deflected my doubts with kisses. The only way to get him to talk, I decided, was to get out in public, where he couldn't distract me with his touch.

When he returned from his meeting, the first thing he did was to search inside the closet where the towels were kept. I wondered if I had missed something, but it was too late now. He didn't ask if I had riffled his things, but I had the feeling that he knew, although he didn't say a word. He never left me alone in the apartment again.

My cousin Alma lived with her mother and sister in an apartment on the second floor of Mami's house on Fulton Street. When they'd lived farther away, I spent more time with Alma, because we made it a point to get together for dinner every so often. Since I'd met Ulvi, however, my friendship with Shoshana had grown stronger, while my relationship with Alma had cooled. There was more to talk about with Shoshana, without the danger that my secret life would get back to Mami.

Alma and I had spent hours talking about getting an apartment together. Our mothers made sure that wouldn't happen. My goal now was to have a place of my own, where I could come and go as I pleased. At twenty years of age, I argued, I was old enough to take care of myself. Mami insisted that the only way she'd let me go was on the arm of a man, preferably a legal husband. Alma, who was a year older, still lived at home, Mami pointed out. With Titi Ana and Mami backing each other up, neither Alma nor I had any chance of getting our way.

Shoshana argued that I was too considerate of Mami's wishes. To become a woman, she asserted, I must rebel against my mother. What she said made sense, and I went so far as to discuss it with Alma, who agreed with Shoshana. Still, I couldn't bring myself to defy Mami, just as Alma didn't oppose Titi Ana, and Shoshana didn't confront her own parents. Alma devoted herself to her work; to her sister, Corazón; to her books. Shoshana and I schemed, planned, dreamed, nurtured secrets. But none of us stood up to our mothers and said, "I'm leaving you. I can stand on my own. It's time for me to claim my life."

We spent as little time at home as possible. Shoshana had Manhattan Community College, a job at a shoe store on 34th Street, and Arthur to keep her busy. I had Children's Theater International, the Advertising Checking Bureau, and Ulvi. Together, Shoshana and I had our dates.

Whether on the street or in a restaurant, Shoshana and I were often approached by men eager to take us out. Most of the time we accepted but followed strict rules for these unexpected dates. We only went to dinner at nice restaurants, never for drinks at a bar. We refused alcohol. We agreed on a curfew, and even if the men were fascinating, left when the time was up. We arrived together and left together. We never left the other one alone with a date. Most of the men were content to talk, but a few offered us money for sex. In that event, Shoshana and I executed a dramatic exit. After the agreed-upon signal, we rose from the table as one and stalked out. Ninety percent of the time, the men were so stunned that they sat with their mouths open while other diners stared after us. Once, a man yelled obscenities as we walked out, which only confirmed our decision to get out of there fast as we could.

We didn't think what we were doing was wrong or that we were cheating on Arthur or Ulvi. They never took us anywhere, as if afraid to be seen with us. The strangers who escorted us to dinner were thrilled to have us by their side, brought us to elegant restaurants, urged us to order the most expensive entrees. We were, we knew, decoration, a line on their expense reports. But we didn't mind. Their conversation, which to their wives or girlfriends might have been stupefying, was fascinating to us, who'd never met an accountant from Peoria or a personnel director from Albuquerque.

The first thing we established about a date was where he lived. We preferred men from out of town, because there was no chance we'd see them again. Then we asked whether he was married, if there were children. If he lied, he only fooled himself. If he shared pictures of his wife and kids, stories about Little League games and school plays, we did his family a service by easing his loneliness and keeping him from actions he might later regret. We had nothing to lose, enjoyed a nice dinner with interesting conversation, and felt virtuous because we were saving a family while still being loyal to our boyfriends.

We learned to spot the boasters and posturers, whose lies and exaggerations added to our mirth the next day, when we traded impressions of the previous evening. As with my sisters and the men we danced with at clubs, the "stocking rippers" and "the octopuses," Shoshana and I had code names for our dates.

First there were the "Groovies," who tried to impress us with their hipness by using adolescent expressions as often as possible. Shoshana and I, both native speakers of other languages, were not as in tune with American slang as native English speakers. Most of the time, a Groovy's use of slang was like another language to us, and we listened in awe of how idioms that sprang from our generation set us apart from them. Because we had learned English as a second language, Shoshana and I were obsessed with its proper usage. We spoke in schoolroom grammar, looked down on the second type, the "YKs," who couldn't put a sentence together without adding "you know" between phrases. A Groovy patronized us, a YK was never specific, let sentences disintegrate into generalities. If we were feeling wicked that day, we prodded YKs to say more, until it was clear to him that no, we didn't know. Shoshana maintained that YKs were threatened by real ignorance, because by saying "you know," they avoided a display of their own.

The third group, Daddies, were older men who, sometime during dinner, compared us to their daughters. "You remind me so much of Lindy," one said to Shoshana, and she prompted him to describe Lindy. Before we knew it, we'd heard the story of his life, with details about in-laws, best friends, alimony payments, visitation rights. Daddies were the most likely to want to see us again, but another of our rules was no repeat dates. Groovies assumed we could find them a drug connection. YKs were the most likely to offer us money for sex.

Shoshana sometimes discussed our dates with Arthur. I kept them from Ulvi, who wasn't interested in my life. Our relationship was a bubble isolated from the rest of our existence, confined to the white walls of his tidy, one-room apartment.

———

Rehearsals for the new Japanese-inspired production for Children's Theater International were on evenings and weekends, while performances of *Babu* took two or three mornings a week. With the exception of Tom and me, most of the actors from the previous season of *Babu* had to be replaced due to other commitments. Allan had joined the Broadway cast of *Fiddler on the Roof*, so a new actor, Jaime, took his place in the repertory.

Like me, Jaime was Puerto Rican, but born in New York. We recognized the irony of two Puerto Ricans playing Indian royalty.

"There's something wrong with this," Jaime complained. "We should be out there fighting for the rights of our people."

Jaime was proud of his heritage, determined to do what he could to preserve Puerto Rican culture in New York. In El Barrio and the Bronx, in parts of Brooklyn, other young Puerto Ricans, some of them members of the Young Lords, campaigned to improve the lives of their *compatriotas*. My cousin Corazón was involved with a group in the Lower East Side that offered art and photography lessons to Puerto Rican high school students. My brother Héctor and my sister Delsa were involved in youth organizations in our neighborhood.

My own social conscience was pathetically underdeveloped. I felt no obligation to "our people" in the abstract, felt, in fact, weighed down by duty to my people in the concrete: Mami, Tata, my ten sisters and brothers.

"That's a cop-out." Jaime charged that I used my family as an excuse to avoid involvement in the Puerto Rican struggle. "And what's with the Indian dance?" he scolded. "We need to champion *our* art and theater. Let the Hindus worry about their own."

My devotion to Indian dance, I argued, wasn't part of a conspiracy to promote their civilization over Puerto Rico's. My love of Indian classical dance and its music didn't extend to any other part of the subcontinent's culture. I didn't like curry or spicy foods, didn't dress in saris, didn't pray to Krishna, Shiva, or Ganesh, sneezed whenever incense burned near me.

"You don't get it," Jaime argued, "if we lose Puerto Ricans to other cultures, we lose Puerto Rican culture."

"What do you think happens to us here?" I contended. "Do you think we're as Puerto Rican in the U.S. as on the island?"

"More," he argued. "We have to work at it here."

I saw his point, but that didn't make me want to rush down to the nearest community center to dance the *plena*. Why should I be less Puerto Rican if I danced Bharata Natyam? Were ballet dancers on the island less Puerto Rican because their art originated in France? What about pianists who performed Beethoven? Or people who read Nietzsche? It was useless to argue with him. Even if I won, Jaime's judgment of me, unsparing and consistent, made me question my loyalty to my people.

In spite of Jaime's accusations that they were a cop-out, I still defined "my" people as Tata, Mami, Delsa, Norma, Héctor, Alicia, Edna, Raymond, Franky, Charlie, Cibi, Ciro. On the periphery there were also Papi, Don Carlos, Don Julio, La Muda, Tía Ana, Alma, Corazón, and the many aunts, uncles, and cousins in New York and back on the island.

For as long as I could remember, I'd been told that I was to set an example for my siblings. It was a tremendous burden, especially as the family grew, but I took the charge seriously, determined to show my sisters and brothers that we need not surrender to low expectations. To avoid the hot-tomato label, I dressed neatly but conservatively. I didn't smoke or drink. If I was in a situation where drugs were being shared, I walked away, so as not to confirm the stereotype of Puerto Ricans as drug abusers. There were enough alcoholics in my family for me to know that it wasn't fun, or pretty, and that whatever a drunk sought to abolish with liquor never went away.

The first Puerto Rican drug addict I met was Neftalí, who paid for it with his life. Maybe he felt good after he injected poison into his veins, just as Tata felt good when she drank beer. From where I stood, sober and straitlaced, the high wasn't worth the low, which for Tata, at least, came earlier every day.

The only people I knew who used drugs were American college students. They held smoky court in a corner of Manhattan Community College or hovered in disheveled groups in the streets of the Village near NYU and the rehearsal studio. They offered to "share" with me, but I refused. I had no desire to alter my consciousness, nor to escape reality. If I took even one "trip," I'd never return. Stubbornly, I observed every second of my ungroovy life, felt every pang of pain, shouldered humiliation, succumbed to joy, leaped into passion.

Mami drilled into me that I had only one asset. I wasn't the prettiest of her six daughters, or the strongest of her children, but I was, she often said, intelligent. It was the power of that intelligence that I trusted. If my one asset was to work for me, my brain needed to remain unfogged and focused. My clear-headed self-absorption kept me sober. It also convinced me that in spite of Jaime's censure, I could be of no help to "my" people until I helped myself.

Jaime and I were too professional to let the prickly relationship we had offstage affect our performance in the happily-ever-after world of children's theater. But we were never as close as I'd been to Allan, who had demanded less and accepted me as I was. With Allan gone from the cast, and to avoid Jaime's frequent rebukes, I drew closer to Tom, the only other actor left from the Broadway production. He was easy to be with, funny, a good actor, a lithe dancer. He made it clear from the beginning that his friendship with me was not as disinterested as Allan's and Bill's. When I told him I was involved with someone, however, he confessed that he was in love with a dancer. "But I had to try," he said, with an impish grin.

For the new play, A *Box of Tears*, Robert De Mora, who'd also worked on *Babu*, designed a spectacular set and elaborate, clever costumes. I played a mermaid who disguised herself as a turtle and was caught in a net by a peasant fisherman. After a series of adventures, he became a prince and I a princess and we lived happily ever after. My mermaid costume was heavily sequined in emerald green and drew applause from the audience when I made my entrance. I wore a wig of long, green hair, made of a material so fine that it floated around me as I moved and gave the impression that we were under water. When I became a princess, my kimonos were traditional in design, my wig elaborately combed and decorated.

A consultant was brought in to show us how to move like Japanese people, including the proper way to bow. She also demonstrated how to put on the three layers of kimonos and gave me some tips on how to walk in the sebutan shoes without falling over (very small steps). During performance, we wore Kabuki-style makeup. I arrived at the theater two hours before curtain to transform myself from Puerto Rican Indian classical dancer to Japanese mermaid. First I applied a thick white paste to my face, which obliterated my features. I then drew in the slanted eyes, straight eyebrows, bow lips in the photograph Kyoko gave me as a guide.

In one of the scenes, I was required to perform for the ocean king in my mermaid costume. Kyoko taught me how to sing "Sakura" in Japanese and choreographed a dance using fans to tell the story of how the fisherman caught the turtle/mermaid. After hearing me sing, Bill and Vera decided that I should just move my lips while Kyoko sang and played the koto.

I loved the play, the extravagant liberties De Mora took with costumes and set, the jokes we played on stage to break each other's concentration. My first words were spoken into a microphone offstage, while I was still a turtle in the hands of Tom as the fisherman. Rather than say my lines as Tom expected, I gurgled watery noises that were magnified through the whole theater. The first time I did that, Tom was disoriented, looked around as if the voice had come from heaven. In a later scene, as I performed my fan dance, Tom had his back to the audience. He often made goofy faces at me, while I struggled to maintain the dignity of a buddha.

My sisters and brothers couldn't come to my performances, because they took place during school hours, but I was enjoying myself so much that I wanted to share it with someone. Well aware that he preferred to keep our private lives private, I still urged Ulvi to come see me perform at the 92nd Street Y. The huge auditorium hummed with children bussed in from schools all over the city. It wasn't until I was putting on my makeup that I envisioned Ulvi in the audience surrounded by fidgety, chatty, precocious New York City schoolchildren. Naturally fastidious, he'd probably notice the pungent smell a roomful of children discharged. He'd frown at their shrill voices, at the way they ran down the aisle to claim a seat next to their best friends. With Ulvi in the audience, it was difficult to concentrate, because I worried that the context for the performance would affect his enjoyment of it.

We'd agreed to meet at his apartment afterward, and when I entered the black-and-white room, he didn't even greet me. He took me in his arms and loved me, and I knew that he knew the performance was for him. That every pore was focused not on the children who were the primary audience, but on the dark scowling face at the back of the theater who now covered my breasts with kisses.

———

Mrs. Davis at the Advertising Checking Bureau called me into a manager's office because she needed to speak to me in private. She'd been informed, she said in her best supervisor's voice, that I was no longer a student at Manhattan Community College. My job was designated as "cooperative education," which meant I received credit for working, but only if I was enrolled in school. Since I wasn't, Mrs. Davis suggested that I take a full-time position elsewhere in the company, so that another student could be hired. Because of my performing schedule, I couldn't work forty hours a week, so I quit the Advertising Checking Bureau. As the holidays approached, however, it was clear that my income from children's theater couldn't keep up with my expenses, even after I dropped dance classes and workshops. Bill and Vera promised there would be more shows in the spring, as well as a tour, but they couldn't say how many dates, nor when the tour might be. Just as the year began, I was forced to leave Children's Theater International and look for a real job. I sobbed my goodbyes to Bill, who was also leaving for San Francisco, to Vera, to Tom and Jaime. It was difficult to imagine that I would no longer wear De Mora's outrageous mermaid costume, that there would be no chain dragging me offstage. In the year and a half I worked in children's theater, I came to love the enthusiastic responses of our audiences, the tension when the hero or heroine was in danger, the giggles at the pranks of the monkey god, the cheers at the end when the prince and princess appeared in their full regalia, their future a cheerful certainty.

My own future didn't look so great. January wasn't the best month to look for work. Everywhere I went I was told business was winding down from the Christmas "rush." The best the employment agencies could do was to send me to do inventory at department stores, whose stock had to be counted before the discount sales began. It was tedious work, and I resented the prospect of counting thousands of shoes, dresses, coats that I couldn't afford to buy, even at a discount.

Shoshana came to my rescue. She had dropped out of college and was about to start a job as a sample model for a manufacturer of junior dresses and skirts. She talked to the owner of the shoe store where she worked and convinced him that he should replace her with me. But I was not good at selling shoes. When a woman asked how white go-go boots looked on her, I tended to be honest —a virtue in life but not in retail. Mr. Zuckerman suggested I find another line of work. After a number of interviews in offices that demanded more skills than I could offer, I was hired at Lady Manhattan. When I told Mami, she was upset. "All this education so that you can work in a factory?" she wailed, and I assured her I'd be in an office, not at machines.

Now that I was employed nine to five, Ulvi and I changed our trysts from afternoons to evenings and weekends. When I wasn't with him, I saw Shoshana or went to the movies or met Alma for dinner. Alma had just started a job as a secretary at NBC, where most of the pages I knew had graduated to better-paying work as assistant producers and writers. She admired her boss, who was said to be headed for great things in the company. I met him once at her office. He looked like a younger version of Mr. Rosenberg, the producer of the Yiddish theater where I was an usher, only more high-strung.

My boss at Lady Manhattan was Iris, a woman in her thirties with kind hazel eyes, cropped auburn hair, and a body type Shoshana described as *zaftig* — not fat, but not quite skinny either. As her assistant, I merited my own office outside hers, where my job was to maintain her files, answer her phone, keep track of her appointments, order her lunch, get her coffee, handle her correspondence. When she interviewed me, Iris didn't give me a typing test, and it wasn't until a week into my job that she realized she should have. It took me an entire morning to type a simple one-paragraph letter with duplicate. Every time I made a mistake, I took out the original and the carbon copy behind it and started over so that both would be perfect. Iris took one look at the pile of Lady Manhattan letterhead and carbon paper crumpled in the wastebasket and shrugged her shoulders.

"Never mind," she said. "I'll type it myself."

In her office, Iris had a wall-size bulletin board on which she pinned swatches of color for the previous, current, and two upcoming fashion seasons. Her job was to purchase the fabrics that the designers used for the blouses Lady Manhattan manufactured. She was good at her job, Iris told me without prompting, and if I was smart and paid attention, I could learn a lot from her. She had me sit in on meetings, ostensibly to take notes, but she admitted it was so that I could "learn the ropes." Together we came up with the names of the next season's colors. I suggested "Teal" — she called it "Mediterranean Blue." Never having seen that sea, I couldn't argue with her. When I offered "Dark Orange" she countered with "Pumpkin Spice." If I saw navy blue, she envisioned midnight. It was clear to everyone else at Lady Manhattan, but not to generous Iris, that I didn't have the poetic or hyperbolic instincts necessary for success in the garment industry.

The office building where I worked was seven blocks from the Broadway theater where Allan was in *Fiddler on the Roof,* starring Harry Goz. Allan was in the chorus and also understudied the role of the idealistic student who married one of the daughters, at that time played by Adrienne Barbeau. One day he called my office to let me know he was taking over the role that evening and that he could get me a ticket to see him. I called Ulvi to cancel our time together. He didn't ask why, and I didn't go into details.

I'd seen *Fiddler on the Roof* when Allan was first cast. It was wonderful to see how he had grown in the role. He lent a boyish charm to the romantic part, an innocence that endeared him to the audience. Afterwards, I met him backstage, and he introduced me to Adrienne and to Harry Goz; to Florence Stanley, whom I'd met in *Up the Down Staircase* and who played Yenta in *Fiddler*; to Bette Midler, who portrayed the oldest daughter. After they signed autographs at the stage door, we walked across the street to eat at a long, tunnel-like restaurant whose walls were decorated with signed photographs of Broadway actors. The bar was smoky, crowded with garrulous actors still high from a performance. In the juke box, Diana Ross proclaimed someday we'll be together, its chorus repeated over and over again by a mushy group in a corner bidding goodbye to one of its members.

It was very late when I arrived home. Mami raised her head from her pillow, waved me in, went back to sleep. The next day, I was exhausted at work, and while Iris went to a meeting in New Jersey, I asked the switchboard operator to handle calls, locked myself in Iris's office, and slept for two hours on the floor. When I checked, there were several messages from Ulvi. He was home, and, even though it wasn't one of our nights, he insisted that I come to his apartment because he needed to talk to me. He was furious, I could hear it in his voice.

"What's the matter?" I wondered, but he refused to talk about it over the phone. "Come after work," he said.

He prepared dinner for me, as he often did. His concoctions were simple — sautéed vegetables sprinkled with feta cheese, salad, steamed spinach with a soft-boiled egg in the center, roasted eggplant. I came to appreciate the subtle, delicate flavors of fresh vegetables — seldom served at home, staples in Ulvi's diet. This time he cooked steamed cauliflower with generous helpings of store-bought Hollandaise sauce, my contribution to his diet. He wasn't as fond of the dish as I was, and it made an impression that he bothered to make it for me. We ate in silence on the leather-topped coffee table. I could tell something was wrong, felt the tension in the room as solid as the four walls. As soon as we cleared the dishes, he led me to the pull-out sofa bed, sat on one corner, pointed to the other, where I sat, one leg folded under me.

"Chiquita," he began. "Where were you last night?"

I told him about the play, Allan, the rest of the cast, the smoky, noisy restaurant. He listened attentively, asked about Allan. When did I meet him? Where? Was Allan my boyfriend before he met me?

"Oh, no," I laughed, "it's not like that with me and Allan. I love him very much, but not that way. We're friends."

Ulvi nodded, a finger curled to his lips. "Tell me, Chiquita, do you have many men friends?"

"Yes," I answered truthfully.

He stood up and in three strides was at the door. "Get out!" He was so angry he glowed red.

I was stunned, unable to move, speechless. He opened the door and repeated his words with such venom that I had no choice but to push myself off the couch, pick up my purse, and leave the apartment. He slammed the door after me. In the elevator, in the lobby, outside his building, down to Third Avenue, I was carried by the force of his rage. What had I done? What could I possibly have said? I walked to the train station, waited behind a column, my thoughts focused on every word I had uttered in his presence. In channeling my English through Spanish, had something been lost? Did he misunderstand what I'd said as he translated English through German to Turkish? Or had I broken some Turkish taboo by spending an evening out with friends? Turkey was a Muslim country. Followers of Islam didn't drink. Was he offended that I went to a bar? No, he was angry that I had male friends. Was that forbidden to women in Turkey? Is that why he reacted so violently? I held my sobs until I reached home — earlier than usual, Mami noted with raised eyebrows. I locked myself in the bathroom, filled the tub with scalding water, soaked and sobbed for an hour, while outside a sister or brother periodically banged on the door because they had to pee.

It was over, just like that. The most words Ulvi and I had

exchanged since the day of the parade led to our first and only fight. Was it even a fight? Didn't a fight require at least two people? It was so one-sided. I didn't get a chance to defend myself. From what? Had I done anything to deserve the way he'd treated me? His fury was so unexpected, swift as a scorpion's sting, as painful. "Get out," he said. With two simple words he kicked me out of his life. As I tossed in bed next to Delsa that night, I moaned and wailed so loud that Mami came to see what was the matter.

"Something I ate," I said, "made me sick to my stomach." Five minutes later she brought me a cup of chamomile tea with honey. I sipped it in front of her, and from time to time, bent over with sobs, pushed my arms against my stomach to still the hurt that pulsed not there, but a little higher up and to the left.

"For that slave-girl look . . ."

Iris noticed that I looked drawn and exhausted the next morning. She called me into her office and asked what was the matter. It was impossible to contain the tears that lurked so near the surface; they flowed against my will.

"Oh, you poor thing," Iris said. "A man did this." I nodded, my face in my hands. She came around her desk to where I sat and put her arms around me. She rubbed my back, offered me tissues, pushed back the hair matted on my cheeks. But she had no words of womanly wisdom that could help me get over the pain. "He's a dog," she finally said, although she'd never met him. Again I nodded. She gave me the rest of the day off.

I called Shoshana at work, and we agreed to meet for dinner. I left the office and walked briskly up Seventh Avenue to Central Park. It was a cold, drizzly winter day, and my red eyes, swollen face, and occasional sobs went unnoticed by passersby. As I reached the spot where Jurgen had confessed his occupation, my heartache turned to anger. How dare Ulvi throw me out of his apartment with no explanation? What kind of a stupid fool was I to do as he asked? What would have happened if I'd refused to leave, if I'd argued with him? A couple of times I turned toward Ulvi's apartment. But as I played possible scenarios in my mind, they seemed melodramatic, too much like a *telenovela*, too close to what was expected of a passionate Puerto Rican who'd been wronged. I squelched the desire to kill him and walked on, letting the drizzle soak me through until I reached the Metropolitan Museum of Art. I stood in front of the Seurat painting where I had first met Avery Lee and was sorry I'd said no to him. Had I said yes, I'd be living in luxury in El Paso, where it never rained. Avery Lee didn't expect more from me than what I gave Ulvi. And he could speak English. I stared at the painting for a long time but still could find no more meaning in it than the first time I saw it.

At dinner, Shoshana urged another bowl of chicken soup to chase away the sniffles that were no longer caused by tears for Ulvi but by the cold I caught after walking in the rain. By the time I told her the story, it no longer hurt to speak of him.

"I can tell you'll be over him soon," Shoshana predicted. "It's not like you to suffer for long." My head was so heavy I couldn't think fast enough to agree or disagree. On the subway to Brooklyn, I jotted down her words on a scrap of paper and folded them inside my wallet. No, it wasn't like me to hold on to pain for long. Why bother? A new setback was bound to come soon enough.

I missed three days of work. Tata and Mami nursed me with broths and the dreaded *tutumá*, which tasted no better now that I was twenty than when Mami had first invented it in my thirteenth year. I slept, lulled by the whirr of sewing machines. Mami had a business at home now. She brought in cut garments from a factory; then she, Titi Ana, and a couple of other women finished sewing them on the machines set up in the living room. Tata watched Charlie, Cibi, and Ciro, who sometimes wandered into the make-shift *fábrica* to be admired, cuddled, and cooed over by the women.

By Saturday morning I felt better but stayed in bed reading. Shoshana called to see how I was doing. At the end of the conversation she told me the real reason she called.

"I didn't want to say anything the other day, when you felt so bad. . . ." She was returning to Israel to fulfill her military service, which she'd put off for some time. She'd be gone for months. "If the Arabs don't do something crazy, I might make it back," she joked, but I didn't laugh. She didn't have much time, but we arranged to meet for one last dinner. Losing my best friend at the same time as my lover sent me back to bed for another day, but on Monday I dragged myself to work. There was a stack of messages on my desk, most of them for Iris but a few for me. "Ulvi called," the receptionist who handled the calls had written on at least five pink slips. On the most recent one she had scribbled "Urgent!" and in parentheses, "He told me to write that," with an arrow pointing to the word. I didn't call him. Every time I looked at the slips, I remembered his fury, the cruel turn of his lips when he told me to get out of his apartment.

I met Shoshana for dinner, and afterwards we walked on Fifth Avenue as we had done so often, toward the Plaza, intending to retrace our steps to Grand Central and the subways. But in front of the fountain, a man approached us. He was a producer, he said. His film was being screened at the Paris Cinema across the street. Would we like to see it?

It was an inscrutable black-and-white film in a Slavic language neither of us could identify. The subtitles didn't help. Shoshana and I giggled through the whole thing, as serious moviegoers hushed us and the hapless producer walked nervously up and down the aisles peering into the faces of his audience, trying to determine who dared laugh at his masterpiece. We ran out of there as soon as the final credits rolled, no longer able to stifle our laughter. As we walked to Grand Central arm in arm, we knew that our free-spirited adventures ended that night. It would be months before Shoshana could return to the States, and by then who knew where I'd be? We hugged, and Shoshana promised to write as soon as she arrived in Haifa. I didn't remind her that every time she left for Israel, she swore to write but never did. Within minutes of our parting, I felt the loss of the best friend I'd ever had, the only person, I thought, who really knew me.

I hadn't forgotten Ulvi, but in the five days since he had slammed the door behind me, he'd become like the pain left after a cut. Most of the time I didn't feel it until I banged up against it. The day after my dinner with Shoshana, I answered Iris's phone.

"Chiquita?" His soft, tentative voice made me lightheaded, and my first instinct was to hang up. First he apologized for his behavior of the previous week. Then he wanted to see me because he had to explain. "Maybe you don't understand," he guessed, "why I am upset."

The use of the present tense didn't throw me off, because Ulvi frequently confused the present for the past. I insisted we meet in a restaurant, not his apartment. "If you want to talk," I said, "it will be better." When I saw him in front of the Magic Pan on East 57th Street, I almost flew into his arms, restrained myself, let him kiss my cheek, pulled away for fear of losing my resolve.

He thought about what happened last week. "You are a child," he said. "I forget sometimes."

I reminded him that I was twenty and a half years old, not ten. He showed his indulgent smile. "To me, you are my *chiquita*," he said. "Always."

He was angry that night, he continued, because we had a date and I broke it at the last minute to be with another man. I explained that Allan was not "another man" in the sense I understood Ulvi to mean, but my dear friend. The reason for the short notice was that Allan, as an understudy, didn't always know ahead of time when he'd perform.

"Why don't you tell me this?" Ulvi asked.

"Because you didn't ask. You never do. You don't want to know about my private life, remember?" It was impossible to keep the resentment from my voice, the sarcasm that crept into the final three syllables. Ulvi winced. We sat in silence for a few minutes. I felt him struggle with a response. There was no possibility of kissing my emotions away here, in a busy restaurant with fake French food. I couldn't be appeased with promises that he'd never hurt me. He already had.

It took him a long time to formulate what he wanted to say. He thought he was the only man in my life. It disturbed him that I felt free to see other men.

I answered that we'd never talked about our "relationship" in a way that made me feel I couldn't date others. If it made him feel better, I assured him, I hadn't had sex with any other man but him. The relief that swept over his face startled me. What did he expect?

We left the restaurant, circled the block, ended up on his street. He grinned, pulled me close, kissed me, and I dissolved through my thick winter coat. His arms felt familiar, his lips like mine. He was the perfect height, no need for me to stretch or scoot down to place my head on his shoulders, for him to wrap his arm around my waist. We walked with the same purposeful stride, our feet hit the pavement at the same time, synchronized through an internal mechanism neither of us controlled. Our lovemaking was a dance, each part of our bodies attuned to its complement in the other, as if we were not two but one. Afterwards, as I lay content in his arms, he said he wanted me always by his side. It wasn't a promise, a proposal, a declaration of love. But I understood it as all those things.

Over the next few days and nights we drew closer. Reluctantly, Ulvi opened up, talked about himself and his obsession with his film, *Dry Summer*. Its success had surprised him, because the favorite for the top prize at Berlin had been *The Pawnbroker*, with Rod Steiger. "No one expect me to win," he laughed. "Not even me." He became famous overnight, traveled around the world for festivals and competitions, made money. He bought a white Rolls Royce, which he drove from New York to Hollywood. There, he met Kim Novak and Angie Dickinson. The Hollywood producer Sid Solow let Ulvi spend a few weeks in his guest house while Ulvi tried to get a film deal. In spite of his efforts, however, *Dry Summer* couldn't pick up a distributor in North America. Wherever Ulvi went, he was told that the film was lovely but that if he wanted to show it in the United States, it needed more sex and better music. He sold the Rolls Royce, invested the money in the film. He hired the Greek composer Manos Hadjidakis, who'd scored *Never on Sunday*, to create new music for *Dry Summer*. Ulvi found a girl who looked like Hulya Kocigit, the love interest opposite him in the film. They drove out with a cinematographer to Long Island and shot new scenes. He was now reediting the film to incorporate the sex.

"Did Hulya agree to that?" I wondered.

"She's a big star in Turkey now. She doesn't have time."

The editing suite was on the second floor of a rundown office building half a block from Woolworth's, where Ulvi had first seen me. His editor was a long-legged older man with white hair, sad eyes, a deeply lined face that seldom smiled. Hans reminded me of Bela Lugosi, both in the way he looked and in his speech, which was heavily accented. He worked at an upright Movieola, his fingers flying from the editing machine to the ashtray at his side. In a back room was another Movieola rented to another filmmaker.

Every day after work I met Ulvi at the editing room, a few blocks from my office. Once he was done, we went to his place, ate, took long, frigid walks down Fifth Avenue or through Central Park, and talked — or rather, he did. I cherished his every word, his intonation, the pauses and hesitations of his speech. He prefaced many of his confidences with "I don't tell anyone this, Chiquita," which made me feel included in his life, privy to secrets.

Ulvi hired a writer to create new subtitles for the film. He worried that the money he had left was dribbling away into making the movie attractive to American audiences. Evenings, after he walked me to the train station, he went to Manos's apartment above the Acropolis restaurant on West 57th Street to work on the score. Manos didn't like to compose during the day, Ulvi said, so their sessions began after eleven at night and ended in the early hours. It was an exhausting schedule, but Manos claimed his creativity was at its peak late at night. Since Manos had won an Academy Award for *Never on Sunday*, Ulvi felt he must indulge him. He hoped that Manos's score would increase interest in his film.

When I worried about his health because he worked so hard, Ulvi thanked me but said he had no choice. "This is my only chance, Chiquita," he confided.

Over the next few weeks my days, evenings, and weekends were consumed by Ulvi. I didn't spend time with anyone else — not my family, not my friends, not my cousin Alma. Able to afford dance classes again, I stopped going to them after Ulvi and I went to a Satyajit Ray movie.

"That's the kind of dance I do," I told him, referring to the Bharata Natyam sequence at the beginning of the film.

"Is ridiculous dance," was Ulvi's opinion. "Not for you."

The next time I went to a workshop, I watched myself in the studio mirror, self-conscious about the stylized movements, the affected expressions, the atonal music. I looked ridiculous in my sari and ankle bells, the dot in the middle of my forehead.

From then on, every free moment was devoted to him. While Ulvi worked on his film, I read in a corner of the editing room. Sometimes I was sent out for coffee or lunch, or to pick up or deliver a package. Johan, who rented the other Movieola in the suite, asked me to translate his film. He and his brother Fritz had documented an archaeological expedition into the Colombian jungle. Many of the scenes were in Spanish, a language neither Johan nor Fritz understood. I translated the Spanish scenes into English, then translated the whole film into Spanish so that he could have a movie in each language.

While he and Hans edited, I saw scenes with a younger, ardent Ulvi but never viewed the entire movie from beginning to end. The nude scenes were skillfully shot, one in a cornfield, another in front of a loom on which was stretched a half-finished carpet. The actress looked enough like Hulya that, through clever lighting and positioning of her face, the transitions were smooth, if not perfect.

Days in the garment center, I failed to come up with evocative names for primary colors. I couldn't type a letter without wasting ten sheets of stationery. Iris's busy schedule meant that I was often alone in the office, overcome with boredom, willing the phone to ring so that I could take a message. It felt wrong to collect a salary when I had nothing to do, so I decided to improve my secretarial skills. I bought the book *Teach Yourself the Gregg Shorthand Method*, but between Spanish, English, Spanglish, high school French, the Turkish that came backwards and forwards from the Movieola, and the German that Ulvi, Hans, and Johan spoke among themselves, there was no more room in my brain for another language.

Mami no longer asked where I'd been, who I'd been with, what I'd been doing. It was as if, with ten other children to look after, my activities held no interest for her as long as I was home every night. I seldom saw my sisters and brothers, because I made it a point to leave the house as early as possible and returned way past everyone's bedtime. One Sunday, Ulvi couldn't see me because he had to visit friends in Long Island. I planned to stay home that day, but two hours after I woke up, I left the house, suffocated by the clutter and disarray, the confusion, the people running in and out of rooms, up and down the stairs. I longed for Ulvi's quiet, austere room, its systematic order no longer sinister but soothing. Without him there, however, I couldn't go to his apartment. I spent the day at the movies, watched the double feature twice, and came home at the same time as always.

Ulvi surprised me one day. He took me to dinner at an expensive restaurant because he wanted to celebrate meeting some people interested in his film. They had shot a couple of low-budget films in Italy and were interested in Ulvi as a director for another film they wanted to produce. Ulvi said they were impressed by his reputation as an art film director, an image they sought to promote for themselves.

"It is a good possibility," Ulvi said, and as he downplayed it, I knew he was relieved. The burden of financing every aspect of *Dry Summer* was lifted just when he ran out of money. "I only have enough for one month," he told me, and I wondered what might have happened if the partners hadn't come along.

When we returned to his apartment, Ulvi took my hand, kissed it. He asked me to close my eyes and clicked a cuff bracelet on my wrist. It was heavy gold mesh, about one and a half inches wide, with gold braid along the edges. I was speechless, embarrassed by the extravagance of such a gift.

"What's this for?" I stammered

"You have been good girl," he murmured.

"But you can't afford it."

"Don't worry," he said.

Later, naked save for the bracelet, I turned my wrist this way and that to catch the shimmer of the gold against my skin. I wondered what the bracelet was worth, whether hundreds or thousands of dollars.

"I feel funny taking this when I know you need money," I offered.

"I said don't worry," he snapped.

On the way home that night, I pulled the sleeve of my coat over the bracelet so that no one on the train could see it and mug me. Because I knew Mami would notice it, I concocted a story about a friend who wanted to sell it. Was the bracelet worth the $25 she asked? Mami thought the price was more than fair.

I wore the bracelet everywhere, with casual or dressy clothes, because it pleased Ulvi to see it on me. When I showed it to Iris at work, she said it reminded her of shackles. "For that slave-girl look," she added.

Over the next few weeks, Ulvi gave me other expensive gifts. An Hermès leather agenda book, a sterling silver key ring from Tiffany's in the shape of a heart. He also took an interest in how I dressed. He insisted that when we were together, I not wear makeup. "I don't like painted woman," he said. He accompanied me shopping for clothes. Before making films, he had worked as a textile engineer in Germany and was particular about what went next to his skin. When I chose a garment, he rubbed it between his fingers, weighed it on the palm of his hand, turned it inside out to see if the pattern was stamped or woven in, and to check the finish on the seams. He eliminated most of my choices. "This is for cheap girl," he sneered, then picked something else. "This one better for you."

"Cheap girl" was his biggest insult, the exact opposite of "elegant girl," who dressed well and behaved appropriately according to a complicated system of etiquette and demeanor that Ulvi swore I needed to master. "If you are going to be with me, you must learn."

I wanted to be with him, so I attended to his lessons. When we were out, I was to mirror his movements, so as not to embarrass myself. I was to eat if he ate, with the utensil he used, to speak less and listen more, to withhold my opinions. He made me aware of my limitations, promised to help me overcome them. "You are poor girl with small mind," he said once and repeated often. When he noticed I was offended, he explained that he meant not that I was stupid but that I was unsophisticated, because I'd been too well protected.

"It is what I love about you, Chiquita," he told me. "I can teach you everything." He wanted to be Pygmalion, and I became the stone upon which he sculpted Galatea. Whenever it felt as if he controlled too much of my life, I complained, but he shushed me with caresses and a promise. "You will be by my side, but you must do as I tell you." To be with him, I had to discard who I was and evolve into the woman he wanted to be with. "I have thousand girlfriends," he boasted, "but only you I care." It was the closest he could come to saying he loved me, but for me it was close enough.

Gradually, he introduced me to people in his life. Each encounter was a test I had to pass to move on to the next level. First I met Hans, Johan, and Fritz and comported myself well in the stuffy editing room. Then he introduced me to Bruce, the writer who helped him with the subtitles, and to his delicate wife, Diana. Peter, the Iranian cameraman who filmed the sex scenes, and his wife, Barbara, were next. When he introduced me to the man he called his best friend, Tarik, I knew he trusted me. Each little piece of his life I was allowed to share felt like a victory, because I'd earned the right to be with him, by his side.

Manos finished most of the score and planned to record it

with a Juilliard-trained group of musicians who performed under the name *The New York Rock and Roll Ensemble*. I came to the recording studio and met Manos for the first time. He was enormous, with an engaging grin; small hands with short, fat fingers; merry ebony eyes.

After the first couple of sessions in the recording studio, Ulvi told me not to come anymore. The musicians and their girlfriends smoked pot constantly, and Ulvi worried that they were into other drugs. "I don't want you around that," he said, and I was grateful for his concern.

The day he admitted how old he was, I understood why he had kept it a secret for so long. He was thirty-seven, the same age as Mami, seventeen years older than me. I'd studied psychology at Manhattan Community College, was aware that Ulvi was the classic father substitute, but it didn't matter. He took care of me in a way no one else did. In his arms I felt safe and protected. Wrapped in his embrace, I had no responsibilities except to do as he said. "Don't worry," he assured me, "I take care everything." He was clear about what he expected from me. Unlike the other adults in my life, he didn't say one thing and do another. If he didn't want me to drink alcohol, it was because he didn't drink. If he frowned on smoking, he didn't smoke. He didn't want children, so he took care I didn't get pregnant.

He needed a disciple; I needed to be led. I felt myself submerge into his need like a pebble into a pond, with no resistance, no trace I'd ever been anywhere or anyone without him. With Ulvi I wasn't Negi, daughter of an absent father, oldest of eleven children, role model for ten siblings, translator for my mother. I was not Esmeralda, failed actress/dancer/secretary. My head against Ulvi's chest, my arms around his neck, I was what I stopped being the day I climbed into a propeller plane in Isla Verde, to emerge into the rainy night of Brooklyn. After seven years in the United States, I had become what I stopped being the day I left Puerto Rico. I had become Chiquita — small, little one. Little girl.

"It is the way it must be."

In April Ulvi and I took long walks in Central Park along paths that he seemed to know intimately. "I jog here," he said, which surprised me because he'd never told me he was a runner. From time to time he liked to leave the paths and walk on the grass, his eyes scanning the green for four-leaf clovers. It impressed me that he always found one, plucked it, pressed it between the folds of a dollar bill. Later, in his apartment, he taped it flat, carefully cut around it. He sent them to friends, he said, and once gave one to me. "It will bring you good luck," he claimed. I kept it in my wallet as he instructed but noticed no difference in my fortunes.

"Maybe I'm immune to good luck," I joked, but he didn't get it.

Our walks in the park usually ended at the zoo, where we visited the sad, caged creatures who paced back and forth with the same tenacity they'd display if they were going somewhere. We stopped to watch the seals slither in and out of murky water, their coats a-shimmer. A crowd gathered around the pond when they were fed, but I found their silly antics for a dead fish pitiful.

Shanti had taken numerous pictures of me in the zoo, by the monkey cages or on a bench surrounded by pigeons, which an old lady fed from a plastic bucket at her side. Every time I passed those spots, I remembered Shanti's Crayola brown eyes, the way he tilted his head to let me know how I should place mine.

When Ulvi and I walked around the Lake, I remembered

Jurgen's content look as he lifted the oars, dipped them in the water, pulled them toward his chest to propel us across. Ulvi liked to sit in the lobbies of fancy hotels like the Plaza, the St. Regis, the Waldorf. I didn't tell him about the dinners Shoshana and I had had in the restaurants of those hotels, about the lonesome men eager to spend their money and their time on a couple of girls hungry for male attention.

The restaurant in Rockefeller Center where Jurgen and I had first talked still served expensive meals under bright umbrellas, but I didn't tell Ulvi I had once sat in their shade to cry on the shoulder of a stranger because Avery Lee had asked me to be his mistress. Ulvi, who talked as if I'd never remember a word he said, didn't ask about me. The less interest he had in my life, the more ashamed of it I became, ashamed of a life before him, without him.

A few weeks short of my twenty-first birthday, we were walking in the park when Ulvi doubled over. I helped him to a nearby bench, and he sat for a while, refusing my offer to accompany him to an emergency room. "It's nothing, Chiquita. I get this before," he said, and I didn't press him but insisted we take a cab back to his apartment. He lay down for a few minutes, which he said made him feel better. Before I left, he promised to see a doctor.

"I need operation," he told me a few days later.

The only people close to me to have needed operations were Raymond, whose injured foot and subsequent surgeries were the reason for our one-way trip to Brooklyn, and Francisco, Mami's love, my brother Franky's father. Raymond's operations had saved his foot. Francisco had suffered through numerous procedures that couldn't save him. Instinctively, I ignored the successes and focused on the failures of medicine. Like Francisco, Ulvi would go for surgery, and I wouldn't see him again. I wasn't strong like Mami, couldn't survive the months of black despair.

"Don't be so scare, Chiquita," Ulvi took me in his arms, pressed me close while I sobbed into his chest. "It is only hernia operation. Nothing to worry."

But he couldn't convince me. My head filled with images of Ulvi, dead. Ulvi, a ghost to haunt me forever, as Francisco had haunted Mami. It took me a long time to calm down, and then Ulvi told me the rest. It was minor surgery, he wouldn't be in the hospital more than a couple of days; but he didn't have insurance, and his savings had run out. The distributors who wanted to release *Dry Summer* arranged for a hospital and a doctor to perform the surgery at no charge, in Fort Lauderdale.

"Why so far?" I whined.

"It is the way it must be." He waited for me to argue, and when I didn't, he continued. Even though he was in pain, he wanted to finish the film before he left New York. The new subtitles had to go in, the film had to be remixed to incorporate Manos's music and new sound effects. He needed a couple of weeks, and then he'd fly to Fort Lauderdale to have his surgery. He didn't know when, or if, he'd come back to New York. He spoke matter-of-factly in his simple, declarative English, each word carefully chosen. I sat with legs folded under me, my hands pressed between my thighs. For some time, I'd dreaded a conversation like this, had known that one day Ulvi would leave my life as swiftly as he had entered it. I was glad he wasn't going to die; he was just going to Florida. As he spoke, I made myself withdraw, until we were not at opposite ends of his black leather sofa but in different continents.

Once he laid out the plans, Ulvi leaned further into his corner of the couch, pressed his hands together, his fingers to his lips, and spoke so softly I had to strain to hear him. "You can come with me."

I'd waited, hoped for those words, certain I'd never hear them, relieved when he said them. I surprised myself, then, when my response was that my mother would never let me go.

"You must leave her, then," Ulvi declared.

There was no way to explain to Ulvi, who didn't know Mami, why the thought of leaving my mother so that I could go to Fort Lauderdale with my lover terrified me. He hadn't been there when she showed up on Long Island in the middle of a snowstorm to rescue me from sex with Otto. He hadn't heard the pain in her voice when she mourned her unfinished education, young, unmarried motherhood, men who betrayed her. He hadn't been with her at the welfare office, had not stood solemn and scared as she humbled herself before people who would conquer her pride because they couldn't vanquish her spirit. He'd never placed his head on her lap, had never listened as she revealed her dreams for her children, who would, she hoped, be smarter about life than she had been. He hadn't seen Mami's face light up at the thought of me, her eldest daughter, dressed in a white wedding gown en route to a cathedral.

"Maybe if we get married," I suggested, pathetic even to myself.

Ulvi shook his head. "No, we cannot get married."

No explanation followed his refusal, and I didn't seek one. He was somber, patient. His eyes watched me with the same intensity as they had, months ago, when Shoshana and I sat in this room trying to impress him so that he would put us in his movie. This, I knew, was a test of my loyalty. If I refused to follow him to Florida, I would fail.

Over the seven months we'd known each other I'd relinquished my will to his. I'd stopped seeing my friends, stopped dancing, ran from work straight into his arms. But I still went home at night to sleep under Mami's roof. Without saying the words, Ulvi was asking me to give her up too, to choose between them.

In all the time we'd been lovers, it had never once occurred to me that I'd ever have to make such a choice. One day, Ulvi would return to Turkey; or to Germany; or to who knew, who cared where. It would be Ulvi who would leave my life, not Mami. Over the years of watching Mami, La Muda, my aunts and cousins as they loved, lost, loved again, I'd learned that love was something you get over. If Ulvi left, there would be another man, but there would never, ever be another Mami.

"You think about," Ulvi advised when I didn't respond right away. For the first time since the first time, I left his apartment without taking my clothes off once. I rode the train to Brooklyn. The heavy, dusty air of the subways was suffocating, made it impossible to breathe, muddled my thoughts so that I didn't know where I was, where I was going, or why. The express hurtled between Nostrand Avenue, Utica Avenue, Broadway-East New York. I got off the train and switched to the local for one stop, to Liberty Avenue, a block from Mami's house. It was dark, but earlier than I usually came home. Mami and Tata had cooked a vat of *arroz con pollo* and stewed pinto beans.

"Ay, Negi, you're early, that's good," Mami said. "Let me serve you some dinner."

She was cheerful because it was Saturday and she was paid on Friday, which meant there was a big, generous *compra* in the pantry. The sewing machines in the living room were quiet, covered with sheets so that the younger kids knew not to touch them. Héctor, Raymond, and Franky were in the cement backyard, throwing a ball around. A little dog snapped at my ankles. Where had it come from? Did we own it? How long had we had it? I changed into my stay-at-home clothes and sat with Mami and Tata in the kitchen, and the three of us ate their good cooking, while in the next room, the television blared a variety show.

My sisters and brothers sprawled on the floor or on the plastic-covered furniture and laughed and pointed at the outlandish costumes and performers. Somewhere one of the babies cried, another screeched, the dog yipped. Tata lit up a cigarette, opened a beer. Mami screamed at Edna to pick up Ciro so he'd stop crying. I stood up, put my dishes in the sink, and burrowed into the room I shared with Delsa, into the bed I shared with Delsa. Covers pulled over my head to block out the noise, the confusion, the drama of my family's life, I knew, just as Ulvi knew when he asked, that I'd already made my choice.

acknowledgments

This is what I remember, as I remember it. Memorable statements, compelling confessions, and intriguing questions have contributed to the recreated conversations in some scenes.

The names of members of my immediate family are real, but circumstances have forced me to change others. For example, so far, there have been twelve Franks and five Normas in my life. While I can tell one from the other, it was harder to do that on the page. To avoid confusion, I've nicknamed or renamed some people.

Then there are those people whose names I can't recall. Some might be minor characters in a novel, but in real life, if they're remembered, they're not minor at all. I beg forgiveness from those who recognize themselves but whose names are different in these pages. Please understand that, while I may have forgotten your name, I still remember you.

Several individuals have helped shape this book. I am particularly indebted to my editor Merloyd Lawrence, whose confidence and encouragement are the greatest motivators any writer could ever hope for. Whenever I was overwhelmed by the emotions the writing of this memoir evoked, I called my friend and agent Molly Friedrich, whose reassurances kept me on course. My writing buddies Terry Bazes, Ben Cheever, Joie Davidow, Audrey Glassman, Marilyn Johnson, and Mary Breasted generously put aside their own work to read this manuscript at various stages. *Mil gracias*, dear friends.

The Santiago/Cortéz/Martínez clan has been gracious and supportive, even if they sometimes disagree with my version of events. Individually and collectively, my mother, father, sisters, and brothers manifest what respect and *dignidad* mean to a Puerto Rican.

And finally, my husband, Frank Cantor, and our children, Lucas and Ila, have figured out when I need to be alone and when I need a hug. You make me sing. (But don't worry, I won't do it in public.)

readers group guide

About This Guide

The questions, discussion topics, and suggested reading list that follow are designed to enhance your group's reading of Esmeralda Santiago's *Almost a Woman*, the sequel to her moving and powerful memoir *When I Was Puerto Rican*. We hope they will provide you with a number of ways of looking at—and talking about—this vibrant story of an ambitious, headstrong teenager as she moves slowly out of the loving and safe but constricting grip of her Hispanic family and community and into the large and unimaginably different world of Manhattan.

About This Book

At the age of thirteen Esmeralda must leave the familiarity, warmth, and vibrancy of Puerto Rico to live in a three-room apartment in Brooklyn shared by ten family members. Challenged by language barriers, cultural stereotypes, and her strict and fiercely protective mother, Esmeralda begins her triumphant struggle for identity and independence. By day she studies acting at Manhattan's Performing Arts High School and interprets for the family at city welfare offices; by night she accompanies her mother and sister to Latin dance halls, but on such a short leash that she does not have her first date until age twenty. Undaunted, she makes up for lost time in a romantic apprenticeship at once hilarious and heartbreaking. Filled with wisdom and humor, Esmeralda Santiago's story is both universal and personal: the immigrant's search for belonging, the adolescent's search for identity, and the daughter's fight, often at a great cost to herself, for independence from a beloved but too powerful parent.

Questions and Answers

1. "In the twenty-one years I lived with my mother, we moved at least twenty times" [p. 1]. Santiago feels that this fact kept her and her family from attaching too much importance to possessions, or even to friends. What other effects did the family's many moves have on their outlook on life, their relationships to one another and to outsiders, and, in particular, on Esmeralda's developing character?

2. After her discussion with a neighborhood child soon after her arrival in Brooklyn, Esmeralda reflects, "Two days in New York, and I'd already become someone else" [p. 5]. What does the two girls' conversation reveal about categories of identity? Is group identity, in a multicultural place like New York, seen to be primarily racial? National? Linguistic? Regional?

3. What different groups does Esmeralda identify herself with during the course of her narrative? How do her experiences at the Performing Arts High School change her ideas about hierarchy and group identity? How does she define herself at the memoir's end?

4. Mami says that Esmeralda's cousins Alma and Corazon are Americanized. "The way she pronounced the word *Americanized*, it sounded like a terrible thing, to be avoided at all costs, another algo to be added to the list of 'somethings' outside our door" [p. 12]. What does Mami mean by "Americanized," and why does the word have such negative connotations for her? Why is she so afraid of Esmeralda's becoming Americanized too? Isn't it true that she also wishes for Esmeralda and her siblings to enter into American life and to succeed there?

5. Listening to Mami, says Santiago, "had taught me that men were not to be trusted" [p. 14]. The same could be said of Esmeralda's observations of her father, and of some of the other men in her community. What mixed messages about men, women, and love does Esmeralda pick up, as a child, from her parents? How does her mother's example affect her own early relationships with men and boys? Does it make her more passive? Wary? Fearful? Impulsive? Why does she never feel "affection" for any man outside her family until she meets Allan — although she is not in love with him — whereas she has been in love with several other men?

6. What does Esmeralda learn about "another United States — the trim, horizontal suburbs of white Americans" [pp. 26–27] — from Archie comics? How much of the imaginary picture she constructs of the white suburbs is a true one, and how much is simple fantasy? In what ways is Esmeralda's life deeply different from those of real suburban teenagers?

7. How, according to Santiago, do race relations and racial consciousness differ between Puerto Rico and

New York? Have the racial attitudes and stereotypes encountered by Esmeralda in the 1960s changed over the ensuing decades? Are things better, worse, or much the same?

8. How does Mami's trip to the welfare office [pp. 43–44] make Mami look? Does this image that Mami presents to the welfare agent resemble the real Mami that we have come to know from the book? Does this scene, and your knowledge of Mami's character, change or affect your ideas about welfare recipients and the welfare system?

9. Mami has high expectations for her daughters: that they will remain virgins until marriage, that they will find good and responsible husbands, and that they will get married in a church. Esmeralda is not even allowed to date until the age of twenty. Yet the example Mami herself has provided is very different: eleven children by three different men, none of whom has married her. "Whenever we discussed it at home, it was agreed by the adults around the kitchen table that 'the Pill' was nothing more than a license for young women to have sex without getting married. The fact that my mother, grandmother, and almost every other female relative of ours had sex without marriage was not mentioned" [pp. 156–157]. Is Mami entirely unreasonable and exasperating on this subject? Do you have any sympathy for her and the discrepancy between her standards and her behavior?

10. Why, as an actress, does Esmeralda refuse to venture into her deeper self [p. 74]? What is she afraid of finding? Is there any part of her teenage life during which she does not feel it necessary to act a role?

11. Jaime, who acts with Esmeralda in Babu, is a political activist who promotes Puerto Rican culture in New York. What is it in Esmeralda's life and experiences that make her resist his perorations, and to believe that "I could be of no help to 'my' people until I helped myself" [p. 288]?

12. How can you explain the fact that Esmeralda accepts the marriage proposal of Jurgen, a man she has known only a few hours, when by her own admission she is deeply distrustful of men in general?

13. "Why him?" Esmeralda asks after losing her virginity to Ulvi. "Why not Otto or Avery Lee or Jurgen" [p. 272]? Can you answer her question? What of her special needs does Ulvi, alone among all the men she knows, meet? Why does she go along with his dominating manner, his wish to separate her from family and friends, his rules and regulations? Does Iris have a point when she says Esmeralda's bracelet, a gift from Ulvi, reminds her of shackles? Or do you agree with Santiago's own retrospective opinion that Ulvi served as a substitute father for her?

14. "Esmeralda's observations of her own family and community have taught her that "love was something you get over. If Ulvi left, there would be another man, but there would never, ever be another Mami" [p. 310]. Why, then, does she opt to leave with Ulvi? Does this move amount to an out-and-out rejection of Mami? What else is she leaving behind when she leaves her mother and family?

15. How has the lack of a father during her formative years affected Esmeralda's life, her character, and her dealings

with the rest of the world? How might her life have been different if her father had been present? How might she, as a person, have developed differently?

16. The relationship between Mami and Esmeralda is a complex one: in some ways it is the classic mother-daughter story, while other elements of it are more unusual. "I felt guilty," Santiago remembers, "that so much of what little we had was spent on me. And I dreaded the price" [p. 86]. What price does Mami, in fact, try to exact? What does she expect of Esmeralda, and how far is Esmeralda willing to go to please Mami? What concessions does Esmeralda refuse to make when it comes to her own life? Do you find that the relationship between Mami and Esmeralda resembles that between Tata and Mami? In what ways is it different, and why?

Comparing *When I was Puerto Rican* and *Almost a Woman*:

1. Almost a Woman could be described as in essence a search for identity, as Santiago changes from Negi, the little Puerto Rican girl she once was, to the young adult, part Puerto Rican and part American, whose persona she herself has gone far to create. In what ways are little Negi and adult Esmeralda different? What characteristics, on the contrary, does Santiago keep all her life? At the end of Almost a Woman, do you feel that Esmeralda has become the woman she will be, or is her character still in a state of flux?

2. The Santiagos felt that in New York, they would have a "better" life than they had in Macún. In what ways

does their American life turn out, indeed, to be better? In what ways is it a less satisfactory life? Santiago, at the beginning of Almost a Woman, says that Mami would eventually return to Macún after ten years in New York. Do you think that was the right decision for her?

3. How might you compare the Latino experience of assimilation with those of, for example, Chinese, Jewish, Irish, or Haitian immigrants? How might the cultural barriers between these groups and mainstream America differ? What roles do race and language play in the process?

4. In what ways does the Puerto Rican extended family, as represented by the Santiagos, differ from its American counterpart? Does it provide more support, or less? Is the family more constricting? More powerful? More protective? How do the conceptions and ideals of certain roles—mother, father, daughter, son—differ between the two cultures?

5. In Brooklyn, Esmeralda finds that she wants more things, is more ambitious, than she was in Puerto Rico. Why is this? Is this feeling of wanting, of striving, a particularly American state of mind, or is it rather a characteristic of urban culture in general?

Suggested Reading

Isabel Allende: *The Infinite Plan*; Julia Alvarez: *How the García Girls Lost Their Accents*; *íYo!*; Claude Brown: *Manchild in the Promised Land*; Lorene Cary: *Black Ice*; Denise Chávez: *Face of an Angel*; Sandra Cisneros: *The House on Mango Street*; Judith Ortiz Cofer: *The Latin Deli*; Jill Ker Conway:

The Road from Coorain; *True North*; Janet Frame: *An Angel at My Table*; Miles Franklin: *My Brilliant Career*; Cristina García: *Dreaming in Cuban*; Lorraine Hansberry: *To Be Young, Gifted, and Black*; Jamaica Kincaid: *Annie John*; *Autobiography of My Mother*; Oscar Lewis: *La Vida*; Nicholasa Mohr: *Nilda*; Pat Mora: *House of Houses*; Rosario Morales and Aurora Levins Morales: *Getting Home Alive*; Edward Rivera: *Family Installments: Memories of Growing Up Hispanic*; Earl Shorris: *Latinos: A Biography of the People*; Betty Smith: *A Tree Grows in Brooklyn*; Amy Tan: *The Joy Luck Club*.

about the author

Esmeralda Santiago is the eldest of eleven children. She spent her childhood in Puerto Rico, moving back and forth between a tiny village and Santurce, a suburb of San Juan. With her mother and siblings she moved to New York in 1961, at the age of thirteen. She attended junior high school in Brooklyn and Performing Arts High School in Manhattan. After the extraordinary years described in her memoirs, *When I Was Puerto Rican*, *Almost a Woman*, and *The Turkish Lover*, she graduated from Harvard University and received a master's degree from Sarah Lawrence College. Santiago is the also the author of two novels, *América's Dream* and *Conquistadora*, and is coeditor, with Joie Davidow, of *Las Christmas: Favorite Latino Authors Share Their Holiday Memories*. Santiago lives in Westchester County, New York, with her husband and two children.